TRENDS IN CONTENT ANALYSIS

PAPERS OF THE

WORK CONFERENCE

ON CONTENT

ANALYSIS OF

THE COMMITTEE

ON LINGUISTICS

AND PSYCHOLOGY,

SOCIAL SCIENCE

RESEARCH COUNCIL

TRENDS IN CONTENT ANALYSIS

EDITED BY ITHIEL DE SOLA POOL

UNIVERSITY OF ILLINOIS PRESS

URBANA, 1959

A grant from the Ford Foundation has helped to defray the costs of publishing this book.

CONTENTS

In the winter of 1955 the Committee on Linguistics and Psychology of the Social Science Research Council called a work conference on content analysis. It took place at Allerton House of the University of Illinois in Monticello, Illinois. Those present at the conference included the members of the committee, a number of persons currently engaged in using content analysis as a research procedure, and a few invited guests. The proceedings of the conference were tape recorded.

At the end of the conference, the consensus of the participants was that enough of importance had transpired to justify the publication of the main statements. Several of the invitees had prepared papers for discussion at the conference; these and some of the floor discussion seemed to be of wide potential interest to social scientists in various fields.

We were particularly struck by the fact that each of us, working on our own studies in content analysis, had arrived at approaches to it which were quite different from those described in the existing literature, yet quite close to each other's. In a number of important respects we seemed each to have made the same departures from the past traditions of the field, and seemed each to be groping for new solutions to common problems. That fact in itself called for some sort of publication, for if our common experience was a guide, others starting out to use content analysis would undoubtedly cover the same ground over again. The field seemed to have moved beyond the existing codifications, and to call for a new statement of problems and of useful approaches to them.

Bernard Berelson's *Content Analysis,* published in 1952, has been the standard codification of the field. When one reads through to the conclusion of that book, one cannot help but be struck by a note of dubiousness about the entire enterprise of content analysis research. The tone of the last two sentences illustrates the doubts which Berelson came to have after reviewing the area of his professional commitment at the time: "Content analysis, as a method, has no magical qualities — you rarely get out of it more than you

1

put in, and sometimes you get less. In the last analysis, there is no substitute for good ideas."

The disillusionment expressed in that cautious and sound conclusion is not unique. If one listed the persons who were publishing in the field of content analysis in the decade of the 1940's (Lasswell, Leites, Berelson, Lerner, Janis, Pool, etc.), one would have difficulty in finding one of them still engaged in that kind of research. One could easily find among them persons who had quite consciously rejected the field as an unprofitable enterprise, while others, though retaining their faith in the ultimate value of the method, had turned for the present to greener pastures.

It was, therefore, somewhat of a discovery for a group of scholars assembled in the mid-1950's, when content analysis seemed to be in a decline, to find that each one was not alone in the research which he was doing, and that other scholars also had seen unexplored potentials in content analysis if certain new tacks were taken to meet the unsolved problems of the previous decade. The conferees, each starting from different directions and generally unaware of each other's work, did not of course see eye to eye on all issues. The discussions were vigorous. Some of the participants were explicitly critical of what they thought content analysis had been, others hopeful, others, having approached the field from novel directions, somewhat unaware of their predecessors. Issues remained at the end of the conference as well as at the beginning. But the striking fact was the degree of convergence.

It is not for this introduction to attempt to state what the convergences of viewpoint were. That will come out in the rest of the book and in the concluding chapter. Suffice it here to note that they centered above all on two points: (1) a sophisticated concern with the problems of inference from verbal material to its antecedent conditions, and (2) a focus on counting internal contingencies between symbols instead of the simple frequencies of symbols. Both these points arose out of the concern of the analysts to make their elaborate quantitative method produce something beyond what could be produced without its paraphernalia — to produce something that would go beyond the reaffirmation of the obvious.

The concern of the participants with problems of inference led to extensive discussion of a set of problems for which the conferees developed their own jargon. The reader will note, in most of the chapters to follow, comments upon "instrumental" and "representational" communications, models, or approaches. Alexander

George's and George Mahl's chapters are both in part critiques of the so-called "representational model" and defenses of the "instrumental." On the other hand, Charles Osgood's chapter boldly styles itself an instance of the "representational" model. This editor's summary chapter in turn discusses the issue, though with a view to minimizing the distinction to some extent, while not minimizing the problem. Clearly, the reader needs in advance some indication of what was meant by the words "representational" and "instrumental." In a rough way we may say that "representational" means that the important point about the communication is what is revealed by the content of the lexical items present in it; that is, something in the words of the message may have indicatorial validity regardless of circumstances, and it is at the message that the analyst looks. "Instrumental" in a rough way signifies that the important point is not what the message says on the face of it but what it conveys, given its context and circumstances. These rough definitions clearly raise more questions than they answer. For example, the reader may well ask "important point" for whom, for the author of the statement analyzed or for the content analyst? This and a number of other questions remain deliberately vague until the final chapter, for, as will become clear below, there were differences in what the participants meant. Some of the important issues concerning the relationship of communications contents to the motives and intentions of the communicator are clarified as each author attempts to bring out various aspects of the problem.

Osgood, for example, uses representation to refer to the fact that the lexical choices an author makes arise from associational connections in the author's thought processes. In this sense clearly what an author says in some way represents his thought processes. As Osgood put it:

The reader will probably experience some confusion in [my] chapter and the next between two uses of the term "representational." . . . In [my chapter] . . . the representational mediation process . . . refers to the meaningful state that occurs in speaker or hearer when encoding or decoding a sign. . . . In a second sense, as contrasted with "instrumental," the term "representational" seems to refer to the face validity of verbal assertions as a basis for inferring motivational states or purposes of the speaker. The representational model [in that sense] accepts . . . that when a patient . . . asserts "I love my father" this is his actual evaluation, that when he gives behavioral and verbal expressions of fear he is afraid, and so on. This is obviously not justified in many cases — people do lie on occasion.

These problems are not trivial ones. One cannot always assume that what an author says is what he means, yet if we can decipher his "real" meaning (which he has tried to hide) by looking only at the text, then somehow he has "said" what he meant after all. This leaves the indicators which we have used to decode his meaning to be determined. Furthermore, the author's instrumental choices in what he says are clearly limited, for he must remain comprehensible to other users of the language. Finally, he is not capable of manipulating all aspects of what he does. Some of his "instrumental" choices are made unconsciously. Do they not then in some sense "represent" him, and if so, what does the distinction mean? Clearly, the issues are important to the intelligent analysis of language.

These are far from the only issues which the following papers discuss. We single out this problem for discussion in the introduction because the reader needs some prior clarification of the terminology we developed. The papers, however, deal with a variety of topics.

These papers were originally written for the conference, after which each author took his original paper and revised it with the transcript of the conference proceedings in front of him. Thus, many of the insights and remarks which came out in the conference discussions have been incorporated into the papers. Also incorporated into them are results, insights, and information dating from the period since the conference; we have not attempted to make the present volume a static transcript. The final chapter draws from both the papers and the transcript to formulate the new problems which seem to be emerging in content analysis, and to identify the available new insights on how to tackle them. The concluding chapter is thus a summary of the common threads in the conference.

Since the Allerton House meeting a number of the authors have published the studies on which they were then working. Some of the material in this volume has thus already appeared in other places. In each case, however, the publication has been addressed to a specialized audience concerned with the subject matter to which the content analysis was being applied. These publications are not readily available to persons in other fields interested in the method as such. The range of subject matter to which content analysis can contribute is indicated by the table of contents of this volume, touching as it does on history, politics, psychology, psychotherapy, linguistics, literature, and folklore. No one reads across all these fields. It therefore seems worthwhile to bring out the present volume complete in its originally proposed form, even though it includes some materials already published.

In general the structure of the chapters to follow is a combination of theoretical treatment with a report of research results, often in that order. Alexander George rests his comparison of qualitative and quantitative methods upon his study of German wartime propaganda and American intelligence. Charles Osgood is concerned with content analysis research into the basic psychological mechanisms of thought and language, but illustrates his points by reference to a series of studies including those on associations of concepts in the Ford Hour speeches of W. J. Cameron, in psychotherapeutic interviews, and in the Goebbels diary. He also illustrates Cloze and evaluative assertion analyses. George Mahl is concerned with the problem of devising stable indices of the emotional state of a communicator, and he illustrates this with a study of speech disturbances in psychotherapeutic interviews and their correlation with anxiety. Sol Saporta and Thomas Sebeok deal with the applications of the methods of linguistics to content analysis problems and refer specifically to some studies in the field of folklore. Robert Armstrong, who is also interested in folklore, uses his study of Suriname and Dakota stories to illustrate the problems of making content analysis units appropriate to the structure of the material analyzed. John Garraty, dealing with the uses of content analysis in history, surveys possible applications in a field in which relatively little has yet been done, but illustrates what might be done by the use of established methods.

The Allerton House conference was an interdisciplinary one, not in the sense that each person spoke for a discipline, but in the sense that it brought together people who had a common problem without reference to their disciplines. The initial stimulus to the conference came from the field of psycholinguistics. The progress of structural linguistics in recent years has made itself felt in a number of fields. The linguist starts out in most cases excluding problems of meaning from his ken. It is clear that he thereby leaves another area for exploration, that which *is* specifically concerned with the meanings communicated by texts. The psychologist, the propaganda analyst, the critic, all work this field and often with the tool of content analysis. But since they are working on verbal texts, it is also clear that what the linguist discovers about the formal properties of the code must in some ways be relevant to what they are doing. It was to bring these contiguous approaches together that the conference was called.

Of the present authors, Alexander George is a political scientist with the RAND Corporation, Charles Osgood, who was our host and chairman, is a psychologist at the University of Illinois, George Mahl is a psychologist at Yale, Sol Saporta and Thomas Sebeok are both linguists at Indiana University, Robert Armstrong is a folklorist with a background in literature and anthropology, John Garraty is a historian at Columbia University (then at Michigan State University), and the editor is a political scientist at M.I.T.

Also sitting in on this conference, and contributing to the discussion, were the following guests: John B. Carroll, Joseph B. Casagrande, James J. Jenkins, Henry Kahane, William Madow, Dallas W. Smythe, and Wilson L. Taylor. We wish to express our gratitude to the Social Science Research Council for its sponsorship of this conference, to John Gardner and the Carnegie Corporation for its support of the Committee on Linguistics and Psychology, and to the University of Illinois and the staff of Allerton House for providing a perfect setting for our discussions.

We wish to thank the following publishers for permission to reprint material from the indicated publications:

Alfred A. Knopf, for Chapter 6, substantially reprinted from John A. Garraty, *The Nature of Biography*, 1957.

Rowe Peterson, for Chapter 1, substantially reprinted from Alexander L. George, *Propaganda Analysis: A Study of the Inferences Made from Nazi Propaganda in World War II*, 1958.

1

ALEXANDER L. GEORGE
THE RAND CORPORATION

QUANTITATIVE AND QUALITATIVE
APPROACHES TO CONTENT ANALYSIS[1]

In some areas — for example, clinical psychiatry and propaganda analysis — the communication analyzed is often highly goal-oriented. The speaker is engaged, consciously or otherwise, in efforts to further his well-being. The investigator examines the communication for clues to the speaker's intention and other aspects of his state of mind. In brief, content analysis is employed as a diagnostic tool for making specific inferences about some aspect of the speaker's purposive behavior. Such inferences, often highly interpretative, are in the nature of causal imputations in the single case. A number of problems arise in efforts to employ the systematic quantitative variant of content analysis for this purpose. Qualitative analysis of a limited number of crucial communications may often yield better clues to the particular intentions of a particular speaker at one moment in time than more standardized quantitative methods.

Researchers have long debated the respective merits and uses of "quantitative" and "qualitative" approaches to content analysis. Yet in their technical and theoretical discussions they have given little attention generally to the qualitative approach. A standard

---

[1] This chapter is based on a study prepared by the author for the RAND Corporation. For elaboration of the points discussed here, see the author's *Propaganda Analysis: A Study of Inferences Made from Nazi Propaganda in World War II* (Evanston, Ill., 1959), and "Prediction of Political Action by Means of Propaganda Analysis," *Public Opinion Quarterly,* 20 (1956), 334-45. For useful comments on earlier drafts of material presented here, the author is indebted particularly to Hans Speier and to Irving L. Janis, Ithiel Pool, and Abraham Kaplan, as well as to participants in the S.S.R.C. work conference on content analysis.

treatise on content analysis by Lasswell, Leites, and associates,[2] for example, does not explicitly differentiate between the "quantitative" and "qualitative" approaches and discusses only the former.

Berelson,[3] on the other hand, identifies some of the main characteristics of the qualitative approach. But his discussion is insufficiently elaborated and leaves somewhat uncertain the matter of whether there *is* a qualitative method which differs fundamentally from the quantitative approach.

As a matter of fact, most writers on content analysis have made quantification a component of their definition of content analysis. In effect, therefore, they exclude the qualitative approach as being something other than content analysis.[4]

Quantitative content analysis is, in the first instance, a statistical technique for obtaining descriptive data on content variables. Its value in this respect is that it offers the possibility of obtaining more precise, objective, and reliable observations about the frequency with which given content characteristics occur either singly or in conjunction with one another. In other words, the quantitative approach substitutes controlled observation and systematic counting for impressionistic ways of observing frequencies of occurrence.[5]

The term "qualitative," on the other hand, has been used to refer to a number of different aspects of research procedure. These different uses of the term are sometimes blurred in discussions of the respective merits of quantitative and qualitative approaches to content analysis. It is desirable at the outset, therefore, to distinguish between them. The term "qualitative" has been used at various times to designate the following:

1. The preliminary reading of communications materials for purposes of hypothesis formation and the discovery of new relationships   as against   systematic content analysis for purposes of testing hypotheses.

----

[2] H. D. Lasswell, N. Leites, and associates, *Language of Politics; Studies in Quantitative Semantics* (New York, 1949).

[3] B. Berelson, *Content Analysis in Communication Research* (Glencoe, Ill., 1952), pp. 114-34.

[4] Authors who favor or have employed the qualitative approach are listed in Berelson, *Content Analysis,* Chap. 3. Various definitions of quantitative content analysis are considered by the same author (pp. 14-18).

[5] For a brief exposition of quantitative content analysis and some of its uses in the study of political communication, see H. D. Lasswell, D. Lerner, and I. de Sola Pool, *The Comparative Study of Symbols* (Hoover Institute Studies; Ser. C: Symbols, No. 1 [Stanford, Calif., 1952]). These authors' sober assessment of the difficulty of meeting various prerequisites of statistical content analysis is particularly useful.

2. An impressionistic procedure for making observations about content characteristics   as against   a systematic procedure for obtaining precise, objective, and reliable data.

3. Dichotomous attributes (i.e., attributes which can be predicated only as belonging or not belonging to an object)   as against   attributes which permit exact measurement (i.e., the true quantitative variable) or rank ordering (i.e., the serial).[6]

4. A "flexible" procedure for making content-descriptive observations, or "coding" judgments[7]   as against   a "rigid" procedure for doing the same.

FREQUENCY AND NONFREQUENCY CONTENT INDICATORS

While these four distinctions are important in themselves, they do not serve to differentiate between the two approaches to the analysis of communication which we shall compare in this chapter. We therefore introduce a somewhat different distinction which focuses on the aspects of the communication content from which the analyst draws inferences regarding noncontent variables.

1. Quantitative content analysis as we here define it is concerned with the *frequency* of occurrence of given content characteristics; that is, the investigator works with the frequency of occurrence of certain content characteristics.

2. Inferences from content to noncontent variables, however, need not always be based on the frequency values of content features. The content term in an inferential hypothesis or statement of relationship may consist of the mere *presence* or *absence* of a

----

[6] For a detailed discussion, see P. F. Lazarsfeld and A. H. Barton, "Qualitative Measurement in the Social Sciences: Classification, Typologies, and Indices," in D. Lerner and H. D. Lasswell, eds., *The Policy Sciences: Recent Developments in Scope and Method* (Stanford, Calif., 1951), pp. 155-92. See also D. P. Cartwright, "Analysis of Qualitative Material," in L. Festinger and D. Katz, eds., *Research Methods in the Behavioral Sciences* (New York, 1953), pp. 421-70.

[7] These are polar points of a continuum. An extremely "flexible" procedure does not specify the actual words or word clusters which are to be regarded as individual occurrences of the type of content with which one is concerned. Thus, coders are permitted considerable latitude in deciding when an instance of the content category occurs in the communication being analyzed. At the other extreme, a "rigid" procedure attempts to specify explicitly and completely the bases on which coding decisions are to be made, leaving the individual coder no room for the exercise of independent judgment. In practice, of course, there are various intermediate degrees of flexibility and rigidity in coding procedures.

given content characteristic or a content syndrome within a designated body of communication. It is the latter type of communication analysis, which makes use of "nonfrequency" content indicators for purposes of inference, that is regarded here as the nonquantitative or nonstatistical variant of content analysis.

The distinction we have introduced concerns the type of content indicator utilized for purposes of inference. Given the several other referents of the terms "quantitative" and "qualitative," it is desirable to introduce a new set of terms. We employ the term "nonfrequency" to describe the type of nonquantitative, nonstatistical content analysis which uses the presence or absence of a certain content characteristic or syndrome as a content indicator in an inferential hypothesis. In contrast, a "frequency" content indicator is one in which the number of times one or more content characteristics occur is regarded as relevant for purposes of inference.

The distinction between frequency and nonfrequency analysis, it should be noted, is independent of the aforementioned four dimensions to which the terms quantitative and qualitative are sometimes applied. Thus, both in frequency and nonfrequency analysis a distinction can be drawn between the hypothesis-formation and hypothesis-testing phases of research, between impressionistic and systematic types of content description, between flexible and rigid procedures for making content-descriptive judgments.

Nor is the familiar distinction in the theory of measurement between dichotomous, serial, and quantitative *attributes* equivalent to the distinction advanced here. Thus, it is incorrect to assume that statistical or quantitative content analysis is concerned solely with language attributes capable of strict measurement whereas nonfrequency analysis deals exclusively with dichotomous attributes. The point to be emphasized here is that frequency as well as nonfrequency analysis may be concerned with dichotomous attributes, that is, attributes which can be predicated only as belonging or not belonging to an object. This is the case, for example, in the simple word-count type of content analysis in which it is merely a question of deciding whether a certain word or symbol ("democracy," "Germany," "Stalin") does or does not appear in each sentence, paragraph or article, depending upon which of these the investigator has selected as his coding unit.

It is not the case, therefore, that only nonfrequency analysis is concerned with dichotomous or qualitative attributes. Rather, the difference between the two approaches is that frequency analysis, even when it deals with dichotomous attributes, always singles out frequency distributions as a basis for making inferences.[8] In contrast, the nonfrequency approach utilizes the mere occurrence or nonoccurrence of attributes (as against their frequency distributions) for purposes of inference. Thus, for example, on the basis of a quantitative study which shows a sharp decline in number of references to Stalin in *Pravda,* the frequency analyst might infer that the successors to Stalin are attempting to downgrade the former dictator or are trying to dissociate themselves from him. On the other hand, the nonfrequency analyst might make a similar inference from the fact that in a public speech one of Stalin's successors pointedly failed to mention him when discussing a particular subject (e.g., credit for the Soviet victory in World War II) where mention of Stalin would formerly have been obligatory. In one case, it is the frequency distribution of attention to "Stalin" over a period of time on which the inference rests. In the other, it is the mere occurrence or nonoccurrence of the word "Stalin" on a particular occasion which serves as a basis for the inference. Yet in both of these examples the investigator deals with a dichotomous attribute, since he is concerned with the presence or absence of "Stalin" in a given unit of communication, though in one case he makes this determination for a relatively large number of coding units and in the other case for only a single coding unit.

Furthermore, the use of frequency and nonfrequency methods is not determined by the fact of multiple or single occurrence of the content feature in question within the communication under examination. The fact that a content feature does occur more than once within a communication does not oblige the investigator to count its frequency. The important fact about that content feature for his inference may be merely that it occurs at all within a prescribed communication.

It should be noted, finally, that the nonfrequency approach to content analysis is really an older and more conventional way of interpreting communication and drawing inferences from it than is the quantitative approach. The resemblance of the nonfrequency approach to traditional methods of textual analysis, moreover, will

---

[8] An explicit reminder of this is given by the investigators of the RADIR Project: "It is useful in reaching conclusions to remain aware that such totals are a summation of the frequency distribution of qualitative variates even though they may look like quantitative variables" (Lasswell, Lerner, and Pool, *Comparative Study of Symbols,* p. 38).

become obvious when we consider some of the characteristics of this approach.

SOME EXAMPLES OF NONFREQUENCY CONTENT ANALYSIS

Several examples will illustrate the nature of the nonfrequency approach and some of the disadvantages of relying exclusively upon frequency or quantitative content analysis. The examples are drawn from wartime propaganda analyses of German communications made by personnel of the Analysis Division, Foreign Broadcast Intelligence Service, Federal Communications Commission.

1. Following the German disaster at Stalingrad, domestic morale sank in Germany, and rumblings of discontent with the Nazi regime were heard. In this crisis German leaders addressed the nation. Goebbels, in one of his speeches, used the word "counter-terror." From the context in which this word was used, and taking into account the situation itself, the F.C.C. analyst inferred that Goebbels had in mind pogroms against the Jews. The inference rested upon the mere presence of the word "counterterror" in a particular context. The word may or may not have appeared several more times in Goebbels' speech or in other propaganda materials at the time; the F.C.C. analyst was interested only in the presence of the word in a particular linguistic and situational context.[9]

2. In another instance the F.C.C. analyst inferred that the Nazi Propaganda Ministry was attempting to discourage the German public, albeit indirectly, from expecting a resurgence of the U-boats. This inference was also based in part upon a nonfrequency content indicator. Hans Fritzsche, leading radio commentator, had asserted the following in discussing a recent success achieved by German U-boats: " . . . we are not so naive as to indulge in speculation about the future on the basis of the fact of this victory. . . ." In focusing upon this statement, the F.C.C. analyst was not concerned with the frequency of the theme in Fritzsche's talk or in other German propaganda accounts of the same U-boat "victory," or with the question of whether it now appeared more or less frequently than in earlier propaganda on the U-boats. For his purpose it sufficed that the content theme was present even once in the context of Fritzsche's remarks about the latest German U-boat victory.

----

[9] Some indirect support for the correctness of the inference is available in an entry which Goebbels made in his diary shortly after the speech mentioned (see L. Lochner, ed., *The Goebbels Diaries* [Garden City, N.Y., 1948], pp. 177, 261-62, 290).

It is interesting to speculate on what would have happened had a frequency (quantitative) approach been employed in this case. In the first place, it is problematic whether a content category could have been set up that would have precisely caught the meaning of this one phrase in Fritzsche's talk. Secondly, since the phrase (or its equivalent) appeared at best only a very few times in German propaganda at the time, the propaganda analyst, in looking over the quantitative results, might well have dismissed it as a "minor theme" or lumped it together with other items in a "miscellaneous" or "other" category. In other words, if this single phrase from Fritzsche's talk had been subsumed under a frequency indicator, it might well have lost its inferential significance.

3. The third example is quite similar. Mussolini had set up a Republican-Fascist government following his "liberation" by German parachutists. German propaganda gave quite a play to these events and celebrated Mussolini's re-establishment of a pro-Axis Italian government. In looking over this propaganda, the F.C.C. analyst noted that, after a few days, a minor theme of some sobriety was introduced into the otherwise enthusiastic publicity on Mussolini and his new government. Only a few Nazi papers carried the new message and, where it did appear, it was rather well hidden. For example, in the *Volkischer Beobachter*, September 29, 1943, the following sentence appeared: " . . . the battle is not yet won by the changes proclaimed by Mussolini, and the structural changes undertaken by him must not be regarded as a guarantee of future greatness."

The significance of this new theme to the F.C.C. analyst lay in the fact that it appeared at all. In other words, he made use of it as a nonfrequency content indicator. Had this new theme been subsumed under a general frequency-type indicator in a quantitative study, it would probably have passed unnoticed. But when singled out as a nonfrequency indicator, the theme, although repeated only a few times in the total Nazi propaganda on Mussolini, provided the basis for an important inference. The F.C.C. analyst inferred, from the appearance of the theme, that the Propaganda Ministry had decided to moderate the public's expectations regarding a resurgence of Italian fascism. Continuing the chain of inference, the F.C.C. analyst then reasoned that such a propaganda goal must have been adopted as the result of a new, more sober estimate by Nazi leaders of the potential of Mussolini's new government. This inference was subsequently verified on the basis of material appearing in *The Goebbels Diaries*.[10]

SOME DIFFICULTIES IN APPLYING QUANTITATIVE CONTENT ANALYSIS FOR THE STUDY OF INSTRUMENTAL ASPECTS OF COMMUNICATION

We noted at the beginning of this chapter that in such fields as clinical psychiatry and propaganda analysis, content analysis is often used as a diagnostic tool for making causal interpretations about a single goal-oriented communication, and we have surveyed some examples of that use of content analysis. In order to identify and explore some of the special problems which arise in this type of content analysis we shall further examine the case of propaganda analysis. Other communication analyses which operate within the framework of an instrumental model may encounter similar problems. We will discuss the following: (1) the problem of coding irrelevant content, (2) the problem of changes in the speaker's strategy, (3) the problem of an expanding universe of relevant communication, and (4) the problem of structural characteristics of instrumental communication.

These problems arise in part from the characteristics of propaganda communication, in part as a result of the investigator's interest in making specific inferences about some aspect of the communicator's purposive behavior. In any case, the result is that a considerable portion of the research effort must be given to discovering new hypotheses or refining old ones; systematic quantitative analysis for purposes of testing inferential hypotheses is often difficult, infeasible, or unnecessary; and, finally, nonquantitative (nonfrequency) content indicators are often more appropriate and productive than quantitative (frequency) indicators.

THE PROBLEM OF CODING IRRELEVANT CONTENT

A variety of specific goals and strategies are usually pursued in propaganda communications. The propaganda analyst, however, may be interested in making inferences only about one or a few

---

[10] In his diary entry of September 23, 1943, Goebbels described the change in Hitler's opinion of Mussolini after his first contacts with him following the rescue. Noting that Hitler was thoroughly disillusioned with Mussolini and that intelligence reports on the Italian response to the new Fascist government were largely negative, Goebbels drew the conclusion that "we must begin slowly to write off the Duce politically" (*Goebbels Diaries*, pp. 469-71, 479, 481).

matters of policy interest. Accordingly, he must exercise care in considering which passages in the stream of communication are *relevant* to each of the goals or strategies of the communicator.

The difficulty of arriving at such judgments of relevance and the considerable sensitivity and discrimination which are required for this purpose are often reasons for not undertaking elaborate quantitative "fishing expeditions" in any sizable body of propaganda communications. For the advantage of having a convenient and orderly summary of content is outweighed for the propaganda analyst by a risk implicit in this procedure. This is the danger that content features of the original communication relevant to *different* inferential problems might be recorded as instances of the *same* content category. Not all the individual items tabulated under any given content category in such a "fishing expedition" may be relevant to the specific inference which the analyst would like to make about the speaker's state of mind.

We are referring here obliquely to one of the important requirements of statistical content analysis, namely, that it be "systematic" in the sense that "*all* of the relevant content . . . be analyzed in terms of *all* of the relevant categories, for the problem at hand."[11]

But the obverse of this requirement — that none of the *irrelevant* content be analyzed — is equally important and is a weighty reason for not undertaking elaborate quantitative content analyses of the "fishing expedition" variety. The task of determining the relevant content (or sample) that must be analyzed for a given inferential problem is often more difficult than it appears to be at first thought. If too large a body of communication is coded, even under relevant content categories, the danger arises that more data will be obtained than is pertinent to the specific inferential problem.

In some cases the inclusion of irrelevant content in the analysis may be no more than a waste of manpower. But in other cases it may rule out the possibility of making a useful inference or lead to wholly mistaken inferences. The problem may become particularly acute when the investigator engaged in a "fishing expedition" of this sort deliberately selects broad content categories in order to ensure large enough frequencies for purposes of subsequent statistical analysis.[12]

----

[11] Berelson, *Content Analysis*, p. 17. As he notes, quantitative content analysts stress this requirement as a safeguard against "partial or biased analyses in which only those elements in the content are selected which fit the analyst's thesis."

[12] On this point see also p. 24 of the present work.

The danger of coding irrelevant content is minimized when research is designed to test clear-cut hypotheses. For hypotheses usually indicate or imply the realm of relevant content or the appropriate sample to be coded.

However, precise hypothesis formation — the assertion of a relationship between a content indicator and one or more communicator variables — is often difficult in propaganda analysis. This difficulty reflects the rudimentary state of the scientific study of communication. The lack of good hypotheses about relationships between content variables and communicator variables makes it difficult for the propaganda analyst to circumscribe the terms and categories for specific investigations.

This difficulty, of course, is by no means confined to propaganda analysis or to studies working within the framework of other instrumental models. The same difficulty is present in many other applications of the content analysis technique. Thus, for example, in a sober assessment of the results of their large-scale study of symbols as indices of political values, attitudes, and ideological dispositions, the RADIR Project investigators emphasized that the scientific study of political communication was hampered by the absence of relevant theory and hypotheses:

. . . there is as yet no good theory of symbolic communication by which to predict how given values, attitudes, or ideologies will be expressed in manifest symbols. The extant theories tend to deal with values, attitudes, and ideologies as the ultimate units, not with the symbolic atoms of which they are composed. There is almost no theory of language which predicts the specific words one will emit in the course of expressing the contents of his thoughts. Theories in philosophy or in the sociology of knowledge sometimes enable us to predict ideas that will be expressed by persons with certain other ideas or social characteristics. But little thought has been given to predicting the specific words in which these ideas will be cloaked. The content analyst, therefore, does not know what to expect.[13]

Essentially the same deficiency, noted by investigators working in other areas of communication analysis as well, was alluded to in various contexts during the work conference. For example, on one occasion George Mahl deplored the lack of a "theory of the dynamics of content categories selected as indicators." A similar point is implied by two investigators, Auld and Murray, in a recent review of the growing list of content analysis studies of psychotherapy: "The problem of how the verbal behavior of the client,

----

[13] Lasswell, Lerner, and Pool, *Comparative Study of Symbols,* p. 49. See also the same authors' discussion of models of symbolic behavior and the problems of "index ambiguity" and "index instability" (pp. 64 ff., 75-78).

which is taken note of in content analysis, is related to his non-verbal behavior, is a difficulty not only for the D.R.Q. [Dollard and Mowrer Discomfort-Relief Quotient] but also for every other system of content analysis."[14]

In summary, there are relatively few theories or general hypotheses about symbolic behavior available for testing by means of rigorous quantitative content analysis. As a result, some investigators employ quantitative content analysis for purposes of a "fishing expedition"; large quantities of content data are collected without guidance of clear-cut hypotheses in the hope of discovering, at the end of the study, new relationships and new hypotheses. Such studies tend to be time consuming, wasteful, and generally unproductive. Disappointing results with "fishing expeditions" are particularly likely when large quantities of material are processed and the chief investigator has to employ clerical personnel to do the coding. As a result, there is insufficient opportunity to refine categories and it is usually not possible to recode the bulky material as many times as necessary in order to produce content data appropriate for testing interesting hypotheses.

THE PROBLEM OF CHANGES IN THE SPEAKER'S STRATEGY

Due to the circumstances which have been described, the "qualitative" phase of hypothesis formation may properly receive unusual emphasis in propaganda analysis. Similar implications for content analysis procedure derive from the fact that the propagandist's strategy on any single subject may change abruptly at any time. In attempting inferences about the speaker's state of mind on that subject matter, therefore, the propaganda analyst cannot easily draw up a set of content categories which will be appropriate for all possible shifts in the communication strategy of the speaker. The analyst will hesitate to commit himself to systematic quantitative description because he fears that the speaker's strategy may change while the count is being made. If such a change is unnoticed by the analyst, the value of the results of the quantitative tabulation for purposes of inference may be lost. For then such content data might well be ambiguous or inappropriate for purposes of inference.

In propaganda analysis the instrumental use to which communication is put by the speaker is regarded as a highly unstable vari-

---

[14] F. Auld, Jr., and E. J. Murray, "Content-Analysis Studies of Psychotherapy," *Psychological Bulletin*, 52 (1955), 380.

able which intervenes between various other antecedent conditions of communication (e.g., speaker's attitude and state of mind, the conditions and calculations which have affected choice of action) and the content variable itself. In this respect, propaganda analysis has much in common with the analysis of psychotherapy protocols. Both the propaganda analyst and the psychotherapist are sensitive to the possibility that the communication intention and strategy of the speaker can change frequently during the course of an effort to make a systematic count of the content features of what he says. Because of this, except when there is reason to believe that the content features selected as indicators are insensitive to variations in the speaker's strategy, frequency counts may be inappropriate as a means of inferring the speaker's attitudes, his state of mind, and the calculations and conditions which have influenced his choice of a communication strategy or goal.

In propaganda analysis, typically, the investigator is interested in inferring one or more of the following antecedent conditions of the propagandist's communication: his propaganda goals and techniques; the estimates, expectations, and policy intentions of the leadership group for whom the propagandist is speaking which have influenced the adoption of a particular propaganda strategy; the situational factors or changes which have influenced the leadership's estimates, expectations, and policy intentions and/or the propagandist's choice of communication goals and techniques.

The interrelationship between the types of antecedent conditions which the propaganda analyst is interested in inferring may be depicted schematically, in simplified form, as follows:

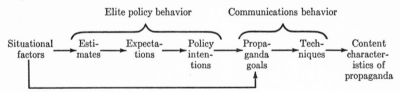

The investigator interested in inferring elite estimates, expectations, policy intentions and/or situational factors which lay behind the adoption of a particular propaganda goal or strategy may employ either of two rather different methods of inference. Thus, he can attempt to find content indicators which directly reflect the component of elite behavior or the situational factor in which he is interested, or he can attempt first to infer the speaker's propaganda goal and then proceed step by step to account for the selection of that goal in terms of elite estimates, expectations, policy intentions and/or situational factors.

The first of these two methods of inference bypasses consideration of the speaker's propaganda strategy. The inferences made with this *direct method* are one-step inferences, as follows:

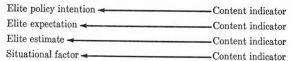

In contrast, the *indirect method* is comprised of an inferential chain of two or more steps, the first of which is always an inference about the speaker's goal or strategy. It may be depicted, in somewhat simplified form, as follows:

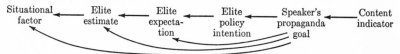

The direct method, which bypasses propaganda strategy, can be successfully employed only if content features can be found which occur *regularly* and *only* when a certain type of elite policy intention, expectation, estimate, or situational factor occurs. The types of regularities or generalizations which the direct method requires as a basis for inferences, therefore, are correlations of a noncausal character. It is important to recognize that the content terms in such correlations must be insensitive to possible variations in propaganda strategy. This is necessary because propaganda strategy is an intervening and relatively unstable variable between elite policy behavior and propaganda content. The direct method is on firm ground only when it employs as content indicators features of the communication over which the propagandist does not exercise control or of whose information-giving value regarding elite policy behavior he remains unaware. Such content features are likely to be symptomatic features of a propagandist's behavior rather than part of his communication intention.[15]

The indirect method, on the other hand, attempts to utilize for purposes of inference the fact that the behavior of the propagandist in selecting communications goals and strategies constitutes an

----

[15] On the difference between interpretation of "intent" and interpretation of "symptoms" in the analysis of communication, see P. Kecskemeti, *Meaning, Communication, and Value* (Chicago, 1952), pp. 60-61.

intervening set of events between elite policy behavior and the dependent variable (content of propaganda). Therefore, the investigator who employs the indirect method attempts to identify content features in the propaganda which are sensitive to and dependent upon the speaker's strategy.

The distinction between content features which are sensitive and insensitive to variations in the speaker's strategy is useful not only in propaganda analysis, but whenever content analysis is used on instrumentally manipulated material. In such cases, obtaining good indices of attitude, value, etc., would seem to require either the avoidance of content features which are likely to be sensitive in the first instance to variations in the speaker's communication strategy or a sophisticated awareness of that strategy.

THE PROBLEM OF AN EXPANDING UNIVERSE OF RELEVANT COMMUNICATION

Another characteristic of propaganda which has procedural implications is the fact that the universe of relevant communication may be expanding while the propaganda analyst is attempting to draw inferences from it. This is the case, of course, when propaganda analysis is employed as a tool for contemporary political analysis. (It is less often the case when propaganda analysis is employed for purposes of strictly historical research.)

In other words, the propaganda analyst often finds himself trying to keep up with the flow of communication which has some relevance to his problem. His position is that of an investigator who has to formulate alternative inferential hypotheses and to select appropriate content categories before he has seen all the communication that may have to be analyzed. Accordingly, as new statements on the topic are made by the source, the propaganda analyst frequently has to revise the set of alternative hypotheses under consideration and his content categories. And, because he must meet "deadlines," the propaganda analyst frequently states inferences which are necessarily in the nature of interim reports, based upon arbitrary and incomplete segments of relevant data.

These circumstances frequently rule out use of the systematic variant of quantitative content description. A familiar prerequisite of quantitative content analysis is that the investigator know what he is looking for before beginning to count. The propaganda analyst cannot very well satisfy this requirement when he must continually reconsider his hypotheses and categories as new statements from the source become available. If a quantitative description of currently available communication is made, the propaganda analyst cannot be confident that the ordered data on content variables which it provides will still be adequate for purposes of inference when new statements on the topic are received from the source. For the most recent communication may throw new light on the inferential problem and, on the basis of these new insights, the propaganda analyst may have to reread and reinterpret the earlier propaganda communications in their original form, before they were transformed into ordered quantitative data.

A similar problem arises, we may note, when information about *noncontent* events bearing upon the inferential problem comes to the attention of the propaganda analyst *after* he has received and analyzed the relevant propaganda communication. Such noncontent events may permit the analyst retrospectively to formulate more discriminating hypotheses about the inferential significance of the propaganda. And, for this purpose, it may be necessary for him to reread and reappraise the propaganda communication in its original form, in the light of the new information available on relevant noncontent events.

The circumstances mentioned above, of course, do not rule out systematic quantitative content analysis in principle. A method of successive codings is often employed in communication analysis. The results of a first coding of the material are examined to see what may have been overlooked; a new code and additional coding rules may be developed to take account of subtleties that were missed, and the material is coded again. The process may be repeated several times to ensure a proper testing of the initial hypothesis or of the more refined hypotheses subsequently formulated. Sophisticated quantitative analysts recognize that even in carefully planned studies the initial processing of the raw material is likely to yield data inadequate in essential respects. The method of successive codings, which is essential to studies that begin as "fishing expeditions," is therefore often necessary also in hypothesis-oriented research.

The necessity to return to the original materials in order to read and reread them, therefore, is itself by no means a unique feature of the qualitative variant of propaganda analysis. Nor is the method of successive codings unknown in propaganda analysis which utilizes the quantitative approach. Rather, it is the aforementioned concern to code only the relevant content and the necessity to cope with an expanding universe of relevant communication which often makes the propaganda analyst reluctant to undertake time-consuming quantitative descriptions. These same considerations partly account for his willingness in many cases to settle for a relatively impressionistic estimate of the frequencies of relevant content features.

THE PROBLEM OF STRUCTURAL CHARACTERISTICS
OF INSTRUMENTAL COMMUNICATION

Propaganda analysis procedures are much influenced, finally, by the necessity to take into account the structure of individual propaganda communications. Different structural types of communication are encountered in the flow of propaganda available for analysis. An article by Goebbels appearing in *Das Reich*, for example, was structurally different from a speech by Hitler; and both, certainly, were structurally different from German radio news broadcasts.

The task confronting the propaganda analyst in this respect, however, is not merely that of avoiding clumsy content comparisons between propaganda communications which are structurally dissimilar. The problem of taking into account structural characteristics is present also in analyzing any single communication (speech, article, news item, editorial, commentary, etc.). The propaganda intention of an individual communication (and its effect as well) often depends not merely on the explicit content of the individual statements or propositions therein contained but also upon the structural interrelationship of these statements within that communication. It is well known that effective persuasion may make use of a more or less subtle manipulation of order, context, and sequence.[16]

Thus, what may be called the "whole-part" problem in content analysis[17] has several important procedural implications. It may affect choice of counting units and categories as well as the decision on the type of content indicator (frequency or nonfrequency) to be employed.

Awareness of the "whole-part" problem often leads the propa-

----

[16] In the funeral oration in Shakespeare's *Julius Caesar,* Mark Anthony achieves his purpose by starting with the predispositions of his audience and praise for Caesar's opponents, gradually proceeding to the new position to which he wishes to move the audience.

[17] J. Goldstein ("Content Analysis: A Propaganda and Opinion Study" [Ph.D. thesis, New School for Social Research, New York, 1942], pp. 38-41) presents a useful discussion of this problem.

ganda analyst to be critical of an important implicit assumption of statistical content analyses, namely, that each individual item counted as falling under a designated content category is of equal significance for purposes of inference.[18] Similarly, the propaganda analyst is often critical of the assumption that the inferential significance of explicit propositions, themes, or statements is dependent upon the precise frequency of their occurrence. Rather, he may find explicit propositions of significance for purposes of ascertaining the strategy of the propagandist because they occur at all or because they occur in a certain relationship to each other within the communication.

In this respect, the implications of structure for the propaganda analyst's procedure appear to be analogous to the situation in linguistics. Thus, as Floyd G. Lounsbury noted:

In the procedure of contemporary structural linguistic analysis, frequency of occurrence (of a given unit in a given context, or of a given contrast) is not a relevant criterion. Only the *possibility* of occurrence — as represented by some one instance or by many instances of it — is relevant. The answers which are sought from data are of a simple yes-or-no type rather than of a how-much type. In statistical analysis on the other hand, frequencies are the immediate goal of analysis, e.g., the probability of occurrence. Statistical procedure usually ignores, however, a matter which is basic to linguistics — the distinguishing of levels of structure. . . .[19]

This does not mean that frequency counts are useless for purposes of propaganda analysis. Frequency tabulation of words, clichés, stereotypes, and slogans may provide an indication of propaganda emphasis and techniques as well as of intentions. But such tabulations in themselves give no clue to the meaning of the content in question. They are of value, therefore, only when the investigator has prior or independent knowledge of their meaning, role, and significance in the system of language habits under study.[20]

In seeking to make inferences, the propaganda analyst of course need not, and does not, limit his attention to the frequency with which certain words, clichés, stereotypes, slogans, etc., are employed. He is also interested in the explicit propositional content of propaganda communications. And the significance of explicit proposi-

---

[18] For an explicit statement of this important (but often ignored) assumption of quantitative content analysis, see Berelson, *Content Analysis*, p. 20.

[19] C. E. Osgood and T. A. Sebeok, eds., "Psycholinguistics: A Survey of Theory and Research Problems," *Journal of Abnormal and Social Psychology,* 49, Supp. (1954).

[20] This point is explicitly discussed by Goldstein ("Content Analysis: A Propaganda and Opinion Study," pp. 26-27, 38-40, 150).

tions (statements, themes, assertions, etc.) for inferring a speaker's purpose, as we have already noted, is not necessarily dependent upon how often they are repeated by that speaker. Rather, it may rest on the fact that such statements do — or do not — occur at all, and on the structural and hierarchical interrelationship between them.

For the latter type of propaganda analysis, then, the usual type of frequency count associated with quantitative content analysis is quite inappropriate. The procedure employed in ascertaining the propositional content of a propaganda communication and in weighing the structural interrelationships of parts therein undoubtedly is often less systematic than in rigorous quantitative content analysis in which coding judgments are closely prescribed. But in principle the reliability of such content observations, too, is subject to investigation.

SOME CHARACTERISTICS AND SPECIAL PROBLEMS OF THE NONFREQUENCY APPROACH

The preceding discussion has already suggested some of the characteristics of nonfrequency analysis of instrumental communications. In this section we recapitulate these characteristics briefly and single out for more extended comment the special problems to which they give rise.

SELECTION OF CONTENT CATEGORIES: THE SEARCH FOR SPECIFIC DISCRIMINATING CATEGORIES

In some quantitative investigations the technical requirement of relatively large numbers for statistical analysis appears to exercise an important influence on the choice of content categories and on the size of the sample of raw material to be coded. Symbols and themes with low frequency of occurrence may be either ignored or grouped together under broader content categories.

The conscious selection of content categories and sample size with an eye to satisfying technical requirements of statistical analysis may be justified when the research objective is to make general inferences. But such a criterion is inappropriate when, as in propaganda analysis, the object is to make specific inferences about events at particular times and places. In the latter case valuable opportunities for making inferences are lost if the investigator ignores or minimizes the value of nonfrequency and low frequency indicators.

The investigator who is aware of the value of nonfrequency indicators tries, rather, to formulate ever more discriminating content categories. He deliberately attempts to "narrow down" the categories and to make them relatively more specific. The fact that this results in low frequencies, in a single occurrence, or in no occurrence at all of the content feature in question is not of concern to him since he expects to employ a nonfrequency indicator for purposes of inference. Thus in certain types of communication research, such as propaganda analysis, it is typical for the investigator to be concerned with establishing slight changes in propaganda line, minute and subtle differences of wording.

EMPHASIS ON HYPOTHESIS FORMATION AS AGAINST HYPOTHESIS TESTING

Perhaps more so than in most frequency analyses the investigator who employs the nonfrequency approach gives unusual attention and effort to the hypothesis-formation phase of research. There are a number of reasons for this emphasis to which we have already alluded: the search for more discriminating categories, the need to exclude irrelevant content, and, of course, the rudimentary state of knowledge and theory about the relationships between content and communicator variables.

RELATIVE EMPHASIS UPON VALIDITY AS AGAINST RELIABILITY OF SEMANTICAL CONTENT DESCRIPTION

The nonfrequency approach places more emphasis upon obtaining valid estimates of the speaker's intended meaning than do many versions of quantitative content analysis. Because he usually deals with relatively large frequencies, the quantitative investigator can work with somewhat lower validity requirements and can (and must) pay greater attention to reliability considerations. The inclusion of a small number of incorrect determinations of the speaker's intended meaning under a content category composed of large frequencies will probably not affect the final analysis greatly. In contrast, just because he works with low frequencies or single occurrences, the nonfrequency analyst cannot afford to risk making any invalid determinations of the speaker's intended meaning.

Given the crucial importance in nonfrequency analysis of validly estimating the one or few meanings which may be of inferential significance, the investigator concentrates upon making an intensive assessment of contextual factors upon which such meanings are likely to depend. This type of assessment, however, is particularly difficult to objectify, for it requires taking into account the situational and behavioral, as well as the linguistic, contexts of given words. Accordingly, the procedure for inferring the speaker's precise intended meanings cannot easily be made fully explicit. Investigators who attempt to infer intended meanings must usually settle for relatively flexible and interpretative procedures of coding content.

Each judgment of an intended meaning is a separate inference arrived at by taking into account not only dictionary meanings and rules of the language, but also all relevant aspects of the context: situational and behavioral as well as linguistic. The concern with inferring intended meaning in this manner does not distinguish the nonfrequency approach from all frequency analysis. But it does serve to differentiate it radically from one variant of the quantitative approach known as "manifest" content analysis.

"Manifest" content analysis is associated particularly with the work of Lasswell and some of his associates. In fact, their definition of statistical, or quantitative, content analysis usually includes the requirement that only the "manifest" content of communication be described, not the presumed intended meanings of the communicator.[21]

Of immediate relevance to our discussion is the fact that in "manifest" content analysis the investigator estimates the meanings of words by applying a set of external criteria as to the usual, customary, or most frequent meaning of the words in question.[22] Such a judgment or estimate of meaning is not a specific inference of the speaker's actual intended meaning. Rather, the usual, customary, or most frequent meaning of words is employed as a rule-of-thumb substitute for inferring intended meaning in each specific instance. Such a rule-of-thumb procedure increases the objectivity of the content-descriptive procedure and facilitates achieving reliability of results. But it may seriously prejudice the validity of results if the intended meanings of the speaker in employing the

---

[21] See, for example, the discussion of these definitions in Berelson, *Content Analysis*, pp. 14-18.

[22] The most explicit statement of the requirements of "manifest" content analysis is the discussion of the "frequency criterion" by I. L. Janis ("Meaning and the Study of Symbolic Behavior," *Psychiatry*, 6 [1943], 433-44, and "The Problem of Validating Content Analysis," in Lasswell, Leites, and associates, *Language of Politics*, p. 58).

words in question differ in too many cases from the meanings which those words ordinarily have.[23]

In coding content for its usual, or "manifest" meaning, the investigator needs to be familiar with the general rules of the language, the customary meanings of words for all users of that language, and — in some varieties of quantitative content analysis — with the usual or most frequent language habits of the communicator.

This type of information is also necessary for inferring a speaker's intended meanings. But in order to make valid inference of intended meaning in each specific instance of communication, the investigator also takes into account the situational and behavioral contexts of that communication. He does so in order to determine which of the possible meanings of the words in question the speaker intends to convey in the instance at hand and the precise shading of his intended meaning. In contrast, only the linguistic context of the words in question is taken into account in "manifest" content analysis.[24]

We can deal only very briefly here with what is meant by situational and behavioral contexts, how they are taken into account and the special problems which arise in doing so.[25]

In taking into account the *behavioral* context of words, the investigator considers the instrumental aspect of the communication in its broad action setting. In order to interpret the precise meaning intended by the speaker in any individual instance he takes into account the *purpose or objective* which the specific communication is designed to achieve.

In taking into account the *situational* context of the communication being analyzed the investigator considers *who* is speaking, *to whom,* and *under what circumstances.* Clues are obtained to the speaker's intended meanings by considering various known characteristics of the speaker and of his audience, and the nature of the

---

[23] The problem of validity noted here arises only when "manifest" content is used as a rule-of-thumb substitute for intended meaning. It does not arise, of course, when the investigator is interested *only* in the usual meanings of words, as in linguistic studies or in studies of effect on a mass audience rather than of intent of the communicator. In other words, depending upon the hypotheses and questions which he wishes to investigate, the analyst may be interested either in "manifest" meaning or intended meaning. And, when interested in intended meaning, he can infer it directly in each instance or employ "manifest" meaning as a rough approximation.

[24] Accordingly, because it avoids assessing situational and behavioral contexts, "manifest" content analysis is more easily objectified.

[25] For additional discussion of these points, see the author's *Propaganda Analysis,* Chap. 10.

speaker-audience relationship. The investigator also takes into account the time and place of the communication and related events preceding or accompanying it. He does so in the expectation that the exact intended meanings of the words employed by the speaker are shaped by (and understood by the audience with reference to) certain aspects of the setting and the stream of related events. This is particularly likely when, as in wartime propaganda, the communication being analyzed is highly situation- or event-oriented.

Such analysis of the instrumental aspect of communications in their situational contexts is not confined to nonfrequency approaches, for it is by no means the case that quantitative, or frequency, analysis always limits itself to coding "manifest" content. As a matter of fact, the criterion of "manifest" content is not generally accepted as essential to the technique of quantitative content analysis. It is explicitly rejected, for example, by Cartwright.[26] Even in the area of political communication research, for which Lasswell's version of content analysis has been primarily developed, many if not most quantitative content analyses do not in practice employ the "manifest" content criterion. Rather, they often attempt to infer intended meanings and employ relatively flexible and interpretative procedures for coding content. If this is a drawback from a scientific standpoint, it is one present in many quantitative studies as well as in nonfrequency analyses. The difference in this respect between frequency and nonfrequency analyses, therefore, seems to be one of degree, stemming partly from the different nature of the two approaches. The nonfrequency approach, by virtue of the limited number of cases with which it deals, requires that all relevant intended meanings always be estimated as validly as possible and, therefore, that full account be taken of situational and behavioral contexts.

The emphasis on validity in the nonfrequency approach is accompanied by less concern with the reliability of the judgments, or inferences, being made of the speaker's intended meanings. Rarely are systematic procedures employed to ensure or to demonstrate the reliability of nonfrequency content descriptions. A possible explanation for this may be suggested. Since the nonfrequency analyst works with a relatively small amount of content data, which he collects himself, he tends to be less self-conscious about the reliability problem and less concerned with it than the quantitative analyst. As a result, he is likely to overlook what the well-trained

---

[26] "Analysis of Qualitative Material," p. 424.

quantitative investigator knows so well and rightly emphasizes, namely, that when the procedure for obtaining content data on intended meanings is highly interpretative, it is all the more necessary to assess in some fashion the reliability of its results.

CLOSE RELATIONSHIP BETWEEN DESCRIPTIVE AND INFERENTIAL PROCEDURES

Some possible circularities of procedure beleaguer the nonfrequency approach to the analysis of communications content. In it content description is intimately intertwined with and overlaps the assessment of inferences from the contents. Inferences as to what the propagandist is trying to say and why he is trying to say it are not neatly discrete.

To illustrate: if one person addresses another as "you old rascal," the analyst who is seeking to interpret the intent validly will want to know if the addressee is an old man or an infant. If it is a baby, one infers that the intent is affectionate and simultaneously describes the content as endearment. There is a mutually interdependent set of assumptions here. One has not established the intent independently and derived the content interpretation from that nor has one established the affectionate meaning of the phrase "you old rascal" independently and derived the intent from that. The two propositions are parts of an interdependent set of inferential hypotheses.

The question arises of whether this aspect of the nonfrequency approach necessarily entails the danger of analytical bias, or "circularity." That is, by not distinguishing more sharply — as in quantitative content analysis — between the descriptive and inferential phases of research, does not the investigator risk the possibility that a hypothesis formulated early in the course of his content description will determine what he subsequently "sees" and regards as significant in the communication?

The danger of circularity in this sense is indeed potentially present in the procedure described above and undoubtedly occurs in many low-grade analyses. However, the disciplined analyst guards against it in several ways. He does not read through the communication material just once, but rereads it as many times as necessary to satisfy himself that the inference favored by him is consonant with all of the relevant portions and characteristics of the original communication material. Similarly, he considers not just one inferential hypothesis when reading and rereading the original communication material, but also many alternatives to it.

He systematically weighs the evidence available for and against each of these alternative inferences. Thus, the results of his analysis, if fully explicated, state not merely (1) the favored inference and the content "evidence" for it, but also (2) alternative explanations of that content "evidence," (3) other content "evidence" which may support alternative inferences, and (4) reasons for considering one inferential hypothesis more plausible than others.

In this fashion the disciplined analyst controls the dangers of circularity present in the overlapping of descriptive and inferential procedures. To the extent that he operates in the systematic, disciplined fashion we have outlined, the nonfrequency analyst follows the accepted scientific procedure of successive approximations.

It is important to recognize that the communication analyst cannot always utilize the preferred scientific procedure of first deriving a hypothesis and a set of relevant categories from one set of communication materials and of then testing that hypothesis by means of a systematic content analysis of a new set (or larger body) of communication materials. This preferred procedure can be employed only when there is reasonable assurance that the raw material for the initial, hypothesis-formation phase of the investigation is a good sample or replica of the material to be utilized for testing the hypothesis. But, as we have seen, such an assumption cannot always be made in interpreting communications which are in historical flux. Propaganda analysis is cumulative in character. "New" content features encountered in the second (or larger) body of communication material may force the investigator to alter his hypothesis or to employ additional or different content categories. Moreover, a skillful propagandist changes his strategy to preclude his future plans' being easily read from the pattern of his past conduct. For these reasons, in the type of applied content analysis being considered here, there is no assurance that an initial body of communication examined for purposes of hypothesis formation will be homogeneous with the body of communication used for testing purposes, or that the former will contain all the content features necessary to enable the investigator to formulate an interesting and useful hypothesis.

The problem of the overlapping of description and inference in the nonfrequency approach appears in a special light when intended (as against "manifest") meanings are used as content indicators.[27] For what we have then is, in fact, an intimate relationship between

----

[27] See pp. 26 ff. of the present work.

two inferential processes: that of inferring the speaker's intended meaning and that of inferring his purpose. We cannot discuss here various reasons for the closeness of the relationship between these two inferential procedures. What the investigator does, ideally, is to consider alternatives for *two* different variables, as it were, simultaneously. He considers alternative combinations of intended meaning plus purpose in the light of whatever else he knows or can reasonably postulate about the behavioral and situational contexts of the communication being examined.

Such mental rehearsals, or "experiments," are capable of being performed relatively rigorously or intuitively. In any case, the inferential results thereby achieved are subject, at least in principle, to systematic assessments of different types. In the first place, the inference derived from content analysis can be compared with more direct evidence of the speaker's intention, his strategy, calculations, state of information, etc. (Thus in the evaluation of wartime propaganda analysis referred to here, an attempt was made to validate inferences of Nazi intentions, etc., by comparing them with historical materials which, left by the Nazi regime and its personnel, became available after the war.[28] Second, inferences from content analysis can be cross-checked with evaluations about the same problems derived from other types of evidence. Third, content analysis inferences may be assessed by an "internal" check on the logic and plausibility of the reasoning on which they rest and by evaluating the degree of confirmation enjoyed by the generalizations used in support of the specific inferences. Finally, in some cases, content analysis inferences of the speaker's intentions, policies, etc., can be made the basis for predicting something about his subsequent actions. If employed with appropriate caution, the confirmation or disconfirmation of such predictions can be taken sometimes as evidence of the validity of the initial content analysis inference.

QUANTITATIVE TESTS OF INFERENCES BASED ON NONFREQUENCY INDICATORS

The relationship between nonfrequency content analysis and quantitative research methods in general may be easily confused unless a distinction is drawn between the character of the content indicator (nonfrequency) and the character of the test (which may be quantitative) for inferences based upon nonfrequency indicators.

---

[28] For illustrative material, see the author's *Propaganda Analysis* and "Prediction of Political Action by Means of Propaganda Analysis."

Consider, as a hypothetical example, the propaganda analysis inference which holds that the single appearance of a certain theme in a speech by a political leader is indicative of a secret change in political policy. This hypothesis could be tested systematically (quantitatively) in principle, by examining all known past instances in which that type of theme appeared in a speech by that leader (or by similarly placed leaders) to see in how many cases there was subsequent evidence of the type of policy change in question.

In practice, however, this type of quantitative test of an inferential hypothesis is often very difficult. There may be no such past instances, or only a few; evidence of policy changes may be fragmentary, inconclusive, or equivocal. In any case, whether or not a systematic test of an inferential hypothesis is feasible, it is important to distinguish between (1) the systematic test (which may be quantitative) of the results of nonquantitative content analysis based upon a nonfrequency indicator, and (2) quantitative content analysis itself, in which inferences are based on frequency indicators.

It may be the blurring of this distinction which sometimes leads proponents of quantitative methods to hold that what is here called nonfrequency content analysis is not really very different from frequency content analysis. Thus, the argument goes, a nonfrequency content indicator can be used with greater confidence for purposes of inference if it is known to have been a valid indicator on other occasions as well. Therefore (*sic*), the value of nonfrequency indicators also depends upon the frequency of their occurrence.

What this argument obscures, however, is that frequency of occurrence in this sense — in many individual inferences — does not make a frequency indicator of a nonfrequency indicator. The fact that a certain nonfrequency indicator has been successfully employed on previous relevant occasions does provide additional support for the new inference. But this does not alter the fact that in each instance the inference is based upon a nonfrequency indicator. That is, the inference — each time it is made — is based on the *presence* of the theme, not the frequency of its occurrence, within each individual communication.

CHARLES E. OSGOOD
UNIVERSITY OF ILLINOIS

THE REPRESENTATIONAL MODEL
AND RELEVANT RESEARCH METHODS

What is it that distinguishes content analysis from other methods of gathering information about people? The chief distinction, as the term implies, is a restriction upon sources of information. When the content analyst studies a person, he is restricted to the "messages" produced by that individual. There is often another restriction, in that he must take such "messages" as are spontaneously produced; usually he is not in a position to manipulate his subjects experimentally although content analysis may be applied to interviews and experimental protocols. Despite these restrictions there is considerable room for variation in the information that "messages" may carry: in face-to-face communication (e.g., the psychotherapist operating as a content analyst) the potential information is maximal — beyond the linguistically coded content of the spoken language there are inflectional patterns, suggestive variations in the pitch and intensity of the voice, and also the entire gestural-visual "band" of facial expression and bodily posture. A tape-recorded message eliminates the gestural-visual information, and a typed transcript, even though literal, eliminates even more information. Most restricted from the information standpoint is the "cleaned-up" text — the final written version of a message — yet this is the material with which most practical content analysis deals.

In this chapter we shall consider methods of content analysis which have developed mainly in the study of the most restricted kinds of messages — "cleaned-up" printed texts — not because these methods are limited to such messages but rather because the kinds of indices or cues upon which they depend are just as available here as in more information-loaded types.

We shall also limit ourselves in this chapter to what purport to be objective and quantitative methods — methods in which the bias of the analyst is at least minimized, in which the essential operations can be made explicit and the conclusions thereby more easily replicated, and in which the findings can be communicated in meaningful numbers. It is realized that such methods are often crude and insensitive in practical application compared to the more intuitive or insightful grasp of the trained analyst (cf. Chap. 1), and they are certainly more laborious, but they also offer certain advantages, as we shall try to show.

CONTENT ANALYSIS AS A PSYCHOLINGUISTIC PROBLEM

We may begin with the reasonable assumption that all of the events which occur in messages are causally dependent upon events or states in the human individual(s) producing the messages. The particular lexical items the speaker or writer selects among possible alternatives, his selection among alternative syntactical constructions, the way he inflects his statements, the pitch, rate, and intensity of his speech, the location and nature of pauses, repetitions, false starts and the like, and the facial expressions, gestures, and posturings which accompany his spoken messages, are all events which we must assume bear definite, if complex, causal relations to the varied psychological states and processes in the source. Many of these message events are presumably under the direct, voluntary control of the source, for example his selection of alternative lexical (meaningful) items or accompanying expressions and gestures; other message events are to a lesser extent under his voluntary control, for example the co-occurrence of certain lexical items in segments of his message or the distribution and nature of his errors and pauses.

Figure 1 outlines some of the relationships between message events and states of the source.

The message system per se is the field of special study for the linguist. Although much of linguistic study so far has been devoted to events on a level too microscopic to be of great interest or use to the content analyst — for example phonemic and morphemic analysis of languages — there are many problems of increasing interest to linguists which are also highly relevant to students of content analysis, such as syntactical structure, voice qualifiers, status tags, pausal phenomena, and the like. One of the methods

Figure 1

	INFERENCES ABOUT SOURCE	INFERENCES ABOUT RECEIVER
Source System	**Message System**	**Receiver System**
alternative encoding habits	lexical items	alternative decoding habits
meanings	lexical contingencies	meanings
associations	syntactical structure	associations
attitudes	other formal characteristics	attitudes
values	voice qualifiers	values
motives	pausal phenomena	motives
specific intentions	errors	specific significances
communication facility (effectiveness)	gestures and expressions	communication facility (comprehension)
	posturings	
	etc.	

Encoding Dependencies   Decoding Dependencies

to be described below (evaluative assertion analysis) illustrates
how linguistics can contribute to content analysis.

Source systems (speakers, writers) and receiver systems (listeners, readers) per se are the objects of study for psychologists
directly and for other social scientists perhaps less directly. Such
investigators are interested in classifying and theorizing about the
habits of language-using organisms, their motives, values, and
attitudes, and also the development of meanings and associations
— to call only part of the roll.

But if we define content analysis as a procedure whereby one
makes inferences about sources and receivers from evidence in the
messages they exchange, then the problem falls precisely in the
field of special interest of the psycholinguist — even though he
probably will not go by that name and may claim affiliation with
sociology, political science, psychology, linguistics, literature, history, anthropology, or some other field entirely. This is because it
is the psycholinguist who, by definition, is concerned with discovering and employing lawful relations *between* events in messages and
processes transpiring in the individuals who produce and receive
them. As shown in Figure 1, when the interest of the content analyst lies in making inferences about the *source* of a message, he
must rely upon *encoding dependencies,* that is, the dependencies of
message events upon psychological processes in speakers and
writers. When his interest lies in making inferences about the
effects of a message upon its receivers, on the other hand, he relies

upon *decoding dependencies,* that is, the dependencies of events in listeners and readers (their meanings, emotions, attitudes, and the like) upon the content and structure of messages. For the most part, content analysts have been more interested in drawing inferences about sources than in making predictions about receivers, but there is no reason why one direction should be more feasible than the other.

INFERENCES AND INDICATORS

Making an inference (or prediction) in content analysis involves at least the following: (1) some indicator or class of indicators that can be identified in the message sequence, (2) some state or process in the individuals producing or receiving the message, and (3) some dependency between these two such that the presence, absence, or degree of the former is correlated more than by chance with the presence, absence, or degree of the latter. The events in messages that *might* serve as indicators (correlate unspecified) are practically infinite — the frequency or locus of occurrences of the first-person singular pronoun "I," the sheer magnitude or rate of output in word or other units, pitch and/or intensity oscillation of the voice in various message segments, the probability level of the syntactical alternatives chosen, and so on ad infinitum. Similarly, the states of individuals that one *might* make inferences about (again, correlate unspecified) are as infinite as the classificatory ingenuity of all of the members of the A.P.A. put together — the intelligence, communicative facility, or racial origin of the speaker, his anxiety, aggressive, or sexuality level, his association, attitude, or value structure, his semantic or formal language habits, and so on. Most (if not all) of the characteristics of an individual, in one way or another, probably influence what happens in his communications. But the rub lies in 3 above — some indicator having a non-chance relation to the characteristic in which we're interested must be isolated — and so far psycholinguistics has had little more than suggestions or hunches to offer.

Driven by demands from superiors for advice on particulars, the practically oriented users of content analysis techniques are likely to be most interested in *specific inferences;* for instance, does country A intend to attack country B and when? Driven by internalized demands for scientific rigor, the academically oriented user of content analysis is likely to be most interested in *general inferences;* for instance, is there a general lawful relationship such that increase in the drive level of the speaker is accompanied by simplification and normalization of his semantic and structural choices? Although in this chapter we shall place more stress on the latter, there is no necessary incompatibility here: just as the validation of many specific inferences by practically oriented users may provide insights into general relations, so the gradually accumulating generalities of the academician may enrich the inference base for the practical content analyst. The ideal situation is probably that in which "tool makers" and "tool users" work in close association.

Of all of the potential source or receiver characteristics which might be inferred from the content of their communications, we will here mention only the following four. (1) *Attention.* This has been measured in the "classic" content analysis methods developed by Lasswell and his associates. It might also be called the "interest in various contents," or even (by implication) "semantic habit strength or prepotency." The indicator is frequency of occurrence of those lexical items judged to be relevant. The underlying assumption is that the greater the source's interest in a given topic, the greater will be the relative frequency with which lexical items associated with this topic are produced. (2) *Attitude.* A type of evaluative assertion analysis will be described below with which one can ascertain the direction and intensity of the source's attitudes toward things mentioned often enough in communications content. The index is essentially the average favorable-unfavorable loading of the evaluative terms which the source associates linguistically with each attitude object. (3) *Association structure.* Here we will be interested in what other ideas tend to be associated with any given idea in the source's thinking to greater-than- or less-than-chance degrees. The indicators are the contingencies between content items in his messages, regardless of either frequency of usage or evaluation. (4) *Language correspondence.* The method developed by Wilson Taylor, and dubbed "Cloze Procedure," will be described. It is designed to index the correspondence *in toto* of the source's system of language habits — including both semantic and grammatical habits — to those of other users of the same language. The index is the average success with which a sample of other users of the language can replace items which have been deleted from the source's messages by the experimenter-analyst.

REPRESENTATIONAL PROCESSES

Individual theorists about language behavior will differ, of course, in their postulations about the nature of those symbolic processes which occur in people when signs are received (decoding) and produced (encoding). I have presented my own views in some detail elsewhere[1] and therefore will give here only the brief review deemed necessary for present purposes.

Young members of any language community grow up in an environment where mature members employ lexical signs in contexts that usually include the objects or situations to which these signs refer. The child will hear "apple" frequently in contexts which include APPLE objects; he will hear "angry" in contexts which include scowling faces, aggressive movements, and the like; and he will see written forms like *alien* in printed contexts that often include other written forms like *dangerous* and *bad*. One of the necessary conditions for the formation of representational processes is association of sign stimuli with referent stimuli. We may assume that referent stimuli are capable of eliciting certain reaction patterns in the language-learning individual, either innately or in terms of previous learning. APPLE objects elicit certain eye and hand movements as well as salivary and other physiological reactions; aggression situations may elicit anxiety or anger reactions depending on the role of the individual; printed signs like *dangerous* and *bad* already have meaning for the young reader when he encounters *alien*. We are therefore dealing with three types of events: *significates* (physical objects and events, e.g., the juicy APPLE itself); *signs* (other physical stimuli associated with significates, e.g., the word "apple"); *symbolic processes* (events within sign-using organisms which develop from the association of signs with significates, e.g., that process set in motion by hearing the word "apple").

The basic assumption I make about the behavioral nature of sign processes or meanings is this: those stimulus patterns we call *signs* (be they perceptual or linguistic) acquire their representing character by coming to elicit some minimally effortful but distinctive portion of the total behavior produced by the things signified. This reduced portion of the total behavior toward things is a *symbolic process*, which I call a *representational mediation process*. It is

----

[1] See particularly Chapters 9 and 16 in the author's *Method and Theory in Experimental Psychology* (New York, 1953), and Chapters 1 and 8 in C. E. Osgood, G. J. Suci, and P. H. Tannenbaum, *The Measurement of Meaning* (Urbana, Ill., 1957).

representational by virtue of the fact that it is part of the very same behavior that is produced by the significate — thus the sign "apple" represents that juicy, edible thing rather than any of a million of other possible things because it calls forth in the language user some distinctive part of the total behavior to APPLE objects. It is *mediational* because the self-stimulation set up in the language user by making this representational reaction can come, through ordinary instrumental learning, to evoke a variety of overt reactions appropriate to the thing signified. Thus the child may run into the kitchen (a nonlinguistic response) when he hears Mother say "apple" and he may himself produce the noise "apple" (a linguistic response) when he perceives one of these objects (the visual image of this object being itself a perceptual sign). By the term *semantic decoding* I refer to the selective association of signs with representational mediation processes; by the term *semantic encoding* I refer to the selective association of representational mediation processes with spoken or written linguistic responses.

At this point the reader may well ask, "What has all this to do with content analysis?" The "representational model" in content analysis assumes (1) that in *semantic encoding by the source* the occurrence of specific lexical items in his messages is indicative of the immediate prior occurrence in his nervous system of the corresponding representational mediation processes; and (2) that in *semantic decoding by the receiver* the occurrence of specific lexical items in messages are predictive of the occurrence in his nervous system of those representational mediation processes which he has developed in association with these signs. This, of course, is merely a more formal way of saying that words "express" the ideas of the speaker and "signify" ideas for the hearer. But expression of these encoding and decoding relations in learning theory terms does permit us to make use of the elaborate machinery of this theory in analyzing psycholinguistic problems in content analysis and elsewhere.

What are some of the ways in which representational processes can vary both within and between individuals, and how may these variations be reflected in messages? (1) *Availability.* For one thing, the habits which associate signs with meanings in decoding and meanings with linguistic responses in encoding are variable. This is close to what we speak of as the familiarity of words; it will affect both the readability of messages and the fluency with which they are encoded. This is part of what Taylor's Cloze measures. For another thing, the range of cues, both external and internal (associational), which are connected with a given representational process will vary, within the individual over time and between individuals. Thus the availability of processes representing "voting" and "Democrat" will be greater in an election year than in other years. Besides these encoding and decoding habits, interest and other motivational states, as drives, affect availability. This is presumably reflected in frequency of usage of lexical items, and hence is indexed by the familiar Lasswellian type of content analysis.

A quite different source of variation is in the (2) *nature of the representational process*, again within the single individual for different signs and between individuals for the same sign. For several years my colleagues and I have been studying meaningful judgments by factor analytic methods. Several basic factors or dimensions have been indicated (including evaluation, potency, activity, stability, receptivity, and some others), and we assume that these represent some of the major ways in which meanings can vary. The factor accounting for the largest proportion of the variance is nearly always evaluation — in other words, an evaluative like-dislike, favorable-unfavorable, good-bad reaction is a dominant aspect of the meaning of most concepts — and we have identified this semantic component with "attitude" as it is usually defined. Although this aspect of the representational process would not be expected to influence the frequency of usage of items, it should influence the assertions constructed about attitudinal items. In other words, the speaker who favors LABOR UNIONS is likely to construct assertions like "The unions have helped working men," "Union leaders are against unnecessary strikes," and "Most labor leaders are anticommunist." *Evaluative assertion analysis* is a content analysis technique designed to isolate and index this component of variation in the meanings of lexical items.

Yet another source of variation is (3) *associations among representational processes*. Quite apart from the association of representational processes with overt acts, each such process is also associated with a hierarchy of other representational processes. Thus when some event elicits the meaningful process correlated with LABOR UNION, this will tend to excite other mediators, for example those which elicit MANAGEMENT, JOB, STRIKE, SECURITY, RADICALS, etc., as may be shown by the responses made in a word-association test. Depending upon the situational and linguistic contexts within which each individual has encountered signs, the structure of his associational hierarchies must vary. LABOR UNION may be associated with STRIKE in one man but with SECURITY in another. *Contingency analysis* is a method of message study designed to index such associational structures in the source.

Similar values for all the variables we have considered — availability of representational processes, their nature, and their association pattern, as well as all grammatical and syntactical habits — contribute to the over-all degree of correspondence between speakers of the same language, and this correspondence is indexed by the *Cloze Procedure.*

INFERENCES ABOUT ATTITUDE: EVALUATIVE ASSERTION ANALYSIS

The practically oriented, nonquantitative content analyst often makes inferences about the attitudes a source may have toward the various social objects (countries, peoples, policies, etc.) discussed. Depending on the type of source, the type of message, and its apparent purpose, he may take the source's assertions at their face value or he may assume an instrumental approach and try to outwit the strategy of the source. Although symbol frequency counts alone do not yield an index of attitude or "valence," Lasswell and others were aware of this need for a description of the valences in a message and tried to adapt frequency procedures to this purpose. In *Language of Politics*, for example, we find a chapter by Janis and Fadner on "The Coefficient of Imbalance." The purpose of the coefficient was to provide an index of the extent to which a topic or symbol was given favorable, neutral, or unfavorable treatment by a source. The method assumed that total messages could be analyzed into countable units — assertions for instance — and that these units could be judged by the analyst to be relevant (to the topic being studied) or irrelevant — and if relevant these units could be judged to be favorable, neutral, or unfavorable. The coefficient was influenced by both the evaluative imbalance and by the proportion of relevant content to total content; for instance, a topic referred to only 5 per cent of the time would have a lower index than one referred to 25 per cent of the time, even though both were consistently favorable in reference. In this characteristic, as well as in the procedures for determining and weighing units, this method differs from that to be described below, but in general the two methods are identical in purpose and similar in operation.

NATURE OF METHOD[2]

The purpose of evaluative assertion analysis is to extract from messages the evaluations being made of significant concepts, with a minimum dependence on the effects of the messages on coders or on their existing attitudes. It begins with a sample of "raw" messages received from some source and ends up with an evaluative scaling of the attitude objects referred to by the source.

The method requires the following assumptions. (1) That reasonably sophisticated users of a language can distinguish between two classes of symbols which we shall call "attitude objects" (AO) and "common-meaning material" (cm) respectively. The former are signs which individuals evaluate with marked difference depending on life experiences, for example SOCIALISM, MY FATHER, SCIENTISTS; the latter are signs upon whose evaluative meanings the users of a language must largely agree if they are to communicate with one another, for example that *atrocity* is something bad, that *people of good will* is something favorable, and so forth. Of course this distinction is one of degree. (2) That reasonably sophisticated users of a language can make reliable and valid judgments as to when two alternative constructions are equivalent or nonequivalent in meaning. For example, it is assumed that coders can judge whether or not (a) /COMMUNISTS/are denounced by/*people of good will*/ and (b) /COMMUNISTS/are/aggressors/ together constitute an evaluative equation with (c) "People of good will denounce these Communist aggressors." It is also assumed that coders can agree to a satisfactory degree on (3) the direction and intensity of assertions (e.g., that /X/*are denounced by*/Y/ is a dissociative assertion of high intensity while /X/*may have been*/Y/ is an associative assertion of weak intensity). Finally it is assumed that coders can agree on (4) the direction and degree of evaluativeness of common-meaning terms (e.g., that /X/is/*a news item*/ has zero evaluativeness, that /X/produces/*authentic reports*/ is slightly positive in evaluation, that /X/is/*a fabricator*/ is quite strongly negative, and so forth). Assumptions 3 and 4 are capable of empirical verification, of course.

----

[2] This method is described in greater detail in C. E. Osgood, S. Saporta, and J. C. Nunnally, "Evaluative Assertion Analysis," *Litera,* 3 (1956), 47-102.

Evaluative assertion analysis involves several stages which can be done serially by a single coder or, preferably, serially by a set of different coders. In Stage I the attitude objects (AO) in the message are identified, isolated linguistically, and then masked (by the substitution of nonsense-letter pairs). In Stage II this masked message is translated into an exhaustive series of evaluative assertions which are standard in structure but semantically equivalent to the original message. In Stage III the assertions and common-meaning evaluations are assigned directions and weights. Finally, in Stage IV, assertions relating to each attitude object are collected and averaged in terms of common-meaning evaluation, thereby allocating each AO to a common evaluative scale. Application of the congruity principle[3] makes possible an internal check on the consistency of the analysis.

Stage I: Identification, Isolation, and Masking of Attitude Objects

In practice, the trained coder will read through the message substituting different arbitrary symbols (AZ, BY, CX, etc.) for everything which would elicit specific attitudinal reactions from a subsequent reader, everything giving information as to who, what, or where. For example, "American delegates to the United Nations condemned the Communist conspiracy on Suez" would become "AZ delegates to BY condemned the CX conspiracy on DW." The problem of categorizing is handled by giving subscripts, for example AZ_1, AZ_2, AZ_3, to AMERICAN PEOPLE, THE UNITED STATES, and THE U.S. GOVERNMENT, and eventually either combining or keeping separate these categories, depending on their evaluative sameness or difference.

However, the training of coders for executing Stage I involves guided practice at the following. (1) *Identification of AO.* The distinction between attitude objects and common-meaning terms seems to be relatively easy in practice. This is in part because most AO's are what in conventional grammar are called proper nouns and identified in the orthography by initial capitals. Occasionally AO's are not capitalized, and here the coder must rely on context; for example, "college professor" may be AO in an editorial on alleged radicals in our educational system but *cm* in "Robert Jones is a college professor." All pronouns standing for AO's are also AO's and receive the same symbol; for instance, in "Secretary

---

[3] Cf. C. E. Osgood and P. H. Tannenbaum, "The Principle of Congruity in the Prediction of Attitude Change," *Psychological Review,* 62 (1955) 42-55.

Dulles made a speech today in which he praised . . ." both *Secretary Dulles* and *he* receive the same arbitrary symbol. Occasionally common-meaning terms are used in place of AO's, such as *the diplomat* for *Sir Anthony Eden,* and this must be masked as well. (2) *Isolation of AO.* The structure of most English sentences is such that an appropriate set of pronouns and relatives can be substituted for everything but verbs and certain function words. For example, for the sentence "(The unruly prisoner in the dock) began shouting that (his rights) were being stolen by (a bunch of crooked lawyers)" we may substitute "(HE) began shouting that (THEY) were being stolen by (THEM)." In practice only the parts of statements that contain an AO are parenthesized. Within such parentheses, the actual AO is then isolated from evaluative common-meaning material, but not from identifying or classifying material; (by the American aggressors) becomes (by the AMERICAN aggressors) with AMERICAN as an AO whereas (by the American delegates) becomes (by the AMERICAN DELEGATES), because the assertion /AMERICANS/are/*aggressors*/ is evaluative whereas the assertion /AMERICANS/are/*delegates*/ is not. The AO's thus identified and isolated are changed to arbitrary symbols.

The between-coder reliability of Stage I procedures (the Masking Technique, following extensive training) was checked by having seven coders mask 18 different messages. The percentage of agreement for each pair of coders on each message was computed by the formula

$$\frac{2 \ (AO_{1,2})}{AO_1 + AO_2},$$

where AO_1 is the total number of AO's isolated by coder 1 (each AO counting as many times as it appeared), AO_2 is the total number isolated by coder 2, and $AO_{1,2}$ is the total number agreed upon by both. The criteria for agreement were rather stringent — exactly the same lexical material had to be included as AO, agreement in substitution of symbols for pronouns was counted, and differences in the exhaustiveness of different coders counted. The average intercoder agreement by this index was 82 per cent over all 18 messages, the lowest value for a pair of coders being 77 per cent and the highest being 88 per cent.

Stage II: Translation of Message into Assertion Form

The purpose of this stage is to translate the message into a set of evaluative assertions, equivalent in meaning to the original but cast in common linguistic form. Depending on the purpose of the analysis, the coder may exhaustively extract assertions relating to all AO's or may extract only those relating to some limited number of AO's.

1. *Identification of evaluative common meaning.* A number of factor analyses of meaningful judgments[4] have provided evidence for a pervasive evaluative or attitudinal factor in human thinking. Although this dimension is best defined by the adjective pair *good-bad,* any common-meaning term will have an evaluative loading to the extent that it projects onto this bipolar dimension elsewhere than at the origin of the semantic space — other adjectives (*fair, dishonest, clean, relaxed, interesting*), nouns formed from adjectives (*kindness, value, security*), adverbs formed from adjectives (*fair-ly, lethal-ly, smooth-ly*), ordinary nouns (*friend, enemy, courage, traitor, peace*), and even many verbs (*lie, respect, lynch*) which include an inherent evaluation regardless of the agent. The simplest test of evaluativeness of a common-meaning element is to use it successively in assertions containing intensely polar actors like HERO and VILLAIN or SAINT and SINNER: it is intuitively clear that "The sinner is a *liar*" is more congruent (expected, normal, etc.) than "The saint is a *liar,*" and that "The hero offers *peace*" is more congruent than "The villain offers *peace*" (where we suspect a trick!), whereas little if any distinction can be made between "The saint was happy (or sad)" *vs.* "The sinner was happy (or sad)" — the last example illustrates the distinction that must be made between evaluation per se and good or bad fortune.

2. *Translation into assertions.* The linguistic construction selected as the most common in English was the ACTOR-ACTION-COMPLEMENT form. The actor is usually a noun (AO), the action is a verb or verb phrase, and the complement may be another noun or an adjective (either a different AO or evaluative *cm*). An assertion is a linguistic construction in which an actor is associated with or dissociated from a complement via a verbal connector (c). Thus all assertions will have the form $/X/c/Y/$ (e.g., /the boy/kisses/the girl/ or /the boy/is/strong/). Letting the attitude object being analyzed be indicated by AO_1, other attitude objects by AO_2, evaluative common-meaning content by *cm* (italicized), nonevaluative common-meaning content by cm (not italicized), and

---

[4] Osgood, Suci, and Tannenbaum, *Measurement of Meaning.*

the verbal connector by c, the following classes of assertions are possible:

a) $/AO_1/c/cm/$; example, /THE GENEVA CONFERENCE/is/*a failure*/

b) $/AO_1/c/AO_2/$; example, /CAESAR/did not love/BRUTUS/

c) $/AO_1/c/cm/$; example, /BOSTONIANS/like/baked beans/

d) $/cm_1/c/cm_2/$; example, /Humility/is/a fine trait/

Classes a and b are counted in evaluative assertion analysis; classes c and d are excluded. In other words, we are only interested in assertions involving both objects of attitude (AO) *and* some sort of evaluation, either in terms of evaluative common meaning or in terms of other attitude objects.

Of course, ordinary messages for analysis seldom consist of strings of simple assertions of this form, and therefore the task of the coder at this stage is to translate the given message (as masked) into this standard form. The paper by Osgood, Saporta, and Nunnally already mentioned gives detailed translation rules — for example, that adj_1 plus adj_2 plus AO = /(adj$_2$) AO/verb "to be" /adj_1/ (example, the *brave*, young AO = /(young) AO/are/*brave*/ — and any reader interested in studying this method or applying it should consult this source. The translation formulas, covering most of the constructions likely to occur in English, serve to transform the original message into a series of assertions on an assertion chart, in which the first column is the AO being evaluated, the second is the connector, and the third is the evaluative material. The following are examples of translation into assertion form:

Example 1. "The extent to which ZY is at war with the finest traditions of BA should be determined."

/BA/has/*fine traditions*/

/ZY/may be to some extent at war with/BA/

/BA/   ⇌   /ZY/

Note the use of the reciprocal sign here to show that the assertion applies equally with the other AO as actor — this is to ensure that all AO's are listed in the first column for later computation purposes.

Example 2. "AZ attacks the expansionist ambitions of both BY and CX."

/BY/has/*expansionist ambitions*/

/CX/has/*expansionist ambitions*/

/AZ/attacks/BY/

/BY/ ⇌ /AZ/

/AZ/attacks/CX/

/CX/ ⇌ /AZ/

Example 3. "Although AZ supported BY's crusade against crime in CY, AZ did not vote for BY in 1948."

/CY/has/*crime*/
/BY/crusaded against/*crime*/
/BY/is/*a crusader*/
/AZ/supported/BY/
/BY/ $\rightleftharpoons$ /AZ/
/AZ/did not vote for/BY/
/BY/ $\rightleftharpoons$ /AZ/

Although there is room for considerable variability in the construction of such assertions, both the averaging of many assertions related to the same AO and the functional equivalence of terms in language permit satisfactory reliability of the terminal values. Since (as will be shown below) the subsequent stages of analysis prove to be extremely reliable, we can best estimate the reliability of this stage by correlating the final evaluative locations of the AO's in a test message as between different coders (where subsequent stages were done by a single analyst to minimize this source of variability). The rank-order correlations for pairs of coders across the ten AO's in a 1,000-word message ranged from .71 to .98, with a median r of .90. The evaluative allocations also displayed high face validity.

Stage III: Assigning Directions and Intensities to Connectors and Evaluators

Working with the assertion chart provided by the previous stage of analysis, the coder now assigns each connector (verb phrase) and each common-meaning evaluator a direction and weight in terms of a seven-step scale running from −3 to +3.

1. *Connectors*. The direction of a connector may be either associative (+) or dissociative (−), depending on whether the verb phrase serves to relate the actor and complement (show them similar, indicate possession, class membership, etc.) or to separate them (show them dissimilar, opposed, etc.). More formally, a connector is associative when it is congruent (appropriate) between signs having the same evaluative direction and dissociative when it is congruent between signs having opposite evaluative directions. Thus, since it is congruent to say "Heroes *strive for* virtuous things" and "Villains *strive for* sinful things," the connector *strive for* must be associative; since, on the other hand, it is congruent to say "Heroes *despise* traitors" but would be incongru-

ent to say "Villains *despise* traitors" (at least in the universe of the simple-minded), the connector *despise* must be dissociative. Connectors like *reasoned with, examined,* and *replied to* will be found to be essentially neutral by this test.

Connectors also vary in the intensity or degree to which they associate or dissociate actor and complement. Although it is difficult to set up formal rules here, coders seem to agree fairly well (perhaps because there are only three degrees in each direction). In general, strong intensity (±3) is carried by the verb "to be" (X *is* a Y), the verb "to have" (X *does not have* Y), and most unqualified simple verbs when used in the present tense (X *loves* Y); moderate intensity (±2) is carried by verbs implying imminent, partial, probable, increasing, etc., association or dissociation (X *plans to* or *is trying to do* Y), by tenses other than the present (X *has favored* Y), and by most modal auxiliary forms (X *used to help* Y); weak intensity (±1) is carried by connectors which imply only possible or hypothetical relation between actor and complement (X *may commit, might agree with, ought to join* Y). Indexing adverbs are also useful guides, for example *absolutely, definitely, positively* (±3), *normally, ordinarily, usually* (±2), *slightly, occasionally,* and *somewhat* (±1).

2. *Evaluators.* Evaluative common-meaning material may be either favorable ($+$) or unfavorable ($-$) in direction. This is usually an easy judgment to make, and in doubtful cases the same congruence test described above can be made; for example, the adjective *careful* seems to be slightly favorable ($+$) because it is more appropriate in "Saints are usually *careful*" than in "Sinners are usually *careful*," and certainly substitution of the opposite, *careless,* leads to the same conclusion. Although there are no formal rules for judging the intensity of evaluation, coders seem to have little difficulty if they keep in mind that the three degrees (3, 2, 1) should be used with roughly equal frequency over large samples of material. We have found that the linguistic quantifiers "extremely," "quite," and "slightly" provide roughly equal units here. Thus *fair play* seems extremely favorable in our culture and *atrocities* extremely unfavorable; *sympathetic* seems quite favorable and *disturbing* quite unfavorable; *interesting* seems slightly favorable and *tense* slightly unfavorable. Again, the use of adverbs as modifiers of adjectives and adjectives as modifiers of nouns often provides helpful cues; for example, X was *extremely honest,* X was a *perfect gentleman.*

To check the reliability of Stage III operations the investigators prepared approximately 15 pages of assertion charts, based on materials from several sources, and these were dittoed. The seven coders judged the direction and intensity of both connectors and evaluators in columns provided for this purpose on the assertion charts. Separate product-moment r's for connectors and evaluators were computed between each pair of coders, the N for connectors approximating 225 and that for evaluators approximating 68. Reliability as to direction ($+$ or $-$) in coding was extremely high: the percentage of entries falling in the error diagonal of the scatterplots was only 4 per cent for connectors and 3 per cent for evaluators. The r's for use of the total seven-step scales ($+3$ to -3), thus including both direction and intensity, averaged .85 (range from .71 to .92) for connector judgments and .90 (range from .82 to .97) for evaluator judgments. We conclude that this sort of coding can be done with considerable intercoder reliability, despite the difficulty one has in stating formal rules.

Stage IV: Evaluative Scale of Attitude Objects

Completion of the preceding stage provides an assertion chart on which each of the connectors and each of the cm elements is coded both as to direction and as to intensity; for example, /ZY/have taken advantage of/-2/human decency/$+3$/. The coder working on Stage IV collects together values of all assertions for each AO, determines the average evaluation score for each AO, and finally assigns each to a common seven-step evaluative scale. The coder uses a computation chart which provides columns for listing AO's (in actor position), values of connectors, values of evaluators, and their products (e.g., -6 for the example above).

The average common-meaning evaluation for each AO is determined first, by dividing the sum of the product column for that AO by the modular sum of its connector column (thus weighing each assertion by the intensity of the connector). In other words, type a assertions (/AO/c/cm/), since they include common-meaning terms, are the initial basis of evaluation.

Then the average evaluation for each AO as just computed is assigned to it wherever it appears as the complement in type b assertions (/AO$_1$/c/AO$_2$/), and all of the assertions of this type for each AO are collected and averaged. In our present example, assuming that the average evaluation of ZY turned out to be -3.0 (i.e., all maximally negative) in common-meaning assertions, this value would be entered in the assertion chart wherever ZY appeared as the complement for other AO's. If these other AO's form associative assertions with ZY, they are thereby lowered in evaluation; if they form dissociative assertions with ZY, they are raised in evaluation themselves.

The final evaluative score for each AO is the grand average for all assertions of both types, and this value, ranging from $+3$ to -3, is entered on a common scale used to represent the source's evaluations of all AO's.

It should be noted that in computing products for assertions the evaluation is plus when connectors and evaluations have the same sign (e.g., when AO is associated with good things or dissociated from bad things) and minus when connectors and evaluations have opposite signs (e.g., when AO is associated with bad things or dissociated from good things). Note also that it is assumed that an intense connector (± 3) is treated as equivalent to an ordinary assertion (± 1) made three times, and similarly for connectors of intermediate strength. These appeared to be the simplest assumptions to make. The original paper discusses certain special treatments for secondary sources — for example, the source says that Eisenhower says Dulles is a good man for his job — and for conditionals. Finally, it should be noted that although evaluations based upon common-meaning assertions and those based on assertions relating one AO to others are usually close on the scale, this is not always the case; for example, a particular source may shun making assertions about people in common-meaning terms, yet may regularly associate them with other either favorably or unfavorably evaluated AO's (the familiar "guilt by association" technique). This is one of the secondary measures that can be derived from the method.

Figure 2 shows the final evaluation chart for an excerpt from the *Progressive Magazine,* an issue devoted to an attack on Senator Joseph McCarthy. The face validity of the analysis is apparent: favorably evaluated, along with universal "goods" like BIBLE, BILL OF RIGHTS, and AMERICAN PEOPLE and COUNTRY, are such AO's as SENATOR BOB LaFOLLETTE, JR., and his father, FIGHTING BOB LaFOLLETTE, as well as the PROGRESSIVE MOVEMENT and PROGRESSIVE MAGAZINE; we find Senator McCARTHY allocated toward the negative pole, along with KLUXISM and COMMUNISTS. It may also be noted that AMERICAN PEOPLE (DW) and COUNTRY (CX) end up with

Figure 2

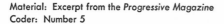

Material: Excerpt from the *Progressive Magazine*
Coder: Number 5

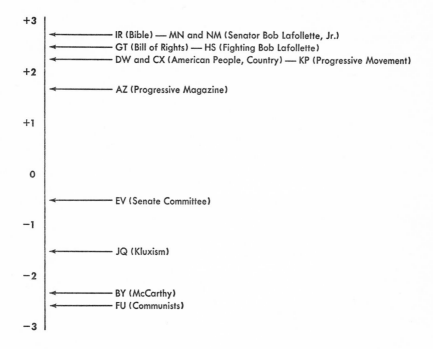

identical evaluative locations; in many analyses these AO's might have been differentiated only by subscripts (CX_1, CX_2) and could be combined into a single AO at this point. If the final evaluations are clearly different, of course, this cannot be done.

Congruity Check

Given the final evaluations for each AO in a message, the logic of the congruity principle allows us to check the consistency of the entire analysis. Going back to the assertion chart, we merely insert a plus or a minus for each AO, depending on its determined evaluative direction on the final scale. Then we check each line of the assertion chart, that is, each assertion, to see if it includes an even number of minuses, 0, 2, 4, etc. Any assertion not meeting this criterion is incongruent; in the example given earlier, ZY should be minus in evaluation for the assertion to be congruent — *BAD AO* (−) *take advantage of* (−) *human decency* (+) is evaluatively congruent. If ZY had turned out plus in the final evaluative scaling, the analyst would know either that there had been an error somewhere in the analysis (which could be checked by reference to the original message) or that the source of the message was actually inconsistent or ambivalent toward this attitude object. The degree of such evaluative inconsistency in sources is another secondary measure derivable from this method.

CRITIQUE OF EVALUATIVE ASSERTION ANALYSIS

By this time the reader will have concluded that what this method gains in rigor and explicitness it loses in terms of laboriousness. In a rough check on the speed with which sets of three coders (one masking, another translating into assertions, and a third giving ratings and computing evaluative locations) could handle material, it was found that it takes about one hour of coder time for each 133 words of material (one triple-spaced page). This is certainly laborious. On the other hand, a set of six well-trained coders working steadily through a 40-hour week should be able to handle about 240 pages of material, and for some problems the dependability of the results may be worth the labor. Furthermore, there are a number of ways in which trained coders can make short cuts; for example, it was found that they could skip the assertion-translation stage by mentally constructing the assertions in a masked message and entering the directions and intensities of evaluations on a computation chart. Although this short cut increased the speed to three triple-spaced pages an hour per coder, average intercoder reliability dropped to about .75.

It must be kept in mind that this is a method for getting at the evaluations explicitly being made in the message itself; it tells the analyst what the message per se says, not what the source may have really intended. It therefore falls completely into the "representational model" described above. For many practical purposes, such as propaganda analysis and interpretation of psychotherapy protocols, where one is concerned with the instrumental use of language, this method would have to be supplemented by or even abandoned in favor of methods which would allow for intuition about language strategy. Because it does accurately reflect evaluations in the message per se, it might yield predictions as to effects on receivers better than inferences as to intentions of sources.

The distinction between representational and instrumental analysis also bears on the Masking Technique employed in evaluative assertion analysis. Its purpose, of course, is to eliminate or at least greatly minimize the potential bias of the analyst's own attitudes and expectations about sources and the like; in this it manifestly succeeds, and this "gimmick" could be applied as a first step, of course, in practically oriented, nonquantitative studies. But if the practically oriented analyst is trying to understand the strategies of his "opponent" and outwit them, one wonders if he could work as effectively with AZ's, BY's, and CX's substituted for attitude objects. This should be worth investigating. It is also possible that training analysts by working under masked conditions would make them more sensitive to the ways in which evaluation or valence can be expressed in language structure.

POTENTIAL USES OF EVALUATIVE ASSERTION ANALYSIS

From the foregoing critique it follows that this method is more likely to find use as a research tool than in practically oriented areas. It can, however, be used as a criterion, for example in selecting alternative coders (i.e., which of a set of coders, using their own nonquantitative methods, best approximates the evaluative scaling of the message provided by quantitative assertion analysis). Also, because the same procedures and scaling units are applied to all messages from all sources, it becomes possible to compare directly across sources and messages. Thus we can say which of several sources best corresponds to some criterion source (e.g., a State Department criterion) in the evaluations being made of particular people and issues; we can say which of several alternative messages best communicates some desired evaluative ordering (e.g., in preparing communication materials); we can say how the evaluative orderings from one or more sources are changing over time. If the issue is important enough to warrant the labor involved, and particularly if interest is more in predicted effects of messages than in inference about source intentions, evaluative assertion analysis may be used in practical situations for these and similar purposes. In conducting experiments on the effects of communications on audiences, the stimulus material may be graded in evaluative intensity and this correlated with amount of audience change or intensity of audience response. A student of biography might profitably use the method to determine how several biographers evaluate the same person and, similarly, how any one biographer evaluates a number of persons.

Finally, beyond the direct allocation of concepts to a common evaluative scale, there are several derivative measures which might be of value in certain cases. We have already noted that an incongruity index can be derived from the number of assertions made by a source which are incongruent with his own over-all evaluative locations. It could be hypothesized, for example, that the more polarized (extreme in evaluation) the attitudes of a source, the fewer the incongruities in his messages. We could also hypothesize that when the source is deliberately constructing untruths, half-truths, and other evasions based on mixed motives, the incongruity index will rise. We have also noted assertion type as a possible secondary measure — the degree to which a source "comes right out and says it in plain language" (*cm* evaluations in assertion type *a*) *vs.* the degree to which a source employs "evaluation by association" (other AO's, assertion type *b*). In psychotherapy this might reflect the degree of conscious awareness and availability on the part of the patient of his evaluations of significant persons; in literature it might be useful in defining different types of character portrayal. The average deviation of a source's AO's from the neutral point of the evaluative scale would serve to index his polarization, a measure probably associated with emotionality about people and issues. Again, this might be useful in such diverse pursuits as psychotherapy and literary study, for instance as an indicator of cathexes in the former case and as a possible index of different literary genres in the latter case. Finally, evaluativeness could be indexed by the sheer density of evaluative assertions, say, per 100 running words of material — the degree to which messages are "propagandistic" as compared with "informative" might be determined on such a basis.

INFERENCES ABOUT ASSOCIATION STRUCTURE: CONTINGENCY ANALYSIS

An inference about the "association structure" of a source — what leads to what in his thinking — may be made from the contingencies (or co-occurrences of symbols) in the content of a message. This inference is largely independent of either "attention level" (frequency) or "evaluation" (valence). One of the earliest published examples of this type of content analysis is to be found in a paper by Baldwin[5] in which the contingencies among content

---

[5] A. L. Baldwin, "Personal Structure Analysis: A Statistical Method for Investigating the Single Personality," *Journal of Abnormal and Social Psychology*, 37 (1942), 163-83.

categories in the letters of a woman were analyzed and interpreted. For some reason this lead does not seem to have been followed up, at least in the published reports of people working on content analysis problems. On the other hand, it soon became evident in this conference that all of the participants had been thinking about the contingency method in one form or other as being potentially useful in their work.

If there is any content analysis technique which has a defensible psychological rationale it is the contingency method. It is anchored to the principles of association which were noted by Aristotle, elaborated by the British Empiricists, and made an integral part of most modern learning theories. On such grounds it seems reasonable to assume that *greater*-than-chance contingencies of items in messages would be indicative of *associations* in the thinking of the source. If, in the past experience of the source, events A and B (e.g., references to FOOD SUPPLY and to OCCUPIED COUNTRIES in the experience of Joseph Goebbels) have often occurred together, the subsequent occurrence of one of them should be a condition facilitating the occurrence of the other: the writing or speaking of one should tend to call forth thinking about and hence producing the other. It also seems reasonable to assume that *less*-than-chance contingencies of items in messages would be indicative of *dissociations* in the thinking of the source. If, in the experience of the source, events A and B (e.g., MOTHER and SEX in a psychotherapy case) have often been associated, but with fear or anxiety, the occurrence of one of them should lead to the inhibition of the other. Such inhibition might be either central (unconscious and involuntary) or peripheral (conscious and deliberate).

AN EXPERIMENTAL TEST OF THE BASIC ASSUMPTIONS OF CONTINGENCY METHOD[6]

In applying contingency content analysis to real problems, such as propaganda study and psychotherapy, we would like to use the data about what things co-occur in messages to make inferences about a person's association structure and also about what things have gone together in his experience — that is, about the experiential basis for his association structure. Unfortunately, however, in such application situations we seldom if ever have any data with

----

[6] This experiment was done by the author in collaboration with Mrs. Lois Anderson. "Certain Relations Between Experienced Contingencies, Association Structure, and Contingencies in Encoded Messages," *American Journal of Psychology,* 70 (1957), 411-20.

which to validate our inferences. Usually we have only the messages produced, not the source who produced the messages (and who could give us other indices of his association structure) and certainly not the past history of his experience. In order to test the basic assumptions of this method, therefore, it is necessary to develop a controlled experimental situation in which (1) the experiential history can be approximately known, and (2) the association structure can be estimated independently of the message structure. The following experiment provides such conditions.

Hypotheses and General Design

Our general assumption is that (1) *contingencies in experience* come to be represented in (2) *an individual's association structure* by patterns of association and dissociation of varying strengths, which help determine (3) *the contingencies in messages* produced by this individual. We require a simple situation in which we can measure (1) $F_a(b) > F_a(c) > F_a(d) \ldots > F_a(n)$ — the varying frequencies (F) in experience with which an event (a) is followed by other events (b, c, d . . . n); (2) $P_a(b)$, $P_a(c)$, $P_a(d) \ldots P_a(n)$ — the varying probabilities (P) with which subjects exposed to the above experience will associate items b, c, d . . . n when *some other person* (the experimenter) gives a, thus providing a measure of association structure (associational probability); and (3) $P_a^*(b)$, $P_a^*(c)$, $P_a^*(d) \ldots P_a^*(n)$ — the varying probabilities with which subjects exposed to the above experience will produce items b, c, d . . . n after *they themselves* have produced a. This provides a measure of message contingency (transitional probability). If we think of the subject in this experiment as a communicating unit in the information theory sense, $F_a(b)$ is the input to the unit and $P_a^*(b)$ is the output. The experimenter determines the input in such a way that $F_a(b) > F_a(c) > F_a(d)$. (It is assumed that previous to this experience the associations between these items are random across subjects, and materials for the experiment are selected to approximate this condition.) The theory which we are testing may be stated more formally as a series of hypotheses.

Hypothesis I. Exposure to a sequence of paired events such that $F_a(b) > F_a(c) > F_a(d)$ will result in a nonchance association structure among these events such that $P_a(b) > P_a(c) > P_a(d)$.

Hypothesis II. Given an association structure such that $P_a(b) > P_a(c) > P_a(d)$ in a set of subjects, sequential messages by these subjects limited to these events will display contingencies (transitional probabilities) such that $P_a^*(b) > P_a^*(c) > P_a^*(d)$.

Hypothesis III. Given exposure to a sequence of paired events such that $F_a(b) > F_a(c) > F_a(d)$ and subsequent production of sequential messages limited to these events, message contingencies will be such that $P_a^*(b) > P_a^*(c) > P_a^*(d)$. This dependency relation between input and output assumes mediation via the subject's association structure.

Hypothesis IV. The dependency relation between association structure and message contingency (described in Hypothesis II) will be greater than the dependency relation between input contingency and message contingency (described in Hypothesis III). This derives from the assumption that message contingencies depend directly upon the association structure of the subject and only mediately upon his experience; to the extent that individual subjects have prior associative experience with the items, these associations will also influence the final structure.

Hypothesis V. The degree of dependence (1) of association structure upon experiential contingency and (2) of message contingency upon experiential contingency will be a direct function of the frequency of experiential contingency, $F_a(b)$. In other words, we assume that modification of association structure (and hence transitional message structure) varies with the frequency with which events are paired in experience — a straightforward psychological association principle. With respect to measurement, this implies that the more frequent pairings in experience have been, the more significant will be the deviations of associational and transitional probabilities from chance.

Hypothesis VI. The degree of dependence between association structure and message contingency will be relatively independent of the frequency of experiential contingency. This assumes that whatever pre-experimental associations between items exist in individual subjects will determine both associative and transitional (message) contingencies; hence dependency relations here should be relatively independent of experimental inputs.

The burden of this analysis, if substantiated in the results, would be that contingency content analysis provides a valid index of the association patterns of the source, but only a mediate and tenuous index of his life history. It is realized, of course, that this "laboratory" approach side-steps many of the problems that arise in practical applications of contingency analysis; some of these will be considered later under a critique of the method.

Method

Two groups of 100 subjects each were shown 100 successive frames of a single-frame film strip. On each frame was a pair of girls' names, for example BEATRICE-LOUISE. There were only ten girls' names altogether, but these were so paired that (1) each name would appear equally often on the left and on the right, (2) the ordering of frames with respect to names was random, and (3) — the main experimental variable — each name appeared with others with different frequencies. The pattern of input pairing shown below for JOSEPHINE was duplicated for each of the ten names (with different specific names, of course):

JOSEPHINE-BEATRICE 6	LOUISE-JOSEPHINE 6
JOSEPHINE-CYNTHIA 3	GLADYS-JOSEPHINE 3
JOSEPHINE-HAZEL 1	ESTHER-JOSEPHINE 1

with SARAH   0
with ISABELLE 0
with VALERIE 0

Subjects were asked simply to familiarize themselves with the names. Following viewing of the 100 frames, two different measures were taken. (1) *Association test.* Each of the girls' names was shown separately on the screen for eight seconds, and subjects were instructed to write down the first other girl's name that occurred to them. Here the experimenter provides the stimulus — associative probability. (2) *Transitional contingency test.* Subjects were given little booklets and instructed to write one girl's name successively on each page, filling in as many pages as they could and not looking back. Here the stimulus for each response is the subject's own previous behavior.

The group that had the associational test first and the transitional last will be referred to as Group I; the one that had the transitional test first and the associational last will be called Group II. Three tables were formed for each group. The *input table*, the same for both groups, gave the relative frequency (per cent) with which each name had been paired with every other name on the presentation frames, without regard to the forward or backward direction of association. Since each name appeared on 20 frames, an item paired six times with another would have this noted as 30 per cent of its appearances, three times, 15 per cent, and one time, 5 per cent. The *association table* gave, for each stimulus name, the relative frequency (per cent) of subjects giving each of the ten possible response names. Thus, if 16 of the 100 subjects wrote BEATRICE when they saw JOSEPHINE, 16 per cent was entered in the appropriate cell. The *transitional table* gave, for each self-produced stimulus name, the relative frequency (per cent) of subjects giving each of the ten possible response names. Thus, if JOSEPHINE appeared in the booklets of 79 subjects and was followed immediately by the name HAZEL in the booklets of 11 of these subjects, 14 per cent was entered in the appropriate cell.[7]

Results

Table 1 gives the correlations obtained among input, association structure, and message contingency. With regard to the first hypothesis, it can be seen that the r between input frequency and associative probability is .58 for Group I and .37 for Group II —

Table 1[a]

Dependency Relations	Group I	Group II
Input/Associational	.58[b]	.37[b]
Input/Transitional	.19	.09
Associational/Transitional	.39[b](.46)[b]	.48[b](.42)[b]

[a] The bracketed values for associational/transitional in this table were computed from the continuous raw data prior to transformation into discrete stepwise values.
[b] Significantly greater than zero at the 5 per cent level or better.

these are both significantly greater than zero and in the expected direction. The fact that the correlation is considerably higher for Group I than Group II may reflect the effect of interpolating the transitional test and the consequent greater remoteness of the stimulus input from the act of producing the association in Group II.

Relations between input frequency and transitional (message) contingency are both in the predicted direction but are not significantly different from zero. Hypothesis III is thus not confirmed at a satisfactory level of significance. It is interesting to note, however, that (1) the input/transitional r is actually lower in Group II, where the transitional test immediately followed the input, than in Group I, and (2) the relation between input and transitional probabilities seems to vary with that between input and associational

----

[7] These tables and certain details of statistical treatment will be found in Osgood and Anderson, "Certain Relations. . . ."

probabilities — as if (as hypothesized) the transitional contingencies depended upon the associative structure.

Regarding Hypothesis II, it may be seen that the r between associational and transitional probabilities is positive and significant for both groups. That the degree of relation between associational and transitional probabilities is approximately the same (particularly when the continuous raw data is correlated, .46 and .42) for both groups substantiates Hypothesis VI; as is shown, despite the gross differences between Groups I and II in degrees of correlation between input frequencies and both measures, the relation with association structure and transitional message structure is the same. With regard to Hypothesis IV, it can be seen that for both groups the correlations between associational probabilities and transitional probabilities are higher than those between input frequencies and transitional probabilities, as anticipated.

Finally, there is Hypothesis V — that the degree of dependency of both associational and transitional probability upon the input frequencies varies with the absolute frequency of input pairing. To test that we examine whether the predictability of a response name from knowing the stimulus name varies with the frequency of pairing in the input. For each subject the number of "correct" responses given in each frequency category was recorded. (A Dixon-Mood sign test was used to determine significance.) For all conditions except the backward direction of association on the transitional test, six pairings yielded significantly more "correct" associations than either three or one pairings. The lower frequencies of pairing, three and one, were not significantly different from each other or from zero pairing. As might be expected in a culture that reads from left to right, "forward" associations were significantly stronger than "backward" associations.

Conclusions

This experiment was designed to test certain assumptions that seem to give value to a contingency method of content analysis: (1) that the association structure of a source depends upon the contingencies among events in his life experience, and (2) that inferences as to the association structure of a source can be made from the contingencies among items in the messages he produces. This experiment provided conditions in which the contingencies among events occurring to human "sources" could be at least partly manipulated and hence known. It also provided conditions in which the resultant association structures of these "sources" could be determined independently of the contingencies in the "messages" (transitional outputs) they produced. Both of the major assumptions above were supported by the results, association being shown to be dependent upon input contingencies and transitional output contingencies upon association structure to significant degrees. The results also indicate that whereas "message" contingencies are dependent upon association structure, they are only remotely dependent upon experienced input within the experiment itself; that is, nonchance associations between items existed prior to the experimental input manipulation and also influenced transitional contingencies. In general, the degree to which input influences both association structure and transitional contingency is a function of the frequency of input pairing.

GENERAL NATURE OF CONTINGENCY CONTENT ANALYSIS

In the application of the contingency method as a kind of content analysis, in contrast to the experimental situation just described, we are limited to events in messages, and from them try to make inferences about the association structure of their source. The message is first divided into units, according to some relevant criterion. The coder then notes for each unit the presence or absence of each content category for which he is coding. The contingencies or co-occurrences of categories in the same units are then computed and tested for significance against the null (chance) hypothesis. And finally, patterns of such greater-than- or less-than-chance contingencies may be analyzed. This may be done by a visual model which gives simultaneous representation to all of the relationships. Let us take up these stages of analysis one by one.

Selection of Units

Often the message materials to be analyzed will fall into natural units. One would normally take each day's entry in a personal diary, for example, as a single unit. Or in analyzing the association structure of "Republicans" *vs.* "Democrats," where a sample of individuals in each class have written letters to an editor, the letter from each individual would be a natural unit. Similarly, in studying the editorials in a certain newspaper, each editorial might be a unit. On the other hand, one may wish to analyze the contingencies in a more or less continuous message, for example in James Joyce's *Ulysses,* and here it would be necessary to set up arbitrary units.

If the unit is too small (a single word, for example), then nothing can be shown to be contingent with anything else; if it is too large (the entire text or message, for example), then everything is completely contingent with everything else. There seems to be a broad range of tolerance between these limits within which approximately the same contingency values will be obtained. Theoretically, the unit should be as large as the temporal span of the stimulus trace — that is, so that the aftereffects of speaking or writing one item can be involved in cuing off an associated item — but this would be impossible to estimate from messages per se. In one small-scale investigation, in which the size of the sampling unit was varied within the same material, we found contingency values to be roughly constant between 120 and 210 words as units, but more needs to be done here.

Selection of Coding Categories

Here, as in most other types of content analysis, the nature, number, and breadth of categories noted depends upon the purposes of the investigator. If the analyst has a very specific purpose, he will select his content categories around this core. In our own work, which has been methodologically oriented, we have merely taken those interesting contents most frequently referred to by the source. The same categorizing problems faced elsewhere are met here as well; for example, whether references to RELIGION in general, CHRISTIANITY, and the CHURCH should be lumped into a single category or kept separate. Of course, the finer the categories used the larger must be the sample in order to get significant contingencies. We do run into one special categorizing problem with the contingency method, however: if one were to code two close synonyms like YOUNG WOMEN and GIRLS as separate categories, he would probably come to the surprising conclusion that these things are significantly dissociated in the thinking of the source; being semantic alternatives, the source tends to use one in one location and the other in another location. If such closely synonymous alternates are treated as a single category the problem does not arise.

Raw Data Matrix

Armed with a list of the content categories for which he is looking, the coder inspects each unit of the material and scores it in a raw data table such as that shown as Figure 3A. Each row in the table represents a different unit (1, 2 . . . n) and each column a different content category (A, B . . . N). The coder may note merely the presence or absence of references to each content category; if pres-

Figure 3

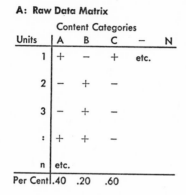

A: Raw Data Matrix

Content Categories

Units	A	B	C	–	N
1	+	–	+	etc.	
2	–	+	–		
3	–	+	–		
:	+	+	–		
n	etc.				
Per Cent	.40	.20	.60		

B: Contingency Matrix

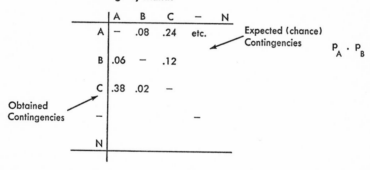

	A	B	C	–	N
A	–	.08	.24	etc.	
B	.06	–	.12		
C	.38	.02	–		
–			–		
N					

Expected (chance) Contingencies $P_A \cdot P_B$

Obtained Contingencies

ent in unit 1, category A is scored plus, and if absent in unit 1, category A is scored minus — how often A is referred to is irrelevant in this case. One may also score in terms of each category being above or below its own median frequency; if above, plus, if below, minus. This method needs to be used when units are relatively large and many categories tend to occur in most units (as can be seen, the presence/absence method in this case would show everything contingent on everything else). In this case one first enters the actual frequencies of reference in the cells of Figure 3A, computes the median for each column, and then assigns each cell a plus or a minus depending on whether its frequency is above or below this median.

Contingency Matrix

The contingency matrix, as illustrated in Figure 3B with entirely hypothetical data, provides the information necessary for comparing expected or chance going-togetherness of categories with actual obtained going-togetherness. The expected or chance contingency for each pair of columns is obtained by simply multiplying together the sheer rates of occurrence of these two categories, that is, p_A times p_B in analogy with the probability of obtaining both heads (HH) in tossing two unbiased coins whose p_H are both .50. We find the probabilities or relative rates of occurrence for each content category in the row labeled "per cent" at the bottom of the raw data matrix. Thus, since A occurs in 40 per cent of the units and B in 20 per cent, we would expect A and B to occur together (be contingent) in only 8 per cent of the units on the basis of chance alone. Extending this to all possible pairs of categories, we fill in the upper right cells of the matrix, A/B, A/C, B/C, etc.

In the corresponding lower left cells of this matrix, for example B/A, C/A, C/B, etc., we then enter the actual or obtained contingencies; these are simply the percentages of units where plusses occur in both of the columns being tested. For example, in the part of the matrix shown in Figure 3A there is one such double plus between columns A and B.

If the obtained contingency is greater than the corresponding expected value (e.g., C/A .38, A/C .24), these events are co-occurring more often than by chance; if the obtained contingency is less than the corresponding expected value (e.g., C/B .02, B/C .12), these events are co-occurring less often than by chance.

Significance of Contingencies

The significance of the deviation of any obtained contingency from the expected value can be estimated in several ways. Baldwin (1942) utilized the chi-square test, in which a two-by-two frequency table (AB, A but not B, B but not A, neither A nor B) is arranged from the data in each pair of columns in the original data matrix and where the total N equals the number of units. This becomes pretty laborious with a large number of units and, furthermore, the frequency of entries in the AB cell may often be below five, a number usually given as a lower limit in applying chi-square. We have used the simple standard error of a percentage,

$$\sigma_p = \sqrt{\frac{pq}{N}},$$

where p is the expected value in the upper right half of the contingency table, q is equal to $1-p$, and N is the total number of units sampled. This gives us an estimate of how much an obtained percentage may be expected to vary about its expected value; for example, if the sigma is .07 then a difference between the expected and obtained of .14 (two sigma) would only occur about five times in a hundred (two-tail test, direction of difference unspecified) by chance alone. With N constant, as it will be for all of the computations in a single analysis, one may easily construct a table showing the size of differences necessary for any given level of confidence for various magnitudes of p (expected). Here again, with large numbers of units, the size of p may become so small that some correction (e.g., an arc-sin transformation) must be made. If the deviation of the obtained value from the expected value proves to be significant at the 5 per cent level (either above or below chance), we may encircle such a case; if it is significant at the 1 per cent level, we may put a heavy square around such a case, and so on.

This method of estimating significance is not altogether satisfactory, and some work on a better method is needed. At least two problems arise in the interpretation of the significance of contingencies as computed above. For one thing, with a large number of significance estimations being made, one would expect 5 per cent of them to be significant at the 5 per cent level by chance alone, 1 per cent at the 1 per cent level, and so on. Therefore, one must also rely on the meaningfulness of the clusters of related (or unrelated) categories. For another thing, as was pointed out by William Madow in this conference, there is a serious question of lack of independence in applying this or any other statistical test of significance across the several columns of the matrix; for instance, the contingency of A with B is not apt to be independent of that between A and C, A and D, and so on. No solution to this problem was suggested. Interpretively, a contingency between two content categories that is significantly above chance is treated as evidence for *association* in the thinking of the source; a contingency significantly below chance is treated as evidence for *dissociation* in the thinking of the source — these ideas are related, but in such a way that the occurrence of one is a condition for the nonoccurrence of the other.

Representation of Results

There are a number of ways in which the results of a contingency

analysis can be represented, all of them being matters of conven-
ience and efficiency in communicating rather than rigorous quantitative procedures in themselves. (1) *Table of significant contingencies.* The simplest summary picture is a table which simply lists,
for each category, the other categories with which it has significant
associations or dissociations. (2) *Cluster analysis.* From the total
contingency matrix, one may by inspection select sets of categories
which form clusters by virtue of all having either significant plus
relations with each other or at least include no significant minus
relations. All such sets may be represented in an ordinary two-
dimensional surface as overlapping regions (see Fig. 5, the Goebbels
diary data). (3) *Models derived from the generalized distance
formula.* Where the plusses and minuses in the raw data matrix
represent frequencies above and below the median frequencies for
each column, one may use the generalized distance formula

$$D = \sqrt{\Sigma d^2},$$

where d represents the difference in each unit between values ($+$
or $-$) in any two columns (0 where they have the same sign, 2
where different signs). If all signs between two columns are identical, D equals zero; if there is no correspondence, D is maximal.

We may now construct a new matrix similar to the contingency
matrix (Fig. 3B) in which we enter D for every pair of categories.
If no more than three factors are required to account for the relations in the D matrix, the entire set of distances can be represented
in a solid model (see Fig. 4, the Ford Sunday Evening Hour data).
If more factors are involved, a three-dimensional model can only
approximate the true distance relations (even though the values in
the D matrix are valid for any number of dimensions).[8] (The reason
the D method cannot be applied where mere presence and absence
is recorded is that in this case pairing of minuses between columns merely indicates lack of relation or independence between
categories.)

ILLUSTRATIVE APPLICATIONS OF CONTINGENCY METHOD

Cameron's Ford Sunday Evening Hour Talks

A sample of 38 talks given by W. J. Cameron on the Ford Sunday
Evening Hour radio program, each talk running to about 1,000

---

[8] For more details on this procedure, see C. E. Osgood and G. J. Suci,
"A Measure of Relation Determined by Both Mean Difference and Profile
Information," *Psychological Bulletin,* 49 (1952), 251-62.

words, was studied by this method.[9] Each talk was treated as a unit. On the basis of a preliminary reading, 27 broadly defined content categories were selected in terms of frequency of usage. The analyst then went through these materials noting each reference to these categories. The median frequency of appearance of each category was computed and a matrix of units (rows) against categories (columns) was filled. A plus was entered for frequency of category above the median for a unit and a minus for frequencies below. Applying the formula for D given above to each pair of content columns, a D matrix showing the distance of each category from every other category was computed. Using four concepts maximally distant from each other as reference points (the solid balls shown), the three-dimensional model shown as Figure 4 was made with sponge-rubber balls and "pick-up" sticks as the best fitting approximation to the distance data in the matrix. This model is an approximation rather than an accurate map because more than three factors would be required in this case for accuracy.

Nevertheless, the conferees familiar with Cameron's talks felt that the pattern of relationships produced here had considerable face validity. References to FACTORIES, industry, machines, production, and the like (FAC) tended to cluster with references to PROGRESS (PRO), FORD and Ford cars (FD), free ENTERPRISE and initiative (ENT), BUSINESS, selling, and the like (BUS), and to some extent with references to RUGGED INDIVIDUALISM, independence (RI), and to LAYMEN, farmers, shopkeepers, and so on (LAY). But when Cameron talked about these things he tended *not* to talk about (i.e., to dissociate them from) categories like YOUTH, our young people (YTH), INTELLECTUALS, lily-livered bookmen, etc. (INT), and DISEASE, poisoned minds, unhealthy thoughts, and the like (DIS), which form another cluster. This relation in Cameron's thinking between YOUTH (always favorable) and DISEASE notions (obviously unfavorable) was unsuspected by the analyst until it appeared in the contingency data, which suggests one of the potential values of the method. Also tending to be dissociated from the FORD, FACTO-

----

[9] It is instructive to compare the results of this contingency analysis with an earlier frequency analysis of speeches by the same speaker. See T. S. Green, Jr., "Mr. Cameron and the Ford House," *Public Opinion Quarterly*, 3 (1939), 669-75. The clusters spotted in the present study seem to have been largely overlooked in Green's more conventional analysis. The studies were independent of each other, for the earlier study was not known to the present author.

Figure 4

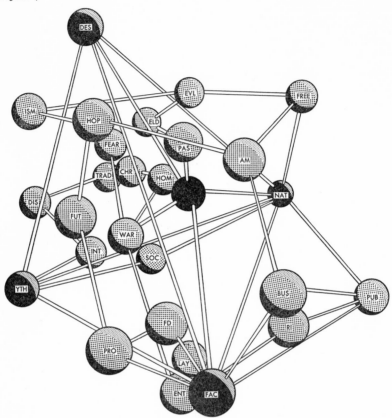

RIES, ENTERPRISE cluster, and more or less independent of the YOUTH, INTELLECTUALS, and DISEASE one, we find an interesting collection of superficially contrary notions: on one hand we have SOCIETY in abstract, civilization (SOC), CHRISTIAN, God, and church (CHR), our ELDERS, mature minds (ELD), TRADITION and basic values (TRAD), and to some extent the PAST of our forefathers (PAS) and our HOMES, fireside, and families (HOM) — all things favorably drawn; but on the other hand, in the same cluster, we find DESTRUCTION and violence (DES), assorted ISMS like Communism, Fascism, and totalitarianism (ISM), FEAR, bewilderment, and dismay (FEAR), and sundry EVILS (EVL). Apparently, when he thinks and writes about the solid, traditional things that hold society together, he immediately tends to associate them with the things he fears, the various isms that threaten destruction of his values. References to the FUTURE (FUT) and to our HOPES and confidence in the New World (HOP) tend to be associated with references to AMERICA (AM), but also ISMS again. The allocation of a few other notions, including references to the general PUBLIC (PUB), to FREEDOM and democracy (FREE), and human NATURE, what is instinctive or natural (NAT), may be studied by the reader himself.

Goebbels' Diary

Using a table of random numbers to select pages and then lines-on-page, 100 samples, each approximately 100 words in length (beginning and ending with the nearest full sentence), were extracted from the English version of Goebbels' diary and typed on cards. An example would be:

#38. Spieler sent me a letter from occupied France. He complained bitterly about the provocative attitude of the French, who continue to live exactly as in peacetime and have everything in the way of food that their hearts desire. Even though this is true only of the plutocratic circles, it nevertheless angers our soldiers, who have but meager rations. We Germans are too good-natured in every respect. We don't yet know how to behave like a victorious people. We have no real tradition. On this we must catch up in the coming decades.

In terms of a rough frequency-of-usage analysis made previously, 21 content categories were selected for analysis. An independent coder (Mrs. Lois Anderson) went through the 100 units in a shuffled order noting simply the presence or absence of reference to these 21 categories, generating a raw data table like that illustrated in Figure 3A. The data were then transformed into a contingency table of the sort shown as Figure 3B, and significance tests were run (utilizing the arc-sin transformation). References to GERMAN GENERALS were significantly contingent upon references to INTERNAL FRICTIONS (in the inner circle about Hitler) at the 1 per cent level; references to GERMAN PUBLIC were associated with those to BAD MORALE at the 5 per cent level, as were contingencies between RUSSIA and EASTERN FRONT; negative contingencies, significant at the 5 per cent level, were obtained between RUSSIA and BAD MORALE, between references to ENGLAND and references to GERMAN SUPERIORITY as a race, and between references to the GERMAN PUBLIC and references to RUSSIA. Such negative contingencies are at least suggestive of repressions on Goebbels' part, that is, avoiding thinking of Russia when he thinks of the bad home-morale situation, avoiding thinking about England when he thinks about the superiority of the German race, and so on. These are merely inferences, of course.

A cluster analysis was made of these data, with the results shown in Figure 5. The content categories included within regions have mainly plus relations and no minus relations. Numerous inferences might be made from this chart. For example: (D) that Goebbels defends himself from thoughts about the HARD WINTER with SELF PRAISE and thoughts about his closeness to DER FUEHRER; (A) that ideas about BAD MORALE lead promptly to rationalizations in terms of the INTERNAL FRICTIONS brought about by GERMAN GENERALS, which in turn bring up conflicts between himself and others in securing the favor of DER FUEHRER; (C) that thoughts about his job of maintaining GOOD MORALE among the GERMAN PUBLIC lead to thoughts

Figure 5

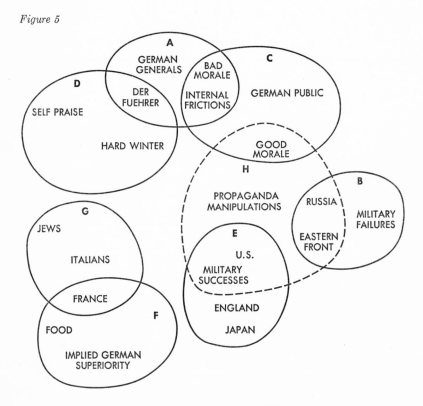

about BAD MORALE and INTERNAL FRICTIONS; (H) that his problem-solving ideas about PROPAGANDA MANIPULATIONS may lead him alternatively to the GOOD MORALE cluster of associations, to the dismal RUSSIA–EASTERN FRONT–MILITARY FAILURES cluster, or to the more encouraging cluster in which his ally, JAPAN, is having MILITARY SUCCESSES against ENGLAND and the U.S.; and finally (G and F), that when he thinks about the subject peoples, JEWS and ITALIANS, and FRANCE, he tends also, particularly in the case of FRANCE, to think about difficulties of maintaining FOOD supplies, leading quite naturally to ideas about GERMAN SUPERIORITY in withstanding hardships, and the like. These are inferences, of course; there are alternative interpretations possible as to why any cluster of symbols shows positive or negative contingency. But the inferences have the advantage of resting on demonstrable verbal behavior which may even be unconscious to the source. They do not necessarily depend upon explicit statements of relation by the source.

A Psychotherapy Case

Fifty-five successive interviews (tape recorded and transcribed) with a young man undergoing therapy with Dr. Hobart Mowrer were analyzed by the contingency method, each interview serving as a single unit. Although no tests of significance were run in this instance, the patterns of associations and relative dissociations displayed in Table 2 are quite interesting and suggestive of the possible use of this technique as a means of producing inferences about a patient that could be checked against clinical insights. First we may note the different ideas that are in nonchance relationship to MOTHER *vs.* FATHER: although both notions are associated with each other and with AGGRESSION, references to the female parent tend to appear with references to his INDEPENDENCE, DRINKING, and RESPONSIBILITIES, whereas references to the male parent tend to occur with VOCATION plans and MILITARY SERVICE. And note that the patient's thoughts about his MOTHER tend to be *dissociated* from (repression?) discussion of HOMOSEXUALITY and MASTURBATION. Judging from the frequency of relations in this table, as well as from frequency in the original interviews, both AGGRESSION and HOMOSEXUALITY were key problems, but they have entirely different associations as well as being dissociated from each other. AGGRESSION comes up in the context of the parents, VOCATION plans, MILITARY

Table 2

Category	Associations	Dissociations
MOTHER	father, aggression, independence, drinking, responsibilities	homosexuality, masturbation, impotence, amnesic recall, military service
FATHER	mother, aggression, vocation, military service	
OEDIPAL RELATION	guilt feelings	vocation
CHILDHOOD	impotence	
HOMOSEXUALITY	heterosexuality, relation to therapist	mother, aggression, progress in therapy
HETEROSEXUALITY	homosexuality	progress in therapy
MASTURBATION		mother, progress in therapy
GUILT FEELINGS	Oedipal relation	
IMPOTENCE	childhood	mother
AGGRESSION	mother, father, vocation, drinking, military service, progress in therapy	homosexuality
INDEPENDENCE	mother	relation to therapist
VOCATION	father, aggression, military service	Oedipal relation
AMNESIC RECALL	military service, relation to therapist	mother
DRINKING	mother, aggression	
RESPONSIBILITIES	mother	
MILITARY SERVICE	father, aggression, vocation, amnesic recall	mother
PROGRESS IN THERAPY	aggression	homosexuality, heterosexuality, masturbation
RELATION TO THERAPIST	homosexuality, amnesic recall	independence

SERVICE, DRINKING, *and* PROGRESS IN THERAPY; on the other hand, HOMOSEXUALITY comes up in connection with its "normal" opposite, HETEROSEXUALITY, and with the patient's RELATION TO THERAPIST. It is also evident that this patient's discourse about PROGRESS IN THERAPY is associated with references to his AGGRESSION but kept dissociated from references to HOMOSEXUALITY and MASTURBATION. A reasonably consistent and meaningful picture of this patient's problem as it is enacted in the therapy situation seems to be derivable from this contingency analysis.

CRITIQUE OF THE CONTINGENCY METHOD

The use of the contingency method is based upon a very general inference about relations between messages and those who exchange them; namely, that contingencies among events in messages are indicative of the association structure in the source and predictive of the association structure that may result in the receiver (given sufficient frequency of repetition). But under what conditions is this general inference likely to be valid? Certainly one cannot make valid inferences about the total association structure of a liberal newspaperman hired to write editorials for the *Chicago Tribune!* In part, at least, the issue here comes down to precisely what question is being asked of the data. When contingencies are significantly above or below chance, there is evidence for structure in the source. If we are dealing with spontaneous informal messages from a single, known source (e.g., personal diaries not intended to be read by the general public, letters to friends and family, extemporaneous speech, as in a psychotherapeutic interview, etc.), then attribution of the association structure to this source is probably most defensible. When dealing with deliberately planned messages, particularly when the "source" is an institution, as is particularly true in propaganda analysis, it would probably be safer to speak of the "policy" of the source rather than its association structure. In other words, here as elsewhere it is necessary for the analyst to take into account the total context from which the message appears.

This leads us to the issue over which the conference members had some of their most spirited discussions — to what extent is the contingency method "representational" in nature and thereby invalidated in many cases? As Alexander George raised the problem, what if you had good reason to believe that Cameron was doing a cynical job of propaganda? How can you assume that contingencies between references to FORD and PROGRESS and ENTERPRISE represent *Cameron's* association structure in this case? Isn't the whole model invalidated in this case? The same argument, perhaps to lesser degree, would apply to Goebbels' diary, since he was probably writing with an eye toward eventual publication. Or, as George Mahl presented the same problem, how can you assume that because a patient repeatedly asserts "I love my mother, I love my mother, I love my mother," this means *mother* and *love* go together, when we know that patients are using language instrumentally, to achieve certain goals?

To what extent does the contingency method fail to allow for such instrumental use of language? It does indeed assume that occurrence of the content items that are recorded depends upon occurrence of appropriate meanings to the speaker or writer. In this sense (which probably must always be true) it is assumed that the source "says what he means." Those who criticize the contingency method as being invalid for instrumental communications because it *cannot* be assumed that the source "says what he means" are obviously using this phrase in a different sense. They refer not just to the meanings which were available in the thinking of the source but rather to the assertions in which he related these meanings. In other words, when a source says "Free enterprise always leads to progress" or "I have always loved my mother" we must assume that the lexical items *free enterprise, progress, love,* and *mother* appear in the message stream because their corresponding meaning-states occurred in the source, but we do *not* need to assume that the assertions *free enterprise leads to progress* and *I love mother* necessarily represent the sources' belief systems. Unlike evaluative assertion analysis, which does proceed on the face value of the assertion made, contingency analysis depends only upon the presence of symbols, not how they are linked. The assertions made are not accepted or rejected for they are indeed not noted.

Viewed in this light, the contingency method is *not* "representational." The fact that references to YOUTH and to DISEASE by Cameron are significantly associated says nothing about the direction of the assertions relating them. As a matter of fact, Cameron's typical statement would be that "Our young people are *not* susceptible to the diseased ideologies of these times." What the method tells us, however, is that there is a greater-than-chance tendency for ideas about DISEASE to occur in the environment of ideas about YOUTH — quite apart from what assertions he may make relating these two. Similarly in the psychotherapy situation, the method gives us evidence that when the patient talked about his MOTHER, he did tend to talk also about AGGRESSION on his own part — quite apart from how he related these two notions in linguistic constructions, or whether he so related them at all. It is quite possible for there to be a significant contingency between two items that are never related in assertions, since the units usually span more than single sentences or even paragraphs.

As a matter of fact, we may define a method of content analysis as allowing for "instrumental" analysis if it taps message evidence that is beyond the voluntary control of the source and hence yields valid inferences despite the strategies of the source. If we think of instrumental analysis in that way, then contingency analysis also seems to suit the purpose. One of its chief advantages, it seems to me, is that a speaker or writer will have great difficulty preventing a contingency from appearing between two ideas that in fact are associated in his thinking. If the idea of INTERNAL FRICTIONS among the Nazi elite regularly and strongly leads Goebbels to think of running to DER FUEHRER for support, he may either produce positive contingencies by expressing some remarks about Der Fuehrer (if this association is not anxiety-producing) or may produce negative contingencies by voluntarily or involuntarily suppressing such remarks (if this association is anxiety-producing). But it would be extremely difficult and unlikely for him to manufacture a chance contingency deliberately.

This has direct bearing on the interpretation of significantly negative contingencies. I think we must assume that a significant contingency, whether positive or negative, is evidence for an underlying association between such content categories. If the contingency is negative (i.e., a significant dissociation) it presumably means that these ideas are associated with some kind of unpleasant affect. If such an undesired association is consciously available to the source, he may deliberately inhibit expressing the associated idea, whereas if repressive mechanisms are operating, he will not be consciously aware of the association yet will still show a negative contingency. The contingency method per se does not indicate whether such dissociation is deliberate or involuntary. The same distinction actually applies to positive contingencies — the source may consciously and strategically express associations (in which case, of course, they are likely to be connected in assertions) or he may display associations without being aware that he is making them. The contingency method provides evidence for nonchance structure; interpretation of this structure is still the job of the skilled analyst.

The question was raised of whether this method takes into

account the intensity of association. It does not take into account the intensity with which assertions are made — if the source says "The French are *definitely* like the Italians in this respect," the method only records an instance of contingency between the French and Italian categories. On the other hand, reflecting the basic psychological principle relating habit strength to frequency of response, the method does indirectly reflect the strength of associations (or dissociations). In other words, the stronger the association between two ideas in the thinking of the source, the more regularly will the occurrence of one be the condition for occurrence (or inhibition) of the other. Thus the magnitude of the contingency relation will index the intensity of association. This does not mean that all significant associations in the thinking of the source will be caught by this method. Contingencies among categories that occur only infrequently across the units studied are difficult to interpret statistically, but they may nevertheless represent significant associations — this is another point at which the sensitive analyst has an advantage over the quantitative method.

In just what sense, we may ask, is this method quantitative and objective? The preliminary steps of selecting categories and judging what to include or exclude from each are highly subjective; it is identical with the Lasswellian frequency methods at this point. From the point where the raw data matrix (categories against units) has been filled in to the listing of significant contingencies (or construction of some cluster chart or model) the method is objective, in the sense that any analyst following the rules must end up with the same association structure. The final stage, in which the analyst interprets the contingency structure, is entirely subjective, of course. The method will thus avoid bias on the part of the analyst in the sense (1) of his being unduly impressed by a single contingency which is actually chancewise over the message as a whole, and (2) of his failing to note certain contingencies that are significant but which are contrary to his expectations. By the same token, there will be a great deal of information which such a method as this will fail to pick up.

Finally, we may note that there was considerable discussion in the conference over whether or not contingency among categories implied similarity of meaning. Certainly, if the meaning of a concept is identified either in terms of what is referred to or in terms of a location in an n-dimensional semantic space,[10] then the fact of

---

[10] Cf. Osgood, Suci, and Tannenbaum, *Measurement of Meaning.*

association is not indicative of semantic similarity. References to COMMUNISM may frequently lead to references to CAPITAL-ISM, but this does not necessarily imply that these concepts are either similar in reference or in psychological meaning. On the other hand, there are certain relationships between association and meaning that should be indicated. First, association between concepts (e.g., GOD and DEVIL, CAPITALISM and COMMUNISM, SOLDIER and SAILOR), even though they may be common opposites semantically, will often reflect the fact that they share certain attributes, are of the same "class," or (linguistically) are alternatives within the same structural frames. Secondly, it may be true that when concepts are repeatedly associated, each will tend to acquire the meaning of the other — a case in point is the effect that the phrase "Fifth Amendment Communist" had upon the meaning of "Fifth Amendment." But it should be carefully noted that in this case there was an implied assertion, "The Fifth Amendment *is used by* (or *protects* or *favors*) Communists," that is, an associative assertion. I suspect that one might express or experience contingencies between COMMUNISM and CAPITALISM indefinitely without semantic assimilation so long as the assertions in which they appeared were consistently dissociative; for example, "Communism *is the antithesis of* Capitalism," "In countries under the domination of Communism . . . *but* in capitalistic societies . . . ," and so on. In other words, the tendency toward semantic assimilation or dissimilation (exaggeration of meaningful contrasts) presumably depends upon the linguistic constructions within which contingencies appear.

POTENTIAL APPLICATIONS OF THE CONTINGENCY METHOD

A number of areas of possible application of this method have already been offered by way of illustrations — application to a type of serial propaganda, to a sample of a personal diary (admittedly somewhat propagandistic), and to the protocols of a psychotherapy case. In the latter connection, the conferees suggested that changes in the contingency structure over successive stages of a psychotherapy case might yield suggestive evidence as to progress in therapy, for example the shift from dissociations to associations among certain critical concepts. This tool would also seem to have a potential role in the study of historical personages via their letters, diaries, and autobiographies. In this connection John Garraty pointed out that one of the values of the method would lie in pointing the finger to unexpected but revealing contingencies in the subject's thinking. Applications of this method to the study of charms and folk tales will be noted by Thomas Sebeok and Robert Armstrong in later chapters. Considerable theoretical interest would also attach to a comparison of contingency findings about the source with those derived from analysis of his speech disturbances and the like — when a patient discusses materials known by the contingency method to involve dissociations, is there a measurable increase in pauses and sentence breaks? James Jenkins pointed out that it would also be possible to analyze the raw data from such pausal analyses in terms of contingencies between units; for example, in what sessions in therapy, or in letters to what people, does the subject display similar patterns of language behavior? In applying contingency analysis to practical problems in content study, the analyst would certainly use it in conjunction with other methods, particularly in conjunction with his own insightful appraisals of the context and strategy of the message.

INFERENCES ABOUT LANGUAGE COMMUNALITY: CLOZE PROCEDURE

The conferees were fortunate to have Dr. Wilson Taylor, developer of Cloze Procedure, sitting in with them. Although not designed or generally used as a method of content analysis in the traditional sense, it is an ingeniously simple operation that has an extremely wide range of potential applications. And, in terms of the general psycholinguistic model suggested earlier in this chapter, it is obviously a technique of content analysis, in that one uses evidence in messages as a basis for making inferences about either sources or receivers. Taylor was invited to discuss his method with the conferees, and what follows is a digest of this discussion.

LOGIC OF CLOZE PROCEDURE

The term "cloze" is a contraction of the Gestalt notion of closure — the tendency in perceptual decoding for observers to fill in or complete familiar forms which are incomplete or obscure as physical events. The same thing happens in the decoding of linguistic signs. Just as the person presented with an incomplete circle tachistoscopically will tend to see it whole, so will the average American reader, when he reads "Chickens cackle but ———— quack," tend to fill in *ducks* as the missing word. In terms of all of the past experience of typical users of our language, *ducks* is the element most probably missing. We may note that filling in *ducks* depends not only upon knowledge of barnyard animals, but also on linguistic facility — given the above structure, the missing word must be a plural noun. To use another example, "The old man ———— down the road," it is clear that the structure of English requires some verb (*flew, limps, crawls, traveled*, etc.), though the tense is not specified by the context; on the other hand, the presence of "old man" and "road" clearly exerts semantic selectivity on the alternatives — *limped* or *hobbled* are certainly more probable semantically than *slept, swam*, or even *ran*.

The essence of Cloze Procedure is as follows. Some source produces a message. It will usually be in written form, but the same procedures with some modification will apply to spoken messages and even to aesthetic messages like paintings and musical compositions. The experimenter (or content analyst) mutilates it by deleting certain items and substituting blanks in their places, and then gives the mutilated form to one or more receivers to fill in. The greater the success these receivers have in replacing the missing items, the higher the Cloze score. In other words, the receiver utilizes what information is there, that is, the context, as a basis for predicting the deleted material.

Why do we call this a measure of language communality? The human source that produces the message has a very complex and hierarchial system of language-encoding habits; these include his semantical meanings (e.g., of *old man*), his associations (e.g., that *day* makes him think of *night*), his syntactical sequencing tendencies (e.g., expecting a noun form following one or more adjectives), his grammatical regularities (e.g., expecting an *s* on a verb following a singular noun), and so on. Similarly, the receivers of his message have equally complex and hierarchial systems of language habits. To the degree that these complex habit systems of source and receiver correspond, one should be able to substitute for the other, that is, should be able to complete his messages. At one extreme, suppose we could take an individual, suddenly split him into identical twins, and have one produce a message and the other fill in a mutilated version of it; we would expect the second twin to yield an almost perfect Cloze score, because all of his language habits, set in motion by the unreeling context, would converge upon the same selections at the same points. At the other extreme, we would expect a receiver that was largely unfamiliar with the

language and culture of the source to have great difficulty. Therefore, it seems reasonable to view the Cloze score as an index of
the over-all correspondence or communality between the language
systems of different individuals. Another way of putting this is
to say that the Cloze score gives us a measure of the ease or difficulty of a particular message for a particular receiver. If the
receiver shares the language system of the source then it is easy for
him to "grasp" the message and to fill in the blanks. If the blanks
in the message are hard for him to fill in then the message is a hard
one for him to "grasp" in the usual sense.

THE MECHANICS OF CLOZE PROCEDURE

As noted above, the essence of Cloze Procedure is very simple —
the investigator takes a message from some source, substitutes
blanks for certain words in it according to some arbitrary rule,
presents this mutilated message to some number of receivers, and
scores them for the correctness of their fill-ins (i.e., the sum or
per cent of blanks correctly filled) — but there are a number of
methodological issues that arise. We can indicate some of these
issues and Taylor's findings with respect to them by asking a series
of questions.

1. Should we delete any words or only difficult words? In one
study Taylor compared the results obtained with three forms of
a test: an "easy" form which took out articles, conjunctions, verb
auxiliaries, and pronouns; an "any word" form; and a "hard" form
which took out nouns, verbs, and adverbs.[11] Although, as would
be expected, the sheer magnitude of Cloze (number of correct fill-
ins) was higher for the easy form than for the hard form, the "any
word" form was found to discriminate among messages and subjects as well as either of the other forms.

2. Should words be deleted at random or by some arbitrary
regular method, such as every fifth word? Taylor has found that
the ranking of difficulty of three standard passages (on which Cloze,
Dale-Chall, and Flesch agree) is exactly the same for four quite
different deletion systems — counting out every fifth word, every
seventh word, every tenth, and finally 10 per cent of the words at
random. This is true despite the fact that each method of sampling
took out entirely different words for the most part. That is, it is not

---

[11] Included in the author's "Aptitude and Comprehension Correlates of
'Cloze' Readability Scores," a paper delivered before the American Psychological Association, Chicago, 1956.

necessary to go through the labor of taking words out at random; merely counting out every nth word will do.

3. How many blanks per passage are needed for a stable score? It is obvious that if all words are blanked out there is no context, whereas if no words are blanked out there is no problem; between these limits there seems to be considerable latitude. Taylor has found empirically that taking out every fifth word yields a sensitive measure of difficulty without presenting an extremely difficult task for the average reader. In an analysis of his data in which increasingly long samples from the same passage were scored, he found that a very stable Cloze score (in terms of the total passage as a criterion) was obtained from as few as 50 blanks. This means that samples as small as about 250 words can be used satisfactorily in applying this method.

4. Should close synonyms or only exact words be scored as correct? The conference members, along with many others, raised this question. Taylor has compared these two methods of scoring directly, that is, on data for the same subjects filling in the same passages. With samples of the size indicated above, he found almost exactly the same ordering of difficulty for passages and ordering of subjects on passages when only the exact word originally used by the source was "correct" as when synonyms were considered "correct." Not only is it very difficult and subjective to judge "close synonymity," but scoring in terms of the exact word is probably more sensitive to fine differences in the styles of different writers. The fact that essentially the same results are obtained probably indicates that the same general variables that influence the probability of getting the exact word also influence the probability of getting a sufficiently close synonym.

5. How many subjects are needed for discrimination among sources? This question has no precise answer, because it will depend upon the grossness of the differences among the messages being measured. If the differences in the readability, comprehension, etc., of the passages is very slight, then a large number of subjects will be required, and vice versa.

SOME ILLUSTRATIVE APPLICATIONS OF CLOZE PROCEDURE

Cloze is a measure applied to messages which serves to index the communality or correspondence between the total language systems of its source and receivers. As such, it can be used (1) to draw inferences about, or make comparisons among, different sources with the set of receivers held constant, or (2) to draw inferences about, or make comparisons among, different receivers with the set of sources held constant. In case 1 we may refer to what we measure as the *readability* (or encoding communicative facility) of the source and in case 2 we may refer to what we measure as the *comprehension level* (or decoding communicative facility) of the receiver.

Readability[12]

The well-known "readability formulas," such as those devised by Flesch or by Dale and Chall, select only a few message indicators (e.g., difficulty levels of individual words, number of pronouns, length of words, length of sentences, etc.) and are necessarily therefore only partial indicators of source-receiver communality. To the extent that communality (or lack of it) depends upon factors other than those tapped by the "formulas," they will break down. To demonstrate that his Cloze Procedure functions as a measure of readability under ordinary circumstances, Taylor first selected three passages from Flesch's book on which both Flesch and Dale-Chall agreed in readability ranking; Cloze Procedure was applied to these passages, and an identical ordering was found. To demonstrate that the other formulas could be "broken down" while Cloze could not, he then selected five more passages, three of them hand-picked "with malice aforethought" — Erskine Caldwell (intuitively very simple, but replete with long sentences), James Joyce's *Finnegan's Wake* (extremely difficult semantically), and Gertrude Stein (little, familiar words and short sentences, but put together in very unconventional ways!). Whereas the Flesch formula rated both Caldwell and Joyce as equally easy (Dale-Chall did show a difference here) and both formulas ranked Stein as the easiest of all eight passages, Cloze ranked these passages as most people familiar with the authors would have done — Caldwell as quite easy, Joyce as quite difficult, and Stein as most difficult. Cloze works where other methods won't, we assume, not because it is a better "formula" but because it is sensitive to just about all of the determinants (semantic, associational, grammatical, and syntactical) which affect encoding by a source and decoding by a receiver.

----

[12] W. L. Taylor, " 'Cloze Procedure': A New Tool for Measuring Readability," *Journalism Quarterly*, 30 (1953), 415-33.

Comprehension

Shifting our attention from source to receiver, it seems reasonable to suppose that the better a reader comprehends the message (in terms of his intelligence, his background of knowledge, etc.) the better he should be able to fill in the missing items. This reasoning was tested in an experiment which used trainees at Sampson Air Force Base, N.Y., as subjects.[13] Two carefully matched comprehension tests had already been developed for a technical article on the Air Force system of supply. Samples, together constituting 20 per cent of the article, were made into Cloze forms. Before even seeing this article, subjects were first given these Cloze forms and then the "before" comprehension test. A week later they read the Air Force supply article, and immediately afterward took the "after" comprehension test and then the same Cloze forms. Intelligence test scores (AFQT) were available for all subjects. High correlations between Cloze and comprehension tests, both "before" and "after" reading the Air Force supply article, indicated that both were measuring essentially the same thing. Cloze scores actually correlated a little higher with the general intelligence test scores than the comprehension test scores, although both were highly significant. Both the comprehension test and the Cloze measure (in terms of increased numbers of correct fill-ins) showed increases after reading the article that were significant at better than the .001 level. Considering the ease of preparing Cloze forms as compared with preparing adequate comprehension tests of the usual type, this experiment indicates one very practical use of the Cloze method. And for our present purposes, it indicates that Cloze is sensitive to individual differences between receivers in their language communality with a single (control) source.

Cloze and Redundancy

It probably will have occurred to the reader that the success with which a set of receivers of a message can fill in its missing parts is a measure of the redundancy of the message. If the context surrounding a blank is such that there is no uncertainty about what the correct word is (and Cloze is 100 per cent), we have complete redundancy; at the other extreme, if the context is such that there is complete uncertainty about the correct word and everyone selects a different alternative (and Cloze is 0 per cent), we have no

----

[13] W. L. Taylor, "Recent Developments in the Use of 'Cloze Procedure,'" *Journalism Quarterly*, 33 (1956), No. 1.

redundancy. To study the relations between Cloze and entropy measures,[14] a continuous 175-word passage was treated as follows: one group of 50 subjects reacted to a form in which the first, fifth, tenth, etc. words were deleted; a second group of 50 subjects received a form in which the second, sixth, eleventh, etc. words were deleted; by using five such groups, each with every fifth word deleted, a continuous profile of both Cloze and redundancy scores for the entire passage could be obtained. The correlation of Cloze score with an information theory measure of redundancy (negative entropy) was .87; in other words, in general a simple measure of per cent correct fill-in correlates highly with an index of the reduction in uncertainty attributable to context.

One may ask why this correlation is not perfect. The answer is that it is possible for an item to yield a Cloze score of 0 per cent correct fill-in and yet have perfect redundancy, in that all receivers supply the same "incorrect" word. An example will make this clear: suppose some writer produces "My aunt willed all her money to a cat and canine hospital" — poor word balance, to be sure; if a blank is substituted for *canine,* all subjects will probably agree in substituting the word *dog,* that is, there is no uncertainty among the receivers but Cloze is zero. In such cases it is apparent that the source has misled the receivers, and it is possible that such discrepancies between Cloze and redundancy scores would indicate deliberate substitutions on the part of the source, for example places where he rejects his own most probable alternative. This discrepancy also highlights the difference between Cloze and redundancy indices — the former uses the actual message of the source as a criterion whereas the latter reflects only the uncertainties of receivers.

CRITIQUE OF CLOZE PROCEDURE

Probably the most serious criticism of Cloze Procedure as a method of content analysis is that it provides answers to other questions than those ordinarily asked by content analysts. For a message as a whole, it gives an index of language behavior communality, the degree to which the communicative habits of the source correspond to those of his readers (readability) or the degree to which the communicative habits of a receiver correspond

---

[14] W. L. Taylor, "Application of Cloze and Entropy Measures to the Study of Contextual Constraints in Samples of Continuous Prose" (Ph.D. thesis, University of Illinois, Urbana, 1954); *Dissertation Abstracts,* 15 (1955), 464-65.

to those of some standard source (comprehension). It may tell us how well a source is "getting through" to his receivers, but it doesn't tell us anything about his motives, his dominant ideas, meanings, or associations. Nevertheless, it is a method of content analysis in the technical sense of that term. Another striking difference of Cloze Procedure from other methods is that it requires samples of subjects; on the other hand, by the same token it eliminates the biases of coders or analysts.

Alexander George raised the question of whether the Cloze score obtained by a subject would always indicate his degree of comprehension of the material — aren't there cases where missing items could be filled in on the basis of immediate context and yet the meaning of the passage as a whole fail to be grasped? An example would be *Gulliver's Travels,* where readers might be able to fill in gaps quite easily and yet not grasp the elaborate satire being developed. This would seem to be an empirical question, in part at least — whether or not a person who comprehends the satire, the irony, the more subtle implications of a piece will score higher than one who doesn't. It is also likely that messages with double or subtle meanings of this sort would produce many discrepancies between Cloze and redundancy scores, places where the receivers agree with each other but not with the author. George also wondered if Cloze would fall down where there is one crucial sentence or paragraph upon whose understanding the meaning of the whole depends. If this crucial material were differentially comprehended by different subjects, it probably would influence their success throughout the whole passage to some degree, and hence should show up in the total score.

POTENTIAL APPLICATIONS OF CLOZE PROCEDURE

Although Cloze Procedure does not provide answers to the questions usually asked by content analysts, the conferees were quick to see many possible uses of the technique. Suggestions came so fast and furiously that it will be best just to list them briefly here:

Kahane: Since the "word" is a very ambiguous unit (albeit a natural one for language users), it might be more interesting to linguists to have morpheme units deleted. This approach would probably indicate that grammatical predictabilities are much higher than lexical predictabilities, for one thing.

Osgood: One could also get at purely structural alternatives in a language by changing the method of scoring, that is, by counting as "correct" any fill-in that is grammatically correct in that location. Thus, if the correct word had been a preposition, any preposition would count toward the subject's score; if the word deleted had been a plural noun, any plural noun would be correct, regardless of whether it made semantic sense or not.

Casagrande: Could we get a measure of cultural or social compatibility with this technique? For example, might it not be likely that messages produced by members of the elite, say, could be filled in quite well by professionals, less well by artisans, and least well by unskilled laborers? This might even provide a more fruitful index of social distance.

Osgood: The same idea might be applied to differences between cultures, although translation problems would be involved. One might, for example, take the folk tales of one group, translate them into a set of other languages (using bilinguals), and then index over-all cultural compatibility by the ease with which members of these various different cultures can fill in the blanks. One is reminded of the difficulties English speakers had with the Indian tale "War of the Ghosts," that Bartlett used in his studies of memory.[15]

Saporta: Following along these lines, wouldn't Cloze provide a feasible index of the degree of bilingualism? That is, if we selected passages in the two languages which are of equal difficulty for monolinguals in those languages and gave them to bilinguals, the relative performance of each bilingual on completing the messages in the two languages should indicate his relative facility in the two — and, furthermore, this measure would be sensitive to the whole gamut of language habits, which most tests of bilingualism are not.

Taylor: Cloze could be used, and some preliminary studies on this have been made, to measure a student's progress in learning any second language, that is, by giving him passages of varying difficulty for monolinguals in the second language. This measure would reflect, of course, acculturation as well as purely linguistic facility.

George: One could select the best translators, say for U.N. proceedings, with this method. Radio monitors "fill in" like this all the time because they have difficulties hearing all that is said.

Mahl: The people working with Harold Kelly have been using a realistic role-playing technique to produce either intense threat of punishment for cheating in students or expectations of easy treat-

---

[15] F. C. Bartlett, *Remembering* (New York, 1932).

ment; the spontaneous speech of these subjects with different emotional states is being transcribed and mutilated in the Cloze fashion, and then given to other subjects to fill in. The results are not yet known. Mahl expects lower Cloze scores for the students under threat (because of increased variability due to emotional disorganization); Osgood predicts higher Cloze scores (because of the effects of increased drive level upon selecting the most probable language sequences).

Jenkins: The data they have been collecting at Minnesota indicates that subjects who give a large number of rare associations both score lower than average on "Clozing" other people's messages and produce lower scores when other people try to "Cloze" their messages. This would be in line with Mahl's predictions, if we assume that such people have a higher anxiety level (as was suggested by their manifest anxiety test scores).

Pool: It would be interesting to compare people in their ability to project themselves into the roles of others by this procedure — would public relations men, for example, fill in the messages of others better than physicists? And on the political propaganda level, it would be interesting to give some Bolshevik or other enemy texts to a group of analysts and see which ones were best able to reproduce the original material under Cloze conditions. Cloze scores might correlate well with ability at inferring enemy thinking or plans.

Garraty: This could also be used as a pretest of propaganda materials. By having a sample of receivers from the target country, for example, fill in the blanks in several alternative messages designed to accomplish the same end, one could predict which message would best communicate the intentions.

George: Another type of application in the political propaganda field would be to determine if the new regime in Russia following Stalin's death really differed significantly from the old. It might be possible to have a set of receivers familiar with the old "line" try to fill in blanks in messages from the new regime — if they were equally successful, it would suggest, at least, that the basic communicative mechanisms had not changed much.

Osgood: Going back for a moment to the area of clinical psychology, would it be possible to diagnose the degree or type of psychic disorder from performance on Taylor's Cloze tests? If we used a set of messages from "normal" people, could the degree of schizophrenic disturbance be shown by the Cloze score the patient obtained? And conversely, would the difficulty "normals" have in replacing missing items from schizophrenic speech indicate the degree of "disturbance of thought" in such cases?

Armstrong: You probably could use this in both music and in line drawing, filling in tones and visual gaps. That is, a measure of redundancy in aesthetic materials.

Taylor: I have been doing some research of exactly this sort — placing a grid over a drawing, for example, and knocking out patches according to some arbitrary procedure. Although this work has not progressed very far as yet, it seems entirely feasible. The better organized the picture, the more easily viewers can fill in missing patches correctly.

Osgood: One of the most general uses of Cloze procedure would be as a means of estimating the distributions of sets of alternatives — in syntactical sequences, in lexical choices, in musical melodic sequences, or what have you. This would be similar to, though easier than, what Miller and Selfridge[16] have done. It is extremely laborious, and requires texts of tremendous size, to estimate directly the transitional probabilities of units of the size of morphemes, words, and the like. One can more easily determine the distribution of alternatives chosen by a set of, say, 100 subjects in completing Cloze forms.

Cloze Procedure is an ingeniously simple tool with a remarkably wide range of potential application, as the discussion at this conference demonstrated. Despite its procedural simplicity, Cloze seems to have the virtue of tapping, or being sensitive to, most of the psychological determinants of encoding and decoding. It thus gives an over-all index of communality between the language systems of sources and receivers. By the same token, it does not give rise to specific inferences of the sort usually sought by content analysts. For this reason, as well as for its dependence upon samples of subjects, it will probably be used more as a research tool than as a procedure in practically oriented content analyses.

----

[16] G. A. Miller and J. A. Selfridge, "Verbal Context and the Recall of Meaningful Material," *American Journal of Psychology*, 63 (1950), 176-85.

3 GEORGE F. MAHL
YALE UNIVERSITY

EXPLORING EMOTIONAL STATES
BY CONTENT ANALYSIS[1]

One of the major aims of content analysis in a wide variety of fields is to infer motivational, emotional, and attitudinal states in speakers or writers. This goal was well represented at the work conference, for five of the seven participants were concerned with it. Garraty wished to investigate the personality of historical figures through the content analysis of their personal documents. George described the effort to determine strategic policies of the Germans in World War II by the content analysis of enemy propaganda. The purpose of Osgood's assertion analysis and contingency methods was to discover the attitudinal states in the message sources. Pool's content analysis of newspaper editorials had a similar aim — the determination of political attitudes and value structures of the Russian Communists. The present author studied the speech of patients in psychotherapy in order to assess their anxiety.

At the work conference, this author contrasted two general viewpoints which can be adopted in using content analysis as a research tool for measuring drives and emotions. One he labeled, rather loosely perhaps, the *representational model,* and the other, the *instrumental model* of language behavior.

The term "representational model" was used by the author to describe the approach which assumes that behavioral states in a speaker are necessarily directly represented in the symbolic content of messages he emits: to cite the example used by Osgood in the preceding chapter, when a person says he is frightened or talks of

[1] The preparation of this chapter and the research reported in it were supported by the Foundations' Fund for Research in Psychiatry and by USPHS Grant M-1052, "The Patients' Language as Expressive Behavior," G. F. Mahl, Principal Investigator.

frightening things that is taken to show that he *is* frightened. In practice the converse is also assumed: that when he is frightened, the words of any message he utters will *necessarily* refer to "fear," "frightening things," or "frightening experiences." Thus, this viewpoint assumes the face validity of the manifest lexical content of a message. Beyond this simple matter of face validity, however, there is a more fundamental and pervasive implication of the representational viewpoint: the implicit assumption that there is an isomorphic relation between behavioral states and quantitative properties of lexical content. This is illustrated in the frequency approaches to manifest content which assume, for example, that the more units of content there are in a language sample about an emotion, the greater the intensity of that emotion in the speaker at the time he uttered the content. The assumption of isomorphism also underlies those interpretations of contingency analyses which conclude that contingencies in messages directly reflect behavioral associations.

Most of the objective studies of psychotherapy interviews that have used content analysis for the measurement of emotional states assumed, implicitly or explicitly, the general validity of the representational model. Many of these studies have been reviewed by Auld and Murray.[2]

The term "instrumental model" emphasizes the instrumental function of language in need or drive gratification, in the implementation of motives and attitudes, etc. Here language functions principally as instrumental behavior and should be regarded as having the basic functional properties of all instrumental behavior. At times language is instrumental by virtue of its symbolic nature, but at other times this is purely by virtue of its signal or stimulus properties. That is, at times language is instrumental because of "intended" encodings and decodings of the linguistic symbols but at other times such processes are irrelevant to the instrumental function of the language behavior.

The thesis of this chapter is that the instrumental model is the more general and valid one for purposes of inferring emotional states from language behavior. People implicitly adhere to this thesis in everyday interaction, but behavioral scientists largely shun it in using content analysis as a research tool. They may do so because the instrumental model seems to imply a more complex and difficult methodology than does the representational model. Per-

---

[2] "Content-Analysis Studies of Psychotherapy."

haps these difficulties have been overestimated. This chapter aims to do two things: to outline some ideas about the instrumental model that were discussed at the conference and subsequently elaborated, and to illustrate briefly the application of certain of these ideas to the language of patients during psychotherapeutic interviews.

INSTRUMENTAL ASPECTS OF LANGUAGE

VARIOUS WAYS IN WHICH LANGUAGE CAN BE INSTRUMENTAL

There are various ways in which messages may function as instrumental behavior. These will be illustrated below, taking hunger as the drive.

The Production of Signals

The earliest instances in an individual's life in which a transmission of information results in hunger gratification are those in which the mother perceives the crying and restlessness associated with increased hunger and thereupon feeds the infant. The crying, etc., will become stable indications of the child's hunger if they are followed by feeding. Eventually they may be accompanied by the utterance of "mama" sounds. Although they become a stable, integral part of the mother-child interaction, these messages are not linguistic in the correct sense of the word. They do not consist of sounds or gestures having a shared and conventionally defined meaning for the mother and child. Rather, they are merely responses of the infant that prompt the mother to gratify his hunger. Thus from the observer's point of view, and later from the child's point of view, they are instrumental responses. They show the properties of all instrumental behavior, nonverbal as well as verbal. For example, their probability of occurrence will increase if they are followed by feeding, and they will extinguish if they are not followed by feeding.

For the purpose of this discussion, the following additional points about the behavior of the infant are of significance: (1) the vocal responses of crying, saying "Mama," etc., do not contain any reference, direct or indirect, to the drive state; (2) they may be nonspecific with reference to the drive state — the same responses, for example, may be effective in gratifying other drives: coldness, wetness, fatigue, fear, colic pains, etc.; (3) other responses may serve the same function in obtaining food, for example sucking on fingers or thumb.

The Use of Symbols That Are Both Representational and Instrumental

Several years later, a hungry child returning home from school may utter at the kitchen door, "Mom, I'm hungry. Would you give me something to eat?" If the mother is tardy in responding to this utterance, the child will repeat it with insistence and with suitable variations. The mother will decode this message and give the child some milk and crackers. At this point the utterance by the child will cease, he will start to eat, and a chain of quite different utterances will take place, dealing with what happened on the school bus, at school, etc.

In this example, too, there are the essential properties of all instrumental behavior, regardless of whether it is linguistic or nonlinguistic. Upon the action of drive and cue stimuli, a response is made which persists until need gratification or drive reduction occurs. We can assume that the occurrence of this response in the presence of these drive and cue stimuli has been rewarded with food frequently in the past. These previous rewards have made it extremely likely that when the child is hungry, he will make the statement he did, and not say "I'm thirsty, may I have a drink of water?"; that he will make his response in the presence of his mother and not to the paper boy or to the bus driver; that his goal-oriented behavior will persist until the reward is forthcoming; and that in this stream of behavior there may be some variations in response from a habit family hierarchy.

The utterance "Mom, I'm hungry. Would you give me something to eat?" is an extremely effective instrumental communication. The "Mom" identifies the audience and arouses her attention. Other components identify the drive state, the drive object, and the action of the mother. The message will be effective at a distance; it is not dependent upon visual elements. There is very little chance left that the drive will not be gratified promptly, assuming the mother is disposed to do so once she has decoded the message.

Of course this type of message may be modified in many ways. The child can specify the degree of hunger (by saying "I'm starving") or a precise object for which there is an appetite. Also, the message may be embellished with elements that will increase the likelihood that the mother will react as desired after she has decoded the message. Thus the child might insert a "please," or utter the words with a pleading or a demanding voice, or he might include words of endearment. All of these variations are possible with language.

The child has encoded his drive state in conventional symbols, but this is not a necessity associated with the use of language and is a secondary factor from the instrumental viewpoint. Of primary importance is the fact that the child has responded with behavior that has been determined by a prior history of reinforcement. As a result of prior rewards, the attributes of the message are molded into a very particular response that is most likely to result in drive gratification in the present situation.

The Use of Symbols That Are Instrumental But Not Representational

Major alterations in the drive-message unit of the preceding example may occur, depending upon the immediate situation and the history of rewards and punishments in similar situations. Two types of alterations will be discussed. They cause the messages to be nonrepresentational, though effective instrumental responses.

1. *Variation in message content.* (*a*) *Abbreviated utterances.* In some child-mother relations, interaction might consist only of the child entering the kitchen door and calling "Mother," whereupon the mother scurries to the kitchen and feeds him. (*b*) *Displaced utterances.* Our hungry child might be confronted with a situation in which direct reference to his hunger and his desire for food does not result in being fed. On occasions in the past, a rejecting but competitive mother may have responded negatively, not positively, to the utterance "I'm hungry, etc." She may have not only failed to feed him, but may have punished him with scolding and spanking as well for even asking for something to eat. In this case, the child's hunger motivates him to make the direct request, but fear of his mother's reaction, which may be stronger than his hunger, impels him to inhibit these direct statements. Displaced responses frequently result from such relatively simple conflicts. As a result of displacement, the child might start to describe how when he got home after school when his grandmother was visiting, she fed him; that his friend next door is coming over as soon as he finishes his snack his mother has given him, and then they are going to play. Such a conversation might arouse competitive responses in the mother which will cause her to feed the child. If so, the probability of occurrence of such rewarded, displaced utterances will increase. (*c*) *"Irrelevant" utterances.* Displaced utterances still contain some

reference, albeit an indirect one, to the speaker's drive state and the corresponding drive objects or aims. If the negative motivation of the mother is strong enough, such indirect references will elicit negative responses just as the direct, undisplaced utterances would. Since a child's hunger is a strong drive, one can expect that if unappeased it will continue to influence his behavior considerably. The use of seemingly "irrelevant" utterances might develop out of a series of situations like this in the past. For example, previous strong negative responses of the mother to both direct and displaced utterances would lead to inhibition of *any* reference by the child to his needs. But the ungratified hunger might lead to hyperactivity, such as "talking a blue streak" to his mother about the day's happenings in school. This is likely to disturb the peace of mind of such a mother to a point where she does something to quiet him down. If she happens to feed him to pacify him, and unintentionally appeases his hunger, such verbal hyperactivity and the class of content would become established as the instrumental response occurring upon future occasions when the child is hungry.

2. *Varying drives with same message content.* A child may use the same message, "Mom, I'm hungry, etc.," for the gratification of various drives. In one instance he might be hungry. But a frightened child may also ask for food. And it is a favorite response of some children to avoid getting to bed on time so they can stay up with their parents. Here again the use of this utterance in particular drive and cue circumstances will depend upon the history of reinforcement in prior interaction.

In short, the utterance "Mom, I'm hungry, etc." is not the only verbal behavior that may be instrumental in bringing about hunger gratification, and it may not be uttered at all by a hungry child. And this utterance may be instrumental in the gratification of quite different drives. The possibilities discussed above are illustrated in Figure 1.

Figure 1

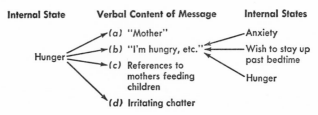

The messages containing symbols may be similar in some respects to the messages consisting of the signals of crying, "mama" sounds, etc., uttered by the infant: they may not contain any reference to the drive state, drive objects, or obvious inducements for the mother to gratify hunger; they may be nonspecific with reference to the drive state; alternative messages may serve the same function; and what appear to be symbols may actually be signals without intended and/or shared conventional meanings.

The examples above have emphasized that the manifest content uttered under given drive conditions is a function of learning. The speaker's past history can vary in many ways that will cause messages to be instrumental but not representational. Representational messages contain direct reference to internal drive and affective states, to drive objects, or to aims. If he is to utter such messages upon any given occasion of mounting drive, the individual's past history must have included (a) instances in which he consciously experienced the corresponding internal sensations; (b) opportunities to learn the relevant conventional vocabulary and grammatical forms; (c) instances in which he used these linguistic forms to identify appropriately his internal state, the objects, or the drive-reducing behavior of the other person; and (d) experiences of reinforcement after having done so.

Two classes of experiences will produce a deficit in these requirements. The first is the simple failure of occurrence — a *deprivation of positive experience*. As a result of overprotection, for example, a child's hunger might never reach sufficient intensity to be experienced by him. A language-poor environment, or limited intellectual capacity in the child himself, could deprive a child of the opportunity to learn adequate language skills. As a consequence of either of the preceding circumstances, step c could not occur. But even if it did, the messages might not be reinforced in such a way that they would be likely to occur in the future. Consistent, complete failure to feed a hungry child after he said "Mom, I'm hungry, etc." illustrates one possibility. Another possibility is that of the overindulgent mother who regularly anticipates the full message and feeds the child upon his abbreviated utterance of "Mother."

The second class of experience consists of those *negative, traumatic emotional experiences* that would cause a, b, and c to become sources of conflict and would lead to their inhibition. The earlier examples of displaced and "irrelevant" messages illustrate this class. They concerned the way in which traumatic experiences would prevent step *c*. If the experiences are intense enough, their effect generalizes so that all language skills are disrupted and so that the affective products of the drive state themselves succumb to repression. In these cases, nonrepresentational messages become "doubly" instrumental, for they may obtain the desired positive gratification and simultaneously circumvent real or imagined dangers.

IMPLICATIONS FOR CONTENT ANALYSIS

If an investigator made purely representational assumptions in the examples summarized by Figure 1, in order to infer the drive state of the speaker, in all likelihood he would do the following. First, he would restrict his analysis to the messages themselves. He would either ignore, not acquire, or be unable to acquire information concerning the situations in which the utterances were made and the pertinent history of prior successes and failures of the utterances in obtaining drive gratification. Secondly, with respect to the messages themselves, he would restrict his analysis to the *lexical* content of the messages. He would probably use typescripts even though original tape recordings of the interaction were available. He would thus not use the additional information available in the vocal aspects of the utterances. Finally, he would assume that the functional relations between the lexical content of the messages and the drive states were representational. His frame of reference would not allow for the divergent and convergent relations pictured in Figure 1.

On these bases, the investigator would conclude (1) that the three children who said "Mom, I'm hungry, etc.," and possibly the one who produced the displaced utterances about eating, were hungry at the time they were speaking, (2) that the child who produced the "irritating chatter" was excited or aggressive, and (3) that the message containing only "Mother" was inadequate for inferring any drive state. The inferential powers of these procedures are obviously not great. Many of the limitations on them arise from the investigator's failure to adopt the instrumental viewpoint and the related reliance on a very restricted segment of the linguistic behavior.

The same limitations arise when one attempts to infer motivational states from segments of nonverbal behavior that are assessed in terms of restricted features and that are taken out of their situational and developmental contexts. The following example illustrates these limitations. A person might glance out his front window and see a boy running rapidly along the sidewalk. Obviously the onlooker cannot tell what is motivating the boy's running: he might be in a race, he might be practicing the Boy Scout "50 paces walking, 50 paces running," he might be aggressively chasing someone, or he might be fleeing in terror from the neighborhood bully. But the observer could choose among these alternatives if he knew what situation had preceded the onset of the running, what factors maintained it, or what events would bring the running to an end. A closer examination of all the boy's immediate behavior, including the running, would also aid in this choice. Later in the discussion these same procedures will be applied to language behavior.

The paucity of information about underlying motives in manifest content is of course familiar to many investigators and prompts them to be cautious in accepting utterances at their face value. One way in which some of them try to obtain greater realism in content analysis coding is to "read between the lines" to get at "what the person really means" or "what the person is trying to say." The assumption is made that one can profitably classify, count, etc., utterances, though in terms of private rather than conventional meanings. There are two difficulties with this procedure. The first is the prospect of poor reliability in the determination of the private meanings. The second difficulty is the theoretical one that this procedure still in some way implies the representational viewpoint, for it assumes that "on some level of organization" the speaker is always motivated to encode his drive, or that the linguistic encoding of drive states is a necessary event, required by behavioral laws.

It is extremely difficult to tell whether or not words have been used with private meaning. The utterances by a hungry child of "Mother" and of the "irritating chatter" can function effectively as instrumental behavior whether they have private but conscious meanings for one or both participants, or whether they function purely as signals, devoid of either unilateral or shared meaning. The abbreviated utterance of "Mother," for example, might be the communication between two very familiar people who understand each other completely. Or it might only be a signal produced by a demanding child that arouses characteristic activity of an anxious, overprotective mother. This would be the unwitting perpetuation of the earliest type of communication mentioned earlier. And the "irritating chatter" might be deliberate strategy by a cunning child which is "seen through" by the mother, that is, they share a private meaning. Or such communication may have developed automatically and outside of awareness for each participant. The child may have no notion of what he is doing in repeating verbal behavior that has resulted in hunger satisfaction in the past. And the mother may not realize that she is gratifying a hungry child. She may understand the situation as one in which she is distracting an irritating child. In short, it is entirely possible that the interaction consists of what Mead[3] calls a conversation of gestures, even though words have been used. If this is so, the questions "What does the person really mean?" etc., may be meaningless.

It is possible to pose and obtain answers to some alternative questions which are significant ones from an instrumental viewpoint. These questions are as follows. (1) What is the external situation at the time the message is started? (2) What events are associated with the continuation or cessation of the messages? (3) What are the nonlexical characteristics of the messages? Answers to these questions coupled with a set of theoretical and/or empirical behavioral principles will improve the accuracy of inferring motive-affective states from messages.

Knowledge of the Situation at the Onset of the Message

This knowledge is useful because it suggests a range of possible motive-affective states that may be reasonably assumed to be operating. Every parent automatically utilizes such knowledge in deciding that the utterance "I'm hungry, etc." by a child in the middle of the afternoon indicates that the child is hungry, but that the same utterance spoken shortly after a big dinner and at the approach of bedtime indicates reluctance to go to bed. At the conference Pool cited Leites' study of the degree of lavishness of praise for Stalin in the speeches of members of the Politburo in Stalin's waning days.[4] Leites inferred that the concealed power positions of the various speakers were inversely related to the degree of lavishness of praise in these speeches. Knowledge of the situation — that the speakers were engaged in a power struggle in a dictatorship — certainly suggested that insecurity could be inferred from the public speeches. Knowledge of techniques likely to be tried in Russia would suggest a class of them, including lavish and fawning praise, that might occur under such motivational conditions.

----

[3] G. H. Mead, *Mind, Self, and Society* (Chicago, 1934).

[4] N. Leites, Elsa Bernaut, and R. L. Garthoff, "Politburo Images of Stalin," *World Politics,* 3 (1951), 317-39.

The following example concerns the usefulness of such knowledge in interpreting the results of content analyses of therapeutic interviews. If one obtains the Discomfort-Relief Quotients[5] of the initial interviews for a sample of patients, the range of these content measures will be restricted to the high end of the scale. If one ignored the fact that these were initial interviews, such results could lead to the conclusion that there was little difference in the tension states between patients at the time of the initial interview. But if the situation is considered, one would naturally surmise that the desire to be admitted into treatment was operating in addition to the tension associated with the patients' illnesses. This desire would cause some patients, who would not otherwise do so because of current tension alone, to utter many distress units and thus narrow the range of the DRQ's. Bearing these considerations in mind, one would not rely upon the DRQ's of initial interviews for inferring individual differences in levels of distress.

Knowledge of Events at the Termination of the Message

This knowledge may be useful for it may suggest a range of possible motive-affective states that may be reasonably assumed to *have been* operating when the message was uttered. This point can be illustrated by reference to our examples of the "I'm hungry" utterances produced by a hungry child, a frightened child, and a child who is maneuvering to stay up at night. Three different events could selectively cause these utterances to cease. In the case of the hungry child they would only cease when he was fed; in the case of the frightened child they would cease if the parent comforted him; and the devious child would stop protesting his hunger if his parents simply said it was all right for him to stay up a little later than usual. On the assumption that these were all instrumental utterances, the cessation of the utterances under these three different conditions would suggest that different motives had been present and would indicate something of their nature.

Analogous observations may be made in the case of the initial therapeutic interviews. Some patients talk and act in a more distressed manner in their initial interviews than they do in subsequent therapeutic interviews. A naïve representational interpretation might assume that the patients' messages reflected the degree of their illness and that these patients had been helped by the first

---

[5] J. Dollard and O. H. Mowrer, "A Method of Measuring Tension in Written Documents," *Journal of Abnormal and Social Psychology*, 42 (1947), 3-32.

interview. While this may happen sometimes, the fact that the degree of "content disturbance" changes markedly with the acceptance of the patient for treatment, which is a critical event after the initial interview, suggests that the messages of the initial interview had been determined more by the patient's uncertainty over being accepted for treatment than by the severity of the illness.

Knowledge of Events Associated with Continuation of a Message

Some acquired drives are not easily satiated and will continue to sustain instrumental behavior for some time while gratification is forthcoming. It is often possible to correlate certain external events with the continuation of messages and thus to infer the nature of the underlying motive or need. A familiar example is the "life of the party," who will continue to "entertain" with jokes and antics as long as he has a responsive audience. In interviews, patients will often continue with accounts of suffering as long as the therapist expresses concern and sympathy. Such relationships, too, imply a possible range of motives and affective states that may be present in the speaker.

Knowledge of the Nonlexical Aspects of Messages

It is common knowledge that the nonlexical attributes of the message may be especially revealing of underlying motive-affective states. This is particularly noticeable in spoken language. "Nonlexical" is used as the general term to include the purely vocal properties of speech, muscular co-ordination features in handwriting, and all the elements that contribute to style of either speech or writing.

The nonlexical attributes would seem to offer a most fruitful source of information for the content analyst wishing to infer drive-emotional states. One reason for this is that they are an inherent part of every message and thus are always present whenever a message exists. Therefore, the possibility of knowledge about them is always present. This is not true in the case of the antecedents, the concurrent events, or the consequences of messages, which are often completely unidentifiable no matter how attentive the investigator is. In the case of enemy propaganda, the antecedents and consequences may be deliberately concealed or they may be known as general knowledge but not as related to any particular piece of propaganda. In psychotherapy, it may be quite clear from the vocal properties of the patient's speech that he is frightened or angry, even though the antecedents of the vocal properties or the events associated with changes in them are obscure (and, of course, even though the manifest content gives no clue either).

Another reason why the nonlexical properties may be very useful is that they may reflect a drive that is of interest to the investigator while the lexical content is being uttered for the sake of another simultaneous drive. This can be illustrated if one imagines that in the messages of the hunger example the investigator is interested in inferring anxiety and not hunger. The hungry child in that example may also be somewhat frightened. He may directly request food in order to gratify his hunger, while the anxiety may only be reflected in the tone of voice. The content analyst is frequently confronted with such multiple drive situations. This is the case, for example, with John Garraty's material, that consists of personal documents of historical figures. A president may write a letter dealing with an administrative or personal matter at a time when he is affected emotionally either by that particular matter or by an irrelevant matter. The lexical content of the letter may implement the one purpose, while only the handwriting or certain features of style may indicate the affect, which would be of most interest to Garraty. Analogous situations arise in psychotherapy and are illustrated in the following section of this chapter.

There may be various reasons why the emotional state of interest is not identified or implemented in the lexical content of the message. (1) It may be of weaker strength than the other drive determining the lexical content. (2) The speaker or writer may not be aware of it. (3) The speaker or writer may not have the vocabulary for producing a representational message concerning it. (4) The source may be consciously or unconsciously motivated to conceal it, but not the other drive. Our culture places a premium on the concealment of many drives and affects, and at the same time our language training and communication habits emphasize the importance of lexical content. Since affects cannot be abolished by the censorship of their expression, and since the nonlexical attributes are not the central targets of cultural or personal control, it is to be expected that the nonlexical features will be more revealing. (5) Simultaneous drives may be of equal strength but the lexical responses they would usually produce may be incompatible, that is, the simultaneous drives may be competing ones. In such cases the resolution is often the expression of one drive in the lexical content, and of the other in the nonlexical content. An angry lover may proclaim his love in one mode, and his anger in the other, but he cannot easily do both in a single mode.

The choice of the appropriate nonlexical indicator will depend upon the type of behavioral state one wishes to assess, as well as the nature of the language material, that is, spoken or written, spontaneous or rehearsed and edited. There are two guides that may be of general value, however, in choosing the suitable nonlexical indicator. They concern the freedom of the indicator from linguistic control and from general social control.

Sol Saporta noted at the conference that the structure of a language itself may impose restrictions on the degree of permissible variation in some nonlexical features, just as it does on permissible variation in the lexicon. This seems to be an important point for the nonlinguist using content analysis, for he is not likely to think explicitly about this point. As this author sees it, the implication is that in the development of nonlexical indices of emotional states, it would be most fruitful to pick those features that are not part of the language, for then there may be less confounding of linguistic and behavioral effects and also greater variability in the attribute due to emotional effects. Word order, for example, plays a definite role in English, but is of much less linguistic significance in German, where similar functions are played by the declensions and conjugations. Much greater variation in choice of word order is permissible by the language, without a breakdown in communication, in German than in English. Accordingly, one would suspect that variation in word order would be a much more sensitive nonlexical indicator of emotional states in German than in English. Pitch, for example, plays a relatively minor role in spoken English from the purely linguistic standpoint, but a major one in Chinese. So it is possible that pitch variations would be more sensitive indicators of emotional states in English than in Chinese.

It was noted above that language training and communication habits focus more on lexical content than on nonlexical features. (This is true even for the nonlexical features of messages that are institutionalized parts of the language. This is shown strikingly by the surprised fascination the novice in linguistic science experiences upon hearing of the many linguistic restrictions that determine his speech or writing: the role of word order, patterns of intonation, stress phonemes, etc.). Since they are response products, however, all nonlexical features are theoretically potential targets for consistent rewards and punishments. Thus they may all acquire instrumental functions and may be subject to the convergent and divergent relations depicted in Figure 1 for lexical content. To the extent that this is so, the value of the nonlexical attributes for the content analyst will decrease. In general, it would seem to be most advantageous for the content analyst interested in drives, motives, etc., to select those nonlexical attributes that are not likely to have been influenced consistently by rewards and punishments in the past. The nonlexical attributes meeting this criterion are those that are most likely to be most remote from awareness in both the speaker and the listener.

To index emotional states, then, it may be advisable to seek out those attributes of messages that are most free from both linguistic and social control.

IMPLICATIONS FOR PSYCHOLOGY

While there is little question about the potential value of the nonlexical indicators, a great deal of research must be done before reliable and valid tools based on them are available for the content analyst. Many things remain to be discovered. Which indicators will be suitable for spoken, spontaneously written, and carefully edited material? In the various type of materials, which, if any, nonlexical indices are specific for distinct drive states? Which are nonspecific indices of generally heightened drive states? Which are inevitable, indirect results of increased drive and which are directly instrumental for specific drives? Are the latter sufficiently universal and removed from voluntary control to be used uninterpretively by the content analyst?

These questions are not ones which can be answered by the content analyst alone. They depend upon psychological knowledge. As Alexander George said at the conference:

Another implication or conclusion one tends to draw from the evaluation we've made at RAND is that many of the problems of content analysis are not really problems of content analysis or content description — they have to do with the rudimentary state of knowledge we have about the problem area concerned. In this case we're concerned with certain types of political behavior, the use of communication as an instrument of policy by totalitarian regimes specifically. We know relatively little that can be formulated into systematic generalizations about how totalitarian regimes use political communications under different conditions. . . . The problems that have been faced in this particular field are not so much ones of content [as ones that have to do with] the development of behavioral models.

George then conjectured that similar conditions existed in other disciplines that are likewise interested in inferring behavioral states from the content of messages.

This author agrees with these comments of George. The work of many investigators from diverse disciplines has shown that it is possible to obtain reliable, quantitative descriptions of many aspects of language content. Adequate content descriptions are of course necessary and legitimate goals for many purposes, including the valid inference of motives, emotions, and attitudes from language samples. We need in addition, however, empirical generalizations or theoretical principles concerning the relationships between message content and behavioral states. These are necessary for the valid interpretation of content descriptions, and they also contribute to the very process of content description itself.

Traditionally, psychology has considered language behavior as an aspect of the "higher mental processes." The symbolic nature of language has been at the focus of attention. Man's uniqueness from the other animals in the development of this mode of behavior is emphasized. The primary purpose of psychological theories of language has been to account for the development and use of linguistic symbols (Mead,[6] Morris,[7] Osgood,[8] Holt,[9] for example). The role of language symbols in problem solving, reasoning, and concept formation has been emphasized. The referential-symbolic aspect of language is of primary importance to communication theory in which encoding and decoding play such a prominent role, for the symbols of course constitute the code. The representational viewpoint is in keeping with the traditional psychological treatment of language, for it treats the manifest verbal content as though it were an encoding of drives, emotions, attitudes, etc., and as though language symbols as conventionally used constituted the code.

For the representational model the referential-symbolizing feature of language is of central importance. But for the instrumental model the more general behavioral function of language is of primary importance. The relationship between behavioral states and messages is a pragmatic one, in Morris' terms. Adherents to the representational viewpoint act as if they implicitly assume that the pragmatic relationship can be discovered by the analysis of only

---

[6] *Mind, Self, and Society.*
[7] C. W. Morris, *Signs, Language, and Behavior* (New York, 1946).
[8] *Method and Theory in Experimental Psychology,* Chap. 16.
[9] E. B. Holt, *Animal Drive* (London, 1931).

the semantics of messages. Therefore they restrict their analysis to the contents of messages, with conventional semantics defining the contents. Adherents to the instrumental viewpoint assume that the pragmatics of language can be determined only on the basis of an investigation of pragmatics themselves, by including the situational and/or the nonlexical contexts of messages in the analysis.

The idea that language functions as instrumental behavior is not a novel one, but this aspect of language has not received the attention, thought, or systematic treatment it merits. It has been excluded by definition from linguistics. Clinical psychologists, psychoanalysts, and psychiatrists are always dealing with the instrumental aspects of language. No general and explicit literature concerning it has developed, however, in spite of the starting points provided by Reich's[10] elaboration of the distinction between the "what" and the "how" of the patients' communications and by Mead's[11] contrast of conversations of gestures and of symbols.

The gap in psychology is clearly shown by the fact that the instrumental aspect of language is not explicitly considered in Miller's excellent text on the psychology of language,[12] in the chapter on psycholinguistics in the recent *Handbook of Social Psychology*,[13] or in the 1954 monograph on psycholinguistics.[14] These observations are intended only as reminders of the theoretical and empirical shortcomings in psychology that handicap the use of content analysis as a research method.

The implications of the ideas presented in the above section of this chapter will vary for the different fields of investigation represented at the conference. The general instrumental viewpoint and certain of the specific ideas outlined above formed the background for this author's research contribution to the work conference. The next section contains some of this research material as well as some additional findings obtained since that time. The following material will illustrate the application of the instrumental viewpoint to the study of recordings and typescripts of interviews and will demonstrate the value of a specific nonlexical indicator for a limited purpose.

----

[10] W. Reich, "On Character Analysis," in R. Fliess, ed., *The Psychoanalytic Reader* (New York, 1948).

[11] *Mind, Self, and Society.*

[12] G. A. Miller, *Language and Communication* (New York, 1951).

[13] G. A. Miller, "Psycholinguistics," in G. Lindzey, ed., *Handbook of Social Psychology* (Cambridge, Mass., 1954).

[14] Osgood and Sebeok, eds., "Psycholinguistics: A Survey of Theory and Research Problems."

ASSESSMENT OF ANXIETY IN THERAPEUTIC INTERVIEWS

There were two reasons why the author started the work described below. First, it seemed to offer a means of determining the nature of certain physiological changes in humans under anxiety in real-life situations. Secondly, there is an obvious need to measure anxiety in patients as it occurs in the patient-therapist interaction. Anxiety is a key behavioral variable for psychodynamics in general and for psychotherapy specifically. No description of changes during the process of psychotherapy or comparisons of the effect of various therapeutic procedures will be complete unless they portray changes in anxiety of the patient. Yet anxiety measurement has been virtually completely ignored to date in the objective studies of psychotherapeutic interviews.[15]

The research goals called for indicators that would sensitively reflect fluctuations in the patient's immediate anxiety, in contrast to measures of his general characteristic state. The patient makes available many behavior attributes that may be regarded as consequences of the anxious state. There are autonomic and skeletal

----

[15] In general, the author conceptualized anxiety from the viewpoint of stimulus-response reinforcement behavior theory, as developed most systematically by J. Dollard and N. E. Miller (*Personality and Psychotherapy* [New York, 1950]).

Anxiety is regarded as an intervening variable consisting of an inferred internal physiological state which has the properties of both responses and stimuli. As a response, it may be "conditioned" to many stimuli including those resulting from ideational events and other internal responses. As a stimulus, other responses, including those that produce ideational events, may be "conditioned" to it. It is assumed that the internal physiological state varies quantitatively, causing parallel quantitative changes in both its stimulus and response properties, and that as the stimulus value increases, the drive properties increase. When this occurs, the innate or learned responses it elicits increase in probability of occurrence and magnitude.

Sensations *may* be experienced when anxiety occurs just as upon any stimulation. Ordinarily these are unpleasant, but this varies with the past learning experience of the individual. Most people, though not all, learn to discriminate these sensations and to label them as "feeling frightened," "anxious," "nervous," etc. The whole problem of the experiential aspects of anxiety is a chapter in itself. The point here is to state that in this report the term "anxiety" refers to the internal physiological state and not to the "experience" per se. And the terms "anxiety level," "intensity," etc., refer to quantitative aspects of the internal state itself. The quantitative aspects are assumed to be indicated by the events conceived to be consequences of the internal state. These may include a variety of "experiences," momentary brief responses, defenses, etc. This is not to deny that the experiential factor is crucial in the psychogenetic vicissitudes of anxiety, that this may also have quantitative properties, or that it may play an important role in any given behavior instance.

physiological responses that play no part as symbols in communication. There are the observable nonvocal responses that function in communication as signals (e.g., tremors) or symbols (e.g., gestures). Then there are the many vocal and verbal facets of the patient's spoken language itself.

The decision was made to focus on measures derived from the patient's spoken language. Linguistic data may be obtained with ease in psychotherapy. The patient's language processes are inherently interesting and linguistic measures of anxiety might have important implications for psychology in general. The neurophysiology of anxiety is not well enough understood to yield ready-made measuring tools for general use. Besides, the original though receding interest required nonphysiological measures in order to investigate this very neurophysiology of anxiety.

Content analysis as usually practiced (see review by Auld and Murray[16]) did not seem to be the most feasible starting point. The general uninterpretive application of content categories ("what" categories) ignores both the motivational factors (the "why" or "how come" or "what for" factors) determining the communication of the content and the nonlexical properties (the "how" features) contained in the language transmitting the content. On both theoretical and empirical grounds it is assumed at the outset that such content analysis will not yield generally valid measures of emotional states, although it may be a very reliable procedure and very valuable for other problems.

More concretely, methods of content analysis could be defined as uninterpretive if they do not include as essential for the classification of any given communication either (1) an evaluation of both the intrapsychic and the interpersonal instrumental aspect of the content at the time it is uttered, or (2) the use of recordings with explicit cognizance of some, and the possibility of being stimulated by many, of the expressive components of speech at the time the content is uttered. Obviously uninterpretive by this definition are methods that propose to assess emotions but categorize isolated and transcribed fragments — passages or pages — of content into affective categories. Also uninterpretive by this definition would be a method that recognized the general motivational aspect of a content or a nonlexical factor but did not recognize the *various* motives that might be manifested or instrumented by it in different people or in the same person at different times. The general classification

---

[16] "Content-Analysis Studies of Psychotherapy."

of silences by all patients at all times in the interview as "anxious" or as "resistive" would be uninterpretive by this definition.

Consider the tempting case of noting and enumerating instances in which previous frightening experiences or reactions are described by the patient. Sometimes a patient will report that he now feels frightened as he thinks of these. Why not assume that this is always the case to some degree even though the patient does not experience or report such feelings in the interview? One can make a theoretical case for the idea that such manifest thoughts are derivatives of concealed anxiety just as one often infers that if a person talks of food or eating this may be an indirect expression of hunger. There are times when such an assumption seems correct, but there are also many instances in which it does not seem correct or at least in which there are alternative explanations. For example, talking of food and eating while at someone's table may be a hostile comparison. Sometimes one is convinced that when patients tell you of frightening experiences they are trying to arouse your sympathy and if you respond with it they will continue with such accounts — feeling protected and safe. A patient started to recount in vivid terms pogroms he had witnessed and experienced as a child. While the therapist reacted with sympathy and concern, the patient continued with ease with further details of these frightening experiences and added a description of fear and "cowardice" by him in battle. The onset of these contents was probably caused by an unconscious fear of the therapist, but it seemed clear subsequently to both the patient and the therapist that the prolongation of the recall was associated with a feeling of comfort when the therapist expressed concern and sympathy. The word content alone of an account of frightening events may not distinguish between the presence or absence of current anxiety.

This is also true for "fearless content." A patient may be expressing content which would not be placed in an anxiety category and yet the communication of such content may well be motivated by anxiety, be eliciting anxiety, and be accompanied by expressive features that are clues of anxiety. For example, a patient frequently attacked his therapist and then made placating statements "sounding" anxious as he did so. The verbal content could easily have been placed in a category of aggression or negative reaction in the first instance, and in one of positive expression in the second. The antecedent of the series was often a statement of the therapist which threatened the patient because it lowered his self-esteem. According to the clinical evaluation of the sequence, the patient's anxiety mounted with the loss of self-esteem and because of the unique learning of this particular patient it motivated the aggressive attack, which elicited still further anxiety that finally motivated the placating maneuver. In short, what may be manifestly anxiety content may be communicated for other motives and be accompanied by expressive signs of comfort; what may not be manifestly anxiety content may be motivated by and elicit anxiety and be uttered with expressive features indicating discomfort.

The basic working hypothesis of the research in progress is that the most generally valid procedure of measuring patient anxiety by means of linguistic analysis will depend upon the treatment of language as an expressive behavior system with instrumental and reactive properties. This assumption determined the selection of the behavior aspects of language as the starting point. It is also one that must be re-examined in the course of the work.

There are many nonlexical attributes of speech that seem to be useful to the therapist in assessing anxiety in the patient. One of these is disruption in the process of speaking that results in what we ordinarily call "jumbled," "confused," or "flustered" speech. It seemed possible that an investigation of this process might yield a partial measure of the patient's anxiety level that would meet the requirements noted above. Some of the findings of such research are presented below.

SPEECH DISTURBANCE

Below are two transcribed excerpts from two psychotherapeutic interviews of the same patient. They are impressive for their confusion. When heard in an interview a therapist immediately wonders, "What is he frightened about?" At other times this patient uttered as fluent speech as the author has heard from patients. (Note the difference in manifest content in the two excerpts and the nature of the therapist's first question in the first excerpt.)

Patient: My uncle had his throat cut.
Therapist: Mmm.
    P: And my uncle . . . ah . . . he wasn't killed, but they tortured him. They took him and they slit his throat right . . . the skin . . . just cut the skin right around like this here.
    T: Who did that? [said in a sudden manner]
    P: Mmm . . . hulligan . . . holigan . . . hulligans, whatever you call them.
    T: The who?

P: The . . . ah . . . you know the . . . ah . . . sss . . . he was in . . .
the . . . he . . . was dri . . . traveling from one town to the oth . . .
next and —

T: Mmmhnn.

P: — he was stopped by a couple . . . ah . . . if you know the situation in the South. . . .

T: Were . . . were they . . . were they Russians or were they Bol-
sheviks?

P: Yes. Yeah . . . mujik . . . mujiks . . . peasants.

. . . .

P: And I told her we had spoken about her and my feelings about
her wishing to move someplace else. And . . . ah . . . at that time
she didn't answer very much. She was quite thoughtful. Ssstill
we've had a whole period now when she's been very cold —

T: Mmmhnn.

P: — to me. [sighs] [half-laugh] Feeling as an un . . . uninvited
guest. And . . . ah . . . she didn't say anything except that . . .
ah . . . my contention was not entirely right that . . . ah . . . the
fact that she wants to move from . . . from . . . from here doesn't
necessarily mean that . . . ah . . . because . . . ah . . . you know
that . . . ah . . . the unhappiness that she . . . ah . . . she has, while
it may be part of her, as I says, still does not mean that . . .
ah . . . she has to be happy here . . . that she doesn't . . . that to . . .
ah . . . have something in common does not necessarily . . . ah . . .
exactly as I put it.

T: Mmmhnn.

P: And then . . . ah . . . Friday night I came home. She asked me
what we discussed. And I said . . . ah . . . "Oh, I don't know,
generalities." And . . . ah . . . we hadn't d . . . I hadn't spoken
about her . . . anything in the discussion about her.

Upon analyzing such instances of extreme speech confusion, it is
found that they consist of a variety of separate identifiable categories of disturbances occurring at a rapid rate. These same disturbances occur at lower rates at times when the patient's speech is
not clinically experienced as confused. It appears that here is an
aspect of speech which has considerable quantitative range, that can
be measured by counting during successive language segments, and
that this is possibly a sensitive continuous measure of anxiety.

The theoretical conceptions concerning speech disturbances are
at present rather crude. They are largely working hypotheses. It is
assumed that one effect of anxiety is to disrupt all finely co-
ordinated ongoing behavior, and that speech is an instance of such
delicate behavior, par excellence. It is also assumed that anxiety
will have this effect regardless of its source, for example if it is
largely evoked by contents of unspoken ideation, by contents that
are being uttered, by purely situational factors, or by the unconscious symbolic significance for the speaker of speech itself.

The Speech Disturbance Categories[17]

The speech disturbance categories used in the exploratory phase of the research are listed below and briefly defined. These were developed empirically by studying recordings and typescripts, and noting disturbances in individual words and in the word-word progression that were sensed as superfluous and/or distorting to the communication of the content.

1. *"Ah."* Wherever the definite "ah" sound occurs, it is scored.
2. *Sentence correction* (SC). A correction in the form or content of the expression while the word-word progression occurs. To be scored, these changes must be sensed by the listener as an interruption in the word-to-word sequence.
3. *Sentence incompletion* (Inc). An expression is interrupted, clearly left incomplete, and the communication proceeds without correction.
4. *Repetition* (R). The serial superfluous repetition of one or more words — usually of one or two words.
5. *Stutter* (St).
6. *Intruding incoherent sound* (IS). A sound which is absolutely incoherent as a word to the listener. It merely intrudes without itself altering the form of the expression and cannot be clearly conceived of as a stutter, omission, or a tongue-slip (though some may be such in reality).
7. *Tongue-slip* (T-S). This category includes neologisms, the transposition of words from their correct serial position, and the substitution of an unintended for an intended word.
8. *Omission* (O). Parts of words, or rarely entire words, may be omitted. Contractions are exempted. Most omissions are of terminal syllables of words.

Real examples of these disturbance categories are contained in the following interview excerpt. In the transcript an asterisk is placed at the point of the disturbance. To the left are the categories in the corresponding line of the excerpt. If there is more than one disturbance in a line, the category names are in sequence with the asterisks. Since the actual scoring is done only when listening as well as reading, some of it may not be completely clear from this written material alone. Poor grammar, inaudibility of the recording, and interruptions by the therapist are not grounds for scoring the categories.

----

[17] This section has been taken from the author's "Disturbances and Silences in the Patient's Speech in Psychotherapy," *Journal of Abnormal and Social Psychology,* 53 (1956), 1-15.

T-S, SC	P:	My impression of my relation to D—— [son] have always been that the reason that I dȯn't . . . didn't seem to feel the love for him that I felt for J—— [daughter] was that during the first sixteen months of his life I was away. I didn't grow up with him. If there was any jealousy of D—— it was in relation to his in-laws. Now that is very possible., Although it's something which
Ah		I also suppressed. Ah . . . and the reason I say it's pos-
2 St		sible 'cause it sort of well le. le. leaves
Ah, R		a . . . ah . . . a sort of memory. When I [?] I. . . .
	T:	You're jealous of his in-laws?
	P:	Of his in-laws, yeah. Because he was brought up with
R		them till . . . until I came home. He was born in their
T-S, O, SC		hou . . . hospital and came to their house, and my wife lived with her parents.
	T:	Ho . . . how do you mean you're jealous of his in-laws?
Ah	P:	Well . . . ah . . . when I first came home, and for the first
Ah		year or so, or more than a year . . . ah . . . D—— was more prone to turn to his grandfather and grandmother than he was to me.
	T:	Mmmhnn.
	P:	And although I understood it, there was a certain
Ah		amount of . . . ah . . . well not bitterness, I wasn't bitter
SC		about it, but a certain amount of . . . a sort of resent-ment, a mild type of resentment.
	T:	You make this sound so . . . ah —
	P:	Well —
	T:	So diluted.
	P:	Well it was diluted. I mean it wasn't something which I felt keenly enough to be angry at his grandparents, let's say, or with D—— himself. I mean I realized that he had grown up with them.
	T:	Mmmhnn.
Inc	P:	And therefore, it was more natural for him to . *. . until
SC, St, Ah		he became . . . completely o. overcame his . . . ah . . . strange-
Ah		ness to me, and it took quite a long time. Ah . . . then
R		there was . . . there was a certain amount of resentment.
IS, O (?)		It wasn't directed against the parents or dec . . . was . . .
IS, St		den . . . ac. actually directed against a circumstance
O		which kept me away. And it was a resentment which re . . .
SC, Ah, SC		in a certain . . . ah . . . to a certain extent reflected itself also in the [clears throat] feeling I had toward people who had remained behind and had made money.
	T:	Mmm. Your in-laws make money?
	P:	Yes. My father-in-law made a lot of money from the war.

Reliability of Speech Disturbance Scoring

Three people have learned to score the speech disturbances.

The interobserver reliability for the number of disturbances scored in given language samples has been determined by correlating the total number scored by independent judges in unselected samples of transcript pages (N = 28-65) for several patients (N = 3-5). The average product-moment correlation was .94. This may be taken as the interobserver reliability of the speech disturbance ratios discussed below. The *exact* agreement in scoring — both as to category and placement in the script — is also of interest. This was determined for two independent scorers with a moderate amount of training and experience. They agreed exactly on 69 per cent of all the disturbances both had scored. Of course they agreed to an even higher degree on the nonoccurrence of disturbances. It was found that 95 per cent of the disagreements were due to the failure of one or the other person to perceive all of the disturbances or to a difference in comprehension of what was actually said, in spite of very good recordings. The exact agreement has never been determined after more experience in scoring. There seems to be enough "editing out" of speech disturbances in the careful listening of even more experienced judges to justify detailed checking of one person's scoring by another. This is the current practice in this research, and was the procedure for virtually all of the material discussed below.

Some General Properties of Speech Disturbances

1. *Frequency of the disturbances.* From a purely quantitative standpoint, the normal speech disturbances constitute a very prominent aspect of speech uttered under the somewhat stressful conditions indicated. The following statements summarize data presented elsewhere.[18] (*a*) There was, on the average, one disturbance for every five seconds of actual patient talking time in initial interviews. Comparable rates occur in subsequent therapeutic interviews. (*b*) For three interviewers who conducted the 31 initial interviews just mentioned, the following average rates were obtained. Interviewer A made one disturbance every 4 seconds he actually talked; Interviewer B made one every 6.5 seconds he talked; and Interviewer C made one disturbance every 12 seconds he talked. (*c*) Undergraduates speaking in a stressful role-playing situation averaged one disturbance every 4 seconds of actual talking. (*d*) Psychiatry and psychology faculty members taking part in seminar discussions

----

[18] G. F. Mahl, " 'Normal' Disturbances in Spontaneous Speech: General Quantitative Aspects," a paper delivered before the American Psychological Association, Chicago, 1956.

on the validity of the Rorschach test averaged one disturbance for every 5 seconds they actually talked.

2. *Awareness of speech disturbances.* Anecdotal observations have been made concerning the reactions people have when they see their own speech disturbances typed verbatim in interview protocols (sometimes scored in red pencil), or those of other people, including one's own patients. These observations have been made by the author on himself, on professional colleagues, secretaries and assistants who have worked with typescripts and tapes, and on five of the undergraduate role players. Reactions of these people were rarely neutral. They included surprise and interest, scorn in the case of someone else's speech, but despair, shame, and anger in the case of being confronted with one's own speech. These observations have strongly suggested that the vast majority of the speech disturbances are "unintended" and escape the awareness of both speakers and listeners, in spite of their very frequent occurrence.

3. *Variability in speech disturbance.* Research described elsewhere[19] has shown that there are (*a*) striking individual differences in the frequency of speech disturbances and in the relative predilections for the individual categories of disturbance, and (*b*) significant variations in the disturbance levels *between* therapeutic interviews for an individual, and also from time to time *within* initial and therapeutic interviews. Illustrations of the within-interview variations are presented later.

The preceding material demonstrates that the nonlexical dimension of speech reflected in the speech disturbances is a prominent one, that it is largely outside of awareness, and that it is subject to sensitive fluctuations in degree that are lawful. Obviously these disturbances are linguistically irrelevant, in the sense that they are not an institutionalized part of our language. They have no conventional semantic function. They can vary within rather wide limits without causing a failure, or noticeable deficit in communication. The evidence warrants the conclusion that the measurement of this nonlexical property of speech is potentially a useful tool for the content analyst.

The next important question — what is the evidence for believing that these speech disturbances reflect anxiety — is considered in the following material.

----

[19] Mahl, " 'Normal' Disturbances in Spontaneous Speech."

SPEECH DISTURBANCES AND ANXIETY

The Speech Disturbance Ratio

A useful measure of the level of speech disturbance can be obtained by identifying the various disturbances in a verbatim transcript and then computing the following ratio for any given language sample:

$$\text{Speech disturbance ratio} = \frac{N \text{ speech disturbances}}{N \text{ "words" in sample}}$$

The "word" count includes the number of completed words, the number of incomplete words, the number of distinct "sounds" caused by stuttering and incoherent sounds, and the number of "ah's." The value placed in the denominator can just as well be some other measure of the amount of talking done by the patient. The requirement is only to have a disturbance measure that is independent of the verbal output by the speaker. In a sample of 31 interviews, measures obtained by using the number of "words" in the denominator were very highly correlated with measures based on the "number of seconds of talking" by the speakers, $r = .91$.

Speech disturbance ratios for successive two-minute intervals of interviews, for larger time periods of variable duration, and for entire interviews taken as a unit are considered in the studies of anxiety to be described below.

Three approaches to the relationship between anxiety and speech disturbances have been followed: *ad hoc* clinical evaluations of therapy interview proceedings, controlled clinical evaluations of therapy interview proceedings, and correlating anxiety ratings of initial interviews with speech disturbance ratios for these interviews.

Ad Hoc Clinical Evaluations of Interview Proceedings

Figures 2 and 3 contain graphs of speech disturbance ratios determined from the patient's speech for successive two-minute intervals of two therapeutic interviews for the same patient. These graphs illustrate how the two-minute ratios may rise and fall during the course of individual interviews, and how the patterns may vary from interview to interview.

The purpose of the *ad hoc* clinical evaluations is to see if one can reasonably account for the vicissitudes of these successive two-minute ratios in terms of the changes in anxiety level that would be inferred on psychodynamic grounds.

At the outset, it might be useful to quote from a general formulation of Patient Z that was written for other purposes about a year before the present linguistic work was started.

This patient, who has now completed approximately 100 hours of treatment, is a 40-year-old married businessman with two children who sought treatment because of peptic ulcer symptoms and repeated attacks of panic and fear that he would die from a heart attack as his father had done. The symptoms were of approximately five years' duration. He presented a clinical picture of peptic ulcer but radiologists disagreed as to the roentgenogram confirmation.

His interpersonal relations were permeated with a need to be approved of, loved, and supported. When these needs were not gratified or when their gratification was threatened (by his wife's leaving for a week-end visit or an interruption in therapy, for example) the patient usually reacted with intense anger and/or severe anxiety attacks. The latter seemed to be elicited by his hostile reactions as well as the threat of dependency deprivation. His awareness of the importance of his passive-dependent needs varied, as did his insight into the cause of the related hostility and anxiety reactions. The patient was ashamed of this entire reaction pattern.

Z's Fifteenth Interview

The following pertinent background information is important in evaluating the speech disturbance graph for this interview, which is presented in Figure 2. In the thirteenth and fourteenth interviews, occurring in the preceding calendar week, the patient started to talk of his discomforting relationship with his mother. He described her as a possessive and dominating woman who interfered in the personal lives of himself, his wife, his brother and sister. She involved the entire family in a morass of conflicting relationships with her by active (e.g., arguing or criticizing) and passive (e.g., feigning weakness) means. While he resented these things she did, his dependency, the allied anxiety, and devotion were even stronger. He was highly conflicted about her.

The patient had been stimulated to talk about her because of recent conversations with his brother, an anticipated visit from her, and because he believed the therapist expected him to work through his relationship with her. When going home after the fourteenth interview, he had continued to think about his mother. Several important things about her occurred to him which he immediately forgot. When this happened he felt nervous and frightened *that he had forgotten them.*

A week end ensued right after the fourteenth interview and his mother visited him at that time. He would ordinarily have come for his fifteenth hour on the following Monday. Instead, his wife called and said he could not make it because of an unexpected change in his business plans. The patient came for the fifteenth session at the next regularly scheduled time on Wednesday.

The context of the therapist-patient relation at this time was highlighted by conscious conflicting tendencies in the patient to become very dependent and passive with the therapist and to avoid this by not giving in to spontaneous, uncontrolled free associations. These tendencies had been openly discussed in only the twelfth interview, when the patient underlined them by describing how he was repeating to himself as he came to the interviewing room that day, "I am not going to become dependent on him" (i.e., the therapist). In this same interview the patient had alluded to *fears that the therapist would stop seeing him if he couldn't produce important emotional material.*

The graph in Figure 2 has been divided into five time segments to correspond to five large phases of interaction (*a, b, c, d, e*) determined from a study of content and interaction depicted by the typescript and tape recording.

Figure 2[a]

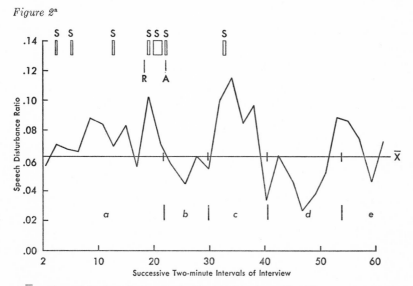

[a] $\overline{X}$ = Mean of the two-minute ratios in Z's eight interviews. N = 242.

S = All silences over ten seconds judged by two observers to be "anxious silences." Judgments were independently made and before any idea of this type of speech disturbance analysis occurred. In order, the durations of the silences are 11, 11, 13, 19, 45, 10, 17 seconds.

R = Repression of fleeting thought.

A = Patient experiences "nervous tics" in buttocks.

a, b, c, d, e = Contentual and interaction phases interpreted in text.

Phase a

Throughout this phase, the patient attempted to describe strong negative feelings he experienced toward his mother during her visit. He described them conflictfully as feelings of antagonism, withdrawal, annoyance, and resentment, and at one time directly denied these feelings only to see the contradiction when the therapist commented on it. In this phase he described several things she did to arouse these feelings and a sense of shame that he overtly manifested his feelings to her.

Intermittently in phase a, the patient indicated an awareness of anxiety when thinking about and discussing these feelings toward his mother. (1) He described a sense of relief at not being here Monday and mounting anxiety as he came to the interviewing room today. (2) He described to the therapist how he was currently tempted to consciously evade talking about his mother by asking the therapist questions about psychology. (3) He described a current sense of inadequacy because he could not use his experience over the week end to understand better his relation to his mother. (4) He reported experiencing a repression of fleeting thoughts about his mother.

As shown in the graph, the patient fell silent for more than ten seconds frequently in this phase and toward the end of it was silent for a long time and experienced "nervous tics" in his buttocks.

Phase a is interpreted as one in which the patient is motivated to think and communicate hostile thoughts which elicit anxiety in themselves ("intrapsychic") and when spoken to the therapist (interpersonal basis). He anticipates rejection by the therapist if he cannot talk of these feelings and this elicits further anxiety. The patient does communicate these thoughts but in a conflictful, partially defending, and oscillating manner — at times expressing them openly, at times exercising control in self-observation, at times defensively being silent or repressed, and finally experiencing anxiety symptoms.

The fact that the two-minute ratios for phase a are almost all oscillating above this patient's general mean two-minute ratio, but not so extreme as they could be, seems highly consistent with the clinical picture if the ratios are regarded as valid measures of anxiety.

Phase b

This phase represented a sudden shift by the patient from the content above to describing an aunt who dominated every phase of his earlier family life in a variety of ways. The items he mentioned included brief references to how she was consulted in the patient's adolescence when he masturbated, propositioned a little girl, and when he was fond of a girl. She destroyed his attraction for the latter girl by merely saying she didn't like the shape of this girl's upper lip. After this last communication, he suddenly stopped and said he couldn't make any connection between his aunt and the "general problem."

This phase is interpreted as being an extended defensive maneuver motivated by the strong anxiety existing at the end of phase a. It is in the form of a displacement — both "away from" phase a and "toward" phase c, to speak loosely. It is clear that a consistently depressed change in the speech disturbances takes place with this maneuver, just as one would expect if it were a valid measure of anxiety. Because of the generalization mechanism, talking about his hostile and fearful feelings toward the aunt rather than toward his mother elicits less anxiety. At the same time he "produces" for the therapist, anticipates to a less degree being rejected, and this further reduces his anxiety.

Phase c

In the last part of the thirtieth minute, the therapist responded to the patient's last comment with an interpretation: "But I wonder if this isn't also the way you feel about your mother? A good many of these things that you just . . . you've just said, you . . . ah . . . you indicated . . . ah . . . applied to your mother too. Last Friday when you were talking about this, you said that your mother was a very possessive person and . . . ah . . . entered into every detail in your life, particularly yours, you said." The patient reacted very reluctantly at first to this statement, saying that he never thought of his mother as dominating, although she is possessive. After he stated that his mother does dominate, not by strength like the aunt, but by her weakness and tears, the therapist pressed the patient by mentioning a consistent incident the patient cited Friday. The patient then related in sequence: how she controls him with tears and protestations of a nagging, weeping nature; how she is anxiety-ridden over his brother's financial condition; and finally how hysterical and frightening to him *she* was when she discovered the time he showed a girl his penis and proposed intercourse when he was 14 years old. Right after a vivid account of "that horrible evening!" and at the end of the thirty-eighth-minute point in the graph, he said that he didn't go out with a girl until he was 24.

As a result of the therapist's interpretation of the defensive maneuver in phase *b*, the patient returned to think and talk about his relation with his mother. With further stimulation from the therapist, the patient now talks of further feelings toward his mother. This is so anxiety-evoking to do that it was previously done only in displaced form. (The motivation to return in this manner is regarded by the writer as due to the transference relation described above and not because of anxiety reduction following the interpretation. Negative evidence of the latter is his initial reluctance and a rather lengthy silence.) The phase of high speech disturbance paralleling this phase *c* is clearly expected if the ratios reflect anxiety in the patient.

Phase d

Right after the last comment of phase *c*, the patient said, "I was afraid of girls." He then immediately proceeded to give an extended account of bashfulness, embarrassment, social gracelessness in "asexual" situations or relations such as club activities, picnics, high school dances, and youthful infatuations. This was all done with great fluency and at times had a flavor of intellectualization. Suddenly, in the interval measured by the fifty-second-minute point in the graph, he said that with one of these girls he had had three opportunities to have intercourse, but he hadn't been able to bring himself to do so. Following this, he was embarrassed. The therapist ambiguously said this did indicate something "strange" in his sexual life.

Here again, the patient suddenly shifts the topic away from his feelings about his mother, selecting something implied in the previous phase but elaborating the least anxiety-evoking aspect of it. But at the close of the phase he has "tricked" himself into an admission that causes him embarrassment. His self-esteem is further threatened by the therapist's comment. The drop in speech disturbance during this phase with the sudden rise in the last interchange is consistent with this interpretation if it measures anxiety. For prior to the end he is uttering less anxiety-evoking contents, yet is meeting the previously verbalized felt demand to produce and understand.

Phase e

At the outset of this phase, the patient suddenly ceased discussing the incident of sexual failure and hurriedly shifted to talk of the circumstance surrounding his marriage — how for him it was not a marriage of love, that it was a case of hero worship on his wife's part, and that he had had an extramarital affair. He alluded to a freedom to talk here about his wife, but reluctance to tell her of what goes on here.

This phase is not clear clinically. At the outset his anxiety is regarded as high as stated above. His lack of love for his wife could be a displacement from his inability to have intercourse. This phase as a whole has the flavor of an obscuring maneuver and it also includes the report of masculine success. Both of these could reduce the anxiety occasioned by his admission and the therapist's comment and so the speech disturbance curve could drop.

Z's Eighty-third Hour

In the eighty-second hour the patient manifested a desire to identify with the therapist by embarrassedly saying that "even though it sounds silly" he had been thinking recently how he would like to return to college and prepare himself to do research in psychology. He described research efforts he had made in the course of conducting his business. Later the patient anxiously expressed positive affectionate feelings for the therapist. He had been thinking of these frequently of late but hesitated to tell him of them. He thought this was because his father's overbearing treatment of him had caused him to bury them with respect to his father.

In the interval between the eighty-second and eighty-third interviews the following things happened. (1) The patient had been ill with intestinal grippe and headaches. (2) The patient and his wife had a very heated disagreement over their life situation one night that involved strong argument and also aroused their dependency needs. (3) They subsequently, on the night before the eighty-third interview, made up by manifesting their felt needs for each other and comforting each other, and (4) finally performing mutually oral-genital and then genital intercourse.

A very obscured and confused description of these charged events, with the last detail being postponed until the end, is what took place in the eighty-third interview. The details of this need not be discussed here, but the following were the major features. The speech disturbance graph is contained in Figure 3.

Figure 3[a]

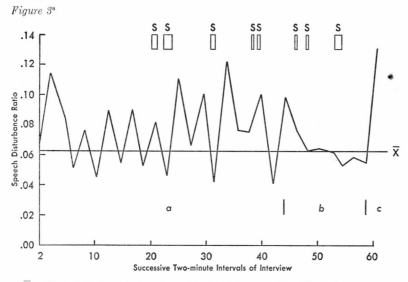

[a] $\overline{X}$ = Mean of the two-minute ratios in Z's eight interviews. N = 242.

S = All silences over ten seconds judged by two observers to be "anxious silences." Judgments were independently made and before any idea of this type of speech disturbance analysis occurred. In order, the durations of the silences are 25, 39, 22, 11, 14, 10, 12, 30 seconds.

a, b, c = Contentual and interaction phases interpreted in text.

Phase a

In the second minute of the hour the patient stated he and his wife had had a very emotional experience and proceeded to describe the argument in detail for the first ten minutes of the hour. After speaking about two minutes in telling of his illness, the patient then related the details of the "asexual" features of their reconciliation, stretching this out until the twentieth minute. The nearest he came to relating anything of a sexual nature was to say that after they expressed their need for each other his wife ". . . was very affectionate and everything else" and ". . . we came to a rapprochement."

He then immediately described a feeling of fear, nervousness, and physical symptoms of anxiety as he got ready to come today and as he was on his way. Following this, and with some unwitting collaboration by the therapist, the patient "swirled" away from the sexual factors and elaborated somewhat on the argument, on his illness, and on his felt dependency needs for his wife. Each of these elicited anxieties themselves because of admissions of dependency and weakness, even though they seemed to start as defensive maneuvers to avoid utterance of the sexual content. All this while the therapist was attempting to find out what had constituted the "rapprochement." This continued until the forty-first minute when the patient started to describe the rapprochement as consisting of "a complete surrender" by his wife when she cried as he comforted her, then as a "giving on her part in her love-making afterwards" and a statement for the first time in the interview that they had had intercourse.

Phase *b*

When the patient then reverted to treating this episode as a "qualitative change" in an abstract way in the forty-fourth minute, the therapist decided to become less active until the patient became less anxious. The patient continued to talk abstractly and intellectually of a "qualitative change," saying that his wife's complete surrendering was most frightening to him and that he had become frightened on his way today when he was thinking of the sequence of events he wanted to tell the therapist. After the long silence, the patient described in detail recent headaches.

Phase *c*

Finally, in the fifty-eighth minute, the therapist commented: "Well, it certainly sounds like a tremendous . . . ah . . . thing happened here. Something of real importance. Ah . . . it's not clear to me exactly what it was. . . ." The patient responded by saying that it was her wholehearted surrender. With the therapist directly asking on the first and successive instances what she had done, the patient — in the last two minutes depicted in the graph — progressively specified that she had shown a lot of emotion in her love-making, had shown abandonment, had been more uninhibited than usual, had performed fellatio. At a point that is beyond the graph, he then described his own cunnilingual activity.

This interview is an excellent example of a sustained strong conflict in the patient over telling of what he perceived as a "shocking, abhorrent," and frightening event — mutual oral-genital contact with his wife. It was further complicated by "lesser" but strong conflicts. The two-minute disturbance ratios reflect this sustained state of conflict.

Throughout the entire session the patient was motivated to describe completely the charged events that had transpired since the preceding interview. Early in phase *a* he had completed a description of all but the sexual elements, and only after progressive-regressive oscillation did he add some of the sexual details to this account. The speech disturbance graph shows that during phase *a* the ratios were relatively unpatterned and were varying about a level distinctly above the general average.

When the therapist decreased his own activity designed to find out what had happened and thus permitted the patient to prolong his defensive maneuvers, the patient entered into phase *b* in which he defensively avoided the feared element by abstraction, a long silence, and a detailed account of his headaches. In this phase, when he was given freedom to be successfully defensive for a relatively long time, the speech disturbance graph shows a flattening at the average level.

When in the last two minutes the therapist intervened and "forced" him to tell what had happened, the patient uttered the contents that previously had evoked anxiety. In the absence of defense the anxiety may be inferred to increase, and the speech disturbance graph suddenly mounts to the very high value shown.

It is worth noting that the patient himself gave independent evidence that the progressive account of the charged events was to be frightening for him when he described his fear at coming and later said it was concerned with the sequence of events he wished to relate. This anticipatory anxiety and the anxiety motivating the many defensive maneuvers in this hour are regarded as primarily interpersonal, that is, fear of the therapist's reaction upon hearing certain contents, and arising out of the strong transference existing at this time. Because of his positive feelings for the therapist, the patient wished the therapist to hold him, in turn, in high esteem — not as one who engages in "shocking and abhorrent" sexual behavior. There may also be inferred irrationally transferred anticipation of overbearing behavior from the therapist similar to that of the patient's father.

The preceding material illustrates how the two-minute speech disturbance ratios seem to reflect changes in the patient's anxiety level during interview proceedings. These evaluations, and others of other interviews, were some of the earliest steps taken in this research. As a matter of research tactics, the author knew what the two-minute graphs looked like at the time the various content or interaction phases were evaluated for anxiety implications. It seemed wisest to proceed with better controlled clinical evaluations only if such *ad hoc* ones suggested that positive results might be obtained in doing so.

Controlled Clinical Evaluation of Interview Proceedings

The preceding paragraphs have illustrated that interviews are divisible into natural segments or phases, each of which can be assigned to a single theme of content or interaction, and that the patient becomes anxious and conflictful in some, but becomes less anxious in others. In the latter, one can often observe that the patient himself has changed the topic or started a new line of interaction with the therapist in such a way that his behavior can be interpreted as a relatively sustained and successful defensive maneuver.

The *ad hoc* judgments of such phases may be contaminated by the knowledge of the speech disturbance measures. The assumption underlying the validation test below is that with adequate context for interpretation of the intrapersonal and interpersonal instrumental significance of content the patient utters and of interaction between the patient and the therapist, it should be possible to judge such phases validly from typescripts only. If so, and if the speech disturbance ratio is a valid partial index of anxiety, then the speech disturbance ratios should be larger in the anxious or conflictful phases than in the low anxious or defensive phases.

A test of these predictions was made using interviews from another patient, Mrs. Y, who had been in treatment for over 100 interviews. The interviews selected for these controlled clinical evaluations were numbers 5, 10, 13, 17, 20, and 26.

With Mrs. Y the first major problem was to prevent contaminated phase judgments. Although the author had been the therapist, the test interviews occurred slightly over two and a half years before this validation test was made. The author had not heard the recordings or studied transcripts of these interviews. After practicing with different interviews, a secretary "edited" verbatim transcripts and prepared clean scripts that did not contain any speech disturbances, any annotations concerning pauses, or any explicit reference to silence by the participants. Of course these "test" scripts were no longer exactly verbatim. Because of these precautions, it is felt that no serious contamination of the phase judgments occurred.

The judgment of the correct anxiety category for the phases of content or interaction required detailed knowledge of the context of each "test" interview. The major reason for this is that the judgment cannot be made solely on the basis of manifest content. The context includes general knowledge of the patient and of the dynamic setting of a given therapeutic session. The development of the context was a major problem. A good deal was known about the patient since the judge had participated in over 100 therapeutic interviews with her. The immediate context of the test hours was obtained by now listening to the recordings for the first 29 interviews, excepting the test hours. Notes made of each of the nontest hours and the complete edited typescripts for the test hours were then reviewed in sequence. Then before finally judging the phases in any given test hour a rough clinical formulation of the therapeutic situation at the time was written.

After the interviews were divided into phases and categorized as to anxiety type, the phases were marked in the original verbatim typescripts in which speech disturbances had been scored by an independent observer. Speech disturbance ratios for the phases were then computed.

A total of 19 defensive and/or low anxiety and 19 anxious or conflictful phases were judged in the five test hours. However, for any given interview there had not always been judged an equal number of each type of phase. To control for the confounding of "hour effects" mentioned earlier, equal numbers of the phase types were randomly selected for each interview. This procedure produced a sample of 15 phases in each group. The results are presented in Table 1. In the anxious or conflictful phases, the mean

Table 1

SPEECH DISTURBANCE RATIOS IN PHASES OF INTERVIEWS

Statistic	Phase		Significance (one-tail test)
	Low Anxious or Defensive	Anxious or Conflictful	
N	15	15	
$\overline{X}$	.038	.049	t = 2.68
			p < .01
SD	.013	.009	

speech disturbance ratio increases by 29 per cent, p < .01 level.

This study is described in more detail elsewhere,[20] including a detailed account of the interview proceedings and the speech disturbances for one of the test hours.

[20] Mahl, "Disturbances and Silences in the Patient's Speech in Psychotherapy."

This study was done to obtain further evidence that the speech disturbance ratio is a valid partial index of anxiety, and to determine the effect of rate of talking, age, education, and hostility on the speech disturbance level.

There was an additional important goal of this study. In work done after the clinical evaluation studies, some question had been raised about the correctness of including "ah" in the speech disturbance ratio for use as a partial measure of anxiety. Evidence on this question was also sought in this study.

The material consisted of the initial interviews of 31 patients applying for treatment at a psychiatric out-patient clinic. There were 20 female and 11 male patients. The recorded diagnoses were: 18 psychoneuroses, 8 character disorders, and 5 schizophrenics. The ages ranged from 19 to 49. The educational levels ranged from completion of the eighth grade through one or more years of college, but no one had officially completed a college course.

Two psychiatric residents and a psychologist conducted and observed the interviews in rotation. One interviewed every third patient in the series, while the other two monitored and observed the interview through a one-way mirror. Immediately after the end of the interview, each person independently rated, on five-point global scales, the degree of anxiety and of hostility manifested by the patient during the interview. Two of the investigators were notably more reliable raters of both anxiety and hostility than the third person was. Consequently, the means of these two raters were taken as the anxiety and hostility measure for each patient. The reliability coefficients for these mean ratings are .82 for anxiety and .73 for hostility.

The interviews had also been recorded, and the tapes preserved and transcribed. The speech disturbances were scored by independent workers. The term "general speech disturbance ratio" is used here to signify the ratio that includes all of the disturbance categories including "ah." The ratio that excludes "ah" is called the "non-ah" ratio, and the "ah" ratio includes only "ah."

Table 2 shows the relationship between the speech disturbance measures and the anxiety ratings. There is a significant positive relationship between the "non-ah" speech disturbances and anxiety,

---

[21] G. F. Mahl, "Disturbances in the Patient's Speech as a Function of Anxiety," a paper delivered before the Eastern Psychological Association, Atlantic City, N.J., 1956.

Table 2

PRODUCT-MOMENT CORRELATIONS BETWEEN ANXIETY RATINGS
AND SPEECH DISTURBANCE RATIOS (N = 31)

Ratio	Anxiety	p
Non-Ah	.36	<.03[a]
Ah	−.30	<.10
General (ah and non-ah)	.08	—
Ah *vs.* Non-Ah	−.23	.21

[a] One-tail test.

a negative correlation between "ah" and anxiety, and the inclusion of "ah" in the speech disturbance measure yields a zero correlation. These findings suggest that "ah" should not be included as an anxiety indicator. The remainder of this discussion deals only with the "non-ah" ratio.

A modest though significant positive correlation between the "non-ah" ratio and the anxiety ratings was what was actually anticipated on the basis of theory and previous work. But a somewhat stronger relationship than is indicated by the correlation of .36 had been expected. In considering the source of this discrepancy, the relative freedom in manifesting affect generally that existed among the women contrasted with the men in this sample, as well as that permitted by our cultural values, was recalled.

Consequently, the correlation between the "non-ah" ratio and the anxiety ratings was determined separately for the 20 women and 11 men. Table 3 contains the results. Here it is shown that the

Table 3

PRODUCT-MOMENT CORRELATIONS BETWEEN SPEECH DISTURBANCE RATIOS (NON-AH)
AND ANXIETY RATINGS IN WOMEN AND IN MEN

Sample	Correlation	p
All 31 Patients	.36	<.03[a]
20 Women	.59	<.005[a]
11 Men	−.47	<.08[a]
Significance of Difference Between Sexes		.006

[a] One-tail tests.

positive correlation of .36 for the sample as a whole concealed an interaction effect. There is a correlation of .59 for the women, and one of −.47 for the men. The difference between the correlations is highly significant.

Correlations of the speech disturbance measure with hostility, education, age, and rate of talking are shown in Table 4. These

Table 4

CORRELATIONS BETWEEN SPEECH DISTURBANCE RATIOS (NON-AH) AND OTHER VARIABLES

Other Variables	All Patients (N = 31)	Females (N = 20)	Males (N = 11)
Anxiety	.36	.59	−.47
Hostility	−.06	−.02	−.04
Education	−.03	.16[a]	−.33
Age	.05	.01	.10
"Words"/Second	.13	−.02	.35

[a] N = 18.

correlations are presented for the group as a whole, and also for the women and men separately. With the exception of speech disturbances and anxiety, none of these correlations are significant. Most of them are impressively near zero. The two exceptions are for educational level and rate of talking in the men. Here there may be a suggestion of decreasing disturbances with increasing educational level, and of decreasing disturbances with slower talking.

The most striking finding of this study is the interaction effect of sex and the anxiety ratings. The actual cause for it is unknown at the present time. Perhaps it reflects a difference in criteria and meaning of the anxiety ratings for the women and for the men. The judges could have been rating manifest anxiety in the women, and defensiveness in the men. Defensive maneuvering indicates both increments and decrements in anxiety. Anxiety must increase to motivate the onset of the defensive maneuvering, but the execution of the defensive process then reduces the intensity of the anxiety. The raters may not have kept this important distinction in mind. Greater defensiveness, that is, less open expression of anxiety, by male patients than by female, especially in the initial interview, is compatible with our cultural definition of masculinity and femininity. It is also possible that male interviewers would violate defensiveness in men less frequently than they would in women when both participants are strangers, as in the initial interview.

A great deal of the exploratory work that preceded the material presented in this chapter was done with the therapeutic interviews of Mr. Z. Either he is the exception among men, or obscure factors were operating in the judges in this study with the initial interviews. The author is of the opinion that the latter is the true state of affairs, but he is alerted to future evidence of a true sex difference. One is also alerted to the importance of distinguishing interpatient and intrapatient comparisons. Even in the absence of uniform regularities across the population in level of anxiety and speech disturbance there may be regular relations between level of anxiety and the departure of an individual from his own speech norms.

The finding concerning "ah" may represent a refinement in the speech disturbance measure. But further data will be needed to determine if "ah" is also detrimental for within-patient comparisons. ("Ah" was included in the study with Mrs. Y, but she happened to use "ah" quite infrequently. On the average only 16 per cent of her disturbances were "ahs," whereas for the initial interviews the mean "ah" was 34 per cent.)

Since the judges in this study based their anxiety ratings on the live interviews, it is possible that the sizable positive correlation for the women is merely a product of a contaminated criterion. Two of the results strongly suggest that this is not the case. The first is the difference in the correlations for the men and the women. This could not have occurred if the ratings were contaminated. The second is the finding that the inclusion of "ah" reduces the correlation for the group as a whole to zero. It is impossible for judges who have not been highly trained in scoring speech disturbances to make discriminations between the various disturbance categories under conditions of live observation. It is extremely difficult for even trained scorers to do so and also follow the interaction. None of the raters were aware of the category set and none had ever identified any of the categories in typescripts. Also, the judges had no basis for believing that "ah's" would be different from the "non-ah" categories so far as anxiety is concerned.

The preceding studies are interpreted as supporting the belief that the speech disturbance measure will be a useful nonlexical indicator of current anxiety in the speaker. But there is obviously a great deal more work to be done. It is especially important to discover the effects that different types of communication situations, different personality structures, and varying emphases on speech in child rearing may have on the anxiety–speech disturbance relationship.[22]

----

[22] Since this chapter was written, Skinner's book on language has been published (B. F. Skinner, *Verbal Behavior* [New York, 1957]). There is considerable similarity between the author's view of language behavior presented above and that part of Skinner's extensive treatment which considers the same problems discussed in the first part of this chapter. The present author has summarized more recent investigations of speech disturbances in "Measuring the Patient's Anxiety During Interviews from 'Expressive' Aspects of His Speech," *Transactions of the New York Academy of Science,* 21 (1959), 249-57.

A recent study (S. V. Kasl and G. F. Mahl, "Experimentally Induced Anxiety and Speech Disturbances," *American Psychologist,* 13 [1958], 349) showed that experimentally induced anxiety, confirmed by palmar sweat measures, increased significantly the "non-ah" ratio, but not the "ah" ratio, in male subjects.

4

SOL SAPORTA AND THOMAS A. SEBEOK
INDIANA UNIVERSITY

LINGUISTICS AND CONTENT ANALYSIS

THE PROBLEM

LINGUISTIC ANALYSIS AND CONTENT ANALYSIS

The linguistic data which the conference generally considered to be most useful, that is, most readily applicable to problems of content analysis, was information about "the different ways in which certain kinds of things can be expressed" (Pool), and statements about the relative frequencies of the alternatives. These data, for example the relative frequencies of equivalent patterns such as the active and passive constructions in English, would be the basis from which any deviations could then be measured. Presumably, deviations from the structural norms in the formal characteristics of messages would then be correlated with differences in the intentions, behavioral states — in short, with some nonlinguistic conditions — in the producer of those messages.

In order to indicate more clearly what the potential contribution of linguistics to content analysis is conceived to be, it seems appropriate to describe (1) a framework within which linguistic analysis and content analysis may be compared, and (2) within that framework to indicate what kind of information linguistic analysis yields.

Although far from meeting with universal agreement in the field, the following statement, representative of a point of view especially prevalent among some American structural linguists, may serve as a useful frame of reference for formulating the problem of what and how linguistic data can be of use to investigators whose concern is content.

The area of "who says what to whom under what circumstances for what purpose and with what effect," which presumably defines the variables in communication analysis, would in general serve as an adequate definition of precisely what linguists are *not* concerned with. Linguistic analysis deals with the code per se; the statements which describe the code enable one to generate an infinite number of utterances, a very high percentage of which will be acceptable to native speakers of the language.[1]

Essentially, the task of the linguist is twofold: the identification of the minimal units in the code — the phonemes and morphemes — and the statement of the permissible sequences of these units.[2]

The phonemic inventory, besides including phonemes in sequence (e.g., the vowels and consonants), considers concurrent phonemes like stress, which in English distinguishes, for example, *billow* and *below*, or *the white house* and *the White House*, and intonation — compare the intonations of "What are we having for dinner, Mother?" and "What are we having for dinner? Steak?" Within linguistics proper there is a restriction, however, on the type of phenomena to be described. Thus, though most speakers of English may agree that "There is a bi:::g bear in the woods" is different from — let's say more emphatic than — "There is a big bear in the woods," the difference in length between [bi:::g] and [big] is not part of the phonemic structure of English (though it may be for other languages). In general, the borderline between phonemes and what have been called voice qualifiers[3] is probably determined by the discrete (or quantized) nature of the former as opposed to the continuous quality of the latter. Thus, if [bi:g] with length is emphatic, then [bi::g] with more length is more emphatic. These features of language have only recently begun to be explored systematically, but one suspects that, within phonology, it is in this area that correlates between the formal characteristics of messages and attitudes of the producers of messages are most likely to be found. The investigation of variation in the use of these voice qualifiers might yield, for example, the "measure that will tell . . .

----

[1] See, for example, C. F. Hockett, "Two Models of Grammatical Description," *Word,* 10 (1954), 232, on criteria for the evaluation of a grammatical description.

[2] Phoneme and morpheme are the basic units in linguistics. For a brief discussion oriented toward investigators in related disciplines, see the presentation by J. Greenberg in Osgood and Sebeok, eds., *Psycholinguistics: A Survey of Theory and Research Problems* (Indiana University Publications in Anthropology and Linguistics, Memoir 10 [Bloomington, 1954], pp. 8-19.

[3] H. L. Smith, Jr., "An Outline of Metalinguistic Analysis," in *Report of the Third Annual Round Table Meeting on Linguistics and Language Teaching* (Washington, D.C., 1952), pp. 59-66.

when the patient is disturbed, regardless of content" (Mahl), if indeed such a measure does exist.

Similarly, on the level of morphemics the analysis of a corpus of material results in the identification and classification of the minimal forms, the morphemes. Thus, comparison of the forms *talks talked talk walks walked walk* yields one class of morphemes including *talk* and *walk*, and a second class including *-s* and *-ed*. The combinatorial possibilities of these forms would be indicated by some statement to the effect that class 1 may occur with or without class 2, but that class 2 may occur only with class 1.

Descriptive linguistics as such does not generally deal with the meanings of morphemes. The distributions, that is, the total combinatorial possibilities, are stated only relative to other morphemes. However, to the extent that distribution and meaning are related, it is possible to use some function of the distributional data as an approximation to the meaning. Under what conditions and to what extent meaning may be considered a function of distribution is discussed later.

THE RELATION BETWEEN UTTERANCE, TEXT, LANGUAGE

A word must be said about the role of the corpus, that is, the particular body of material being analyzed in linguistics as opposed to content analysis. Again the two techniques are quite different. Whereas for linguistic analysis a corpus is adequate to the extent that it is representative of the language as a whole, in content analysis one of the points of interest is precisely in what way the text may be said to differ from the language as a whole. However, though its concern is with the code, linguistics makes its most meaningful statements about relatively short utterances, in general what have traditionally been called sentences. The point has been made most clearly by Harris: "Descriptive linguistics generally stops at sentence boundaries. This is not due to any prior decision. The techniques of linguistics were constructed to study any stretch of speech, of whatever length. But in every language, it turns out that almost all the results lie within a relatively short stretch. . . . That is, when we can state a restriction on the occurrence of element A in respect to the occurrence of element B, it will almost always be the case that A and B are regarded as occurring within the same sentence."[4] There are, of course, some restrictions which

---

[4] Z. S. Harris, "Discourse Analysis," *Language,* 28 (1952), 1-2.

can be stated across sentence boundaries; for example, the choice between a masculine or feminine pronoun may be conditioned by a noun in a previous sentence. In general, however, "descriptive linguistics, which sets out to describe the occurrence of elements in any stretch of speech, ends up by describing it primarily in respect to other elements of the same sentence. This limitation has not seemed too serious, because it has not precluded the writing of adequate grammars: the grammar states the sentence structure; the speaker makes up a particular sentence in keeping with this structure, and supplies the particular sequence of sentences."[5] Thus the linguistic analysis does not reveal anything which is peculiar to the text under consideration. However, a text may be said to deviate from the linguistic norm in two ways: in the relative frequencies of the constituent elements and patterns,[6] and by being further restricted by an additional "structure" beyond that of the language as a whole. The most apparent, but probably the most trivial from the point of view of content analysis, are the phonological restrictions caused by the requirements of rhyme and meter in poetry. The first type of difference — the quantitative difference — might prove to be more pertinent in the analysis of most spontaneous communications including, for example, psychotherapeutic protocols; the second — the qualitative difference — would seem to be more revealing in the analysis of any less casually uttered communications (whether esthetically motivated or not), including such highly structured forms as charms, folk tales, nursery rhymes, and the like.[7] Beside the additional restrictions in structure, the qualitative difference may be manifested in the particular juxtaposition of the constituent elements. It is this feature of certain

----

[5] Harris, "Discourse Analysis," p. 2.

[6] See B. Bloch, "Linguistic Structure and Linguistic Analysis," in *Report of the Fourth Annual Round Table Meeting on Linguistics and Language Teaching* (Washington, D.C., 1953), p. 42, for the following definition of style: "the style of a discourse is the message carried by the frequency distributions and transitional probabilities of its linguistic features, especially as they differ from those of the same features in the language as a whole." See also H. Rubenstein, review of Miller's *Language and Communication*, in *Language*, 28 (1952), 116, who suggests that "style . . . may be best defined by the analogy style: dialect : : personality : (non-linguistic) culture; i.e., style is the individual's modification of his group's non-linguistic culture." The matter of style is thoroughly explored in T. A. Sebeok, ed., *Aspects of Style in Language* (in press).

[7] Alexander George points out that this "basic distinction between types of communication . . . comes close to that referred to in the conference as 'representational-instrumental.'"

messages which suggests the feasibility of a statistical contingency analysis.

DISTRIBUTION VS. MEANING

Although it is perhaps an oversimplification, it may be useful to characterize the difference in the aims and techniques of linguistic *vs.* content analysis as an interest by the former in the distribution of forms, that is, their privilege of occurrence in relation to other forms, as opposed to the latter's concern with the meaning of these forms. We may illustrate the concept of distribution by examining two sets of forms: (1) *oculist, eye doctor, lawyer,* and (2) *sit, chair, door.*[8]

The distribution of a linguistic form means the sum of all its environments. Thus, regarding the members of our first set, we would find a large number of utterances with *oculist*, such as "I've had my eyes examined by the same oculist for twenty years," etc. We would also find identical sentences with *eye doctor*. In short, *eye doctor* and *oculist* may occur in many identical environments. For some occurrences of *oculist* we could not substitute *eye doctor;* for example, "An oculist is just an eye doctor under a fancier name," etc. We then describe the relation in distribution between *eye doctor* and *oculist* by stating that they may be substituted for one another in most environments; the majority of cases where they may not be so substituted are sentences in which both occur. Now, if we compare the occurrences of *oculist* and *lawyer*, we find that for some utterances with *oculist* we find identical utterances with *lawyer* — for example, "I told him to go see a good oculist/lawyer" — but that, in addition, there are many environments in which *oculist* occurs but *lawyer* does not, such as the one above, "I've had my eyes examined by the same oculist for twenty years."[9] Thus,

----

[8] The following is essentially a rephrasing of the discussion by Z. S. Harris, "Distributional Structure," *Word*, 10 (1954), 146-62, who has developed the argument further than most linguists. See, however, S. Saporta, "A Note on the Relation Between Meaning and Distribution," *Litera*, 4 (1957), 22-26. For critical examinations of the notion of distribution, cf. especially P. Diderichsen, "The Importance of Distribution versus Other Criteria in Linguistic Analysis," and H. Spang-Hanssēn, "Typological and Statistical Aspects of Distribution as a Criterion in Linguistic Analysis," *Proceedings of the Eighth International Congress of Linguists* (Oslo, 1958), pp. 156-82, 182-94.

[9] As Harris points out ("Distributional Structure," pp. 156-57), "it is not a question of whether the above sentence with *lawyer* substituted is true or not; it might be true in some situation. It is rather a question . . . of whether we will obtain *lawyer* here if we ask an informant to substitute any

"if A and B have almost identical environments except chiefly for sentences which contain both, we say they are synonyms: *oculist* and *eye doctor*. If A and B have some environments in common and some not (e.g., *oculist* and *lawyer*) we say that they have different meanings, the amount of meaning difference corresponding roughly to the amount of difference in their environments,"[10] so that "if we consider words or morphemes A and B to be more different in meaning than A and C, then we will often find that the distributions of A and B are more different than the distributions of A and C."[11]

If we turn now to our second set (*sit, chair, door*) we find that since *sit* and *chair* are members of different grammatical classes they have no environments in common, that is, they may not be substituted for one another. However, *sit* and *chair* seem to have a similarity in meaning (despite being members of different grammatical classes) which *sit* and some other verb like *slam* do not have, or which *chair* and some other noun like *door* do not have. Now, if we feel that verb 1 is more similar in meaning to noun 2 than it is to noun 3, then we would like to find some feature in their distribution which will correlate with this similarity in meaning. We may compare the respective lists of adjectives which occur with noun 2 and with noun 3 with the adjectives plus *-ly* which occur with verb 1. Thus, if *sit* and *chair* are more similar than *sit* and *door*, we will find that if the sequence *sit comfortably* occurs, then it is more likely that the sequence *comfortable chair* will also occur than it is that the sequence *comfortable door* will occur.

It must be pointed out that in talking about meaning above we have used speculative phrases like "if we feel . . ." and "if we consider . . ." etc. In short, how do we know that *sit* and *chair* are more similar in meaning than *sit* and *door?* One epistemological problem which eventually must be explored is whether some nondistributional method of arriving at the differences in meaning is possible; if not, the argument becomes circular, since the only evidence for difference in meaning turns out to be the distributional

---

word he wishes for *oculist*." The problem can conveniently be formulated in terms of the Cloze Procedure discussed in Chapter 2 of the present work. For some frames informants may fill in any one of the three forms, *oculist, eye doctor, lawyer;* for example, "I told him to go see a good _____."
For other frames only two, *oculist* and *eye doctor,* are likely to be filled in; for example, "I've had my eyes examined by the same _____ for twenty years." In a few frames only *oculist* will be supplied; for example, "An _____ is just an eye doctor under a fancier name."

[10] Harris, "Distributional Structure," p. 157.
[11] Harris, "Distributional Structure," p. 156.

difference. An independent method for determining meaning differences must be feasible before any statement about distributional correlates becomes testable.

Using an admittedly intuitive measure of meaning relationships, we may nevertheless examine certain pairs of forms, consider their semantic relationships and the data which might result from a contingency analysis (cf. Chap. 2 and below), and then determine what kind of distributional facts can be correlated with these semantic relationships.

Consider the following pairs: (1) *Hitler–Der Fuehrer*, (2) *Capitalism-Communism*, and (3) *mother–girl friend*. Let us assume that within some given unit (let us say, arbitrarily, a sentence) our contingency data reveal that in certain propaganda material *Hitler* and *Der Fuehrer* tend not to co-occur; that in some newspaper editorials *Capitalism* and *Communism* tend to co-occur; and that in a particular psychotherapeutic protocol *mother* and *girl friend* tend not to co-occur. We note these hypothetical findings in the first column of Table 1, where plus means greater-than-chance co-

Table 1

Paired Terms	Contingency Analysis	Semantic Relationship
Hitler–Der Fuehrer	−	+
Capitalism–Communism	+	−
Mother–Girl Friend	−	0

occurrence and minus means less-than-chance co-occurrence. (Presumably the chance co-occurrence of two concepts is not of particular interest.) In the second column we turn to the semantic relations of the terms in each pair; plus means, roughly, semantically equivalent; minus means semantically opposite; and zero means neither.

We have then three semantic relationships and we would like to discover how these different relationships are manifested in the relative distributions of the members of each pair.

First let us examine the first two pairs — *Hitler–Der Fuehrer* and *Capitalism-Communism*. In English we would discover that for most utterances with *Hitler* we would find identical utterances with *Der Fuehrer* (except primarily for utterances containing both, for example "He didn't know that Hitler was called Der Fuehrer"). It turns out, however, that for most utterances containing *Capitalism* we would also find identical utterances containing *Communism*. In other words, in a language as a whole certain antonyms are just as likely to have similar distributions as are synonyms. But if we now restrict ourselves to a given text, we will find that whereas for any one speaker at a time *Hitler* and *Der Fuehrer* may still have the same distribution, *Capitalism* and *Communism* do not. Thus, if speaker A says "I don't like Hitler" he is also likely to say "I don't like der Fuehrer"; but if he says "I don't like Communism" it is not equally likely that he will also say "I don't like Capitalism." Thus, if two forms have similar distributions both for the language as a whole and for individual speakers they are synonyms. If they have similar distributions for the language as a whole but not for individual speakers they are antonyms.[12] The forms may be nouns, adjectives, verbs, etc. "My brother Bill is honest" and "My brother Bill is dishonest" both occur in English, but only one will occur with high probability in the speech of one individual within a relatively short time.[13]

Let us consider the two pairs which are negatively associated in the contingency analysis, *Hitler–Der Fuehrer* and *mother–girl friend*. Sentences containing *Hitler* do not also contain *Der Fuehrer;* sentences containing *mother* do not also contain *girl friend*. There is obviously a difference, which can perhaps be clarified by positing an analogy to the linguistic concepts of free variation *vs.* complementary distribution. Harris states the distributional relationships as follows: "If for two elements A and B we obtain almost the same list of particular environments (selection), except that the environment of A always contains some X which never occurs in the environment of B, we say that A and B are (complementary) alternants of each other: e.g. *knife* and *knive-*.[14] If A and B have identical environments throughout . . . we say that they are free variants: e.g. perhaps for /ekənamiks/ and /iykənamiks/ *economics*."[15] From the point of view of at least

---

[12] In this connection, see the mention of the principle of congruity in Chapter 2 of the present work.

[13] There apparently are different kinds of distributional relationships for what are usually called antonyms. Thus a pair of relative terms like *good* and *bad* may share more environments than a pair of absolute terms like *black* and *white*. If the sequence *good sugar* occurs, then *bad sugar* is also likely to occur. However, the occurrence of *white sugar* does not imply the occurrence of *black sugar*.

[14] The X in this case being the plural morpheme; *knive-* occurs only before *-s* whereas *knife* never occurs before *-s*.

[15] Harris, "Distributional Structure," p. 157.

certain aspects of content analysis, synonymous expressions like *Hitler* and *Der Fuehrer* (or *oculist* and *eye doctor*) might be considered free variants.[16] To what extent the analogy may be carried out requires further investigation. In any case, it is tempting to speculate about what kind of X can be postulated whereby utterances with *girl friend* can be converted into equivalent utterances with *mother*. For example, do *mother* and *girl friend* occur in similar environments except that *mother* tends to occur with, say, *father*, whereas *girl friend* tends to occur with some reference to *self?* One might then find pairs of utterances like "My mother and father had a fight last night" and "My girl friend and I had a fight last night."

Thus at least some aspects of the different semantic relationships between (1) *Hitler–Der Fuehrer,* (2) *Capitalism-Communism,* and (3) *mother–girl friend* could be deduced from the distributional data, both in the texts under consideration and in the language as a whole.

THE METHODS OF APPLICATION

INVENTORY VS. FREQUENCY

In general, linguists have tended to consider only the presence or absence of linguistic phenomena, usually ignoring their relative frequencies. Consequently we have very little reliable information on the frequencies of, for example, comparable syntactical patterns. Indeed, even for so well-known a language as English there is probably no definitive information as to what the equivalent patterns are. Presumably these equivalences must first be identified (according to some clear-cut criteria) and norms as to relative frequencies established before deviations can be determined. Only then can deviations in frequency be correlated with the behavioral states of the producers of the message.

MARKED VS. UNMARKED

The systematic description of equivalent lexical patterns (synonyms) would obviously be of interest to the content analyst. In this connection it may be useful to introduce one additional

---

[16] George suggests that it is quite possible for content analysts to entertain certain specific hypotheses in connection with which it might be important to distinguish between the use of *Hitler* and *Der Fuehrer*. For example, *Der*

linguistic concept which seems to have a potential application in the analysis of equivalent patterns. This concept, that is, the opposition between marked and unmarked members,[17] can perhaps be illustrated by a brief discussion of two pairs of synonymous expressions: (1) *he died* vs. *he passed away,* and (2) *he came too soon* vs. *he arrived prematurely.*[18] Of the members of a pair, one, in general the most frequent, may be considered as being relatively neutral in connotation and therefore unmarked, as opposed to the other member, which is marked. Thus, in the first pair, at least in certain subcultures, *he died* may be considered unmarked and *he passed away* marked for euphemism. Wherever a particular expression becomes taboo some more euphemistic equivalent is likely to develop. The relationship between the two members is not necessarily stable, so that it is quite conceivable that the euphemistic term becomes the neutral member and the taboo term then becomes marked; it may have a connotation of vulgarity, for example. The second pair, *he came too soon* vs. *he arrived prematurely,* illustrates that the member considered marked is often chosen depending on the context. In most cases *he came too soon* would be considered the unmarked member and *he arrived prematurely* would be marked, the choice of the latter perhaps being considered elegant, or, in some cases, stilted or pedantic. However, a mother talking about her child is more likely to say that *the baby arrived prematurely,* so that a hearer is more apt to be struck by *the baby came too soon.* In such a context it would be the latter form which would be marked, by having special connotations.

The same framework would appear to be useful in the analysis of

---

Fuerher "might be taken as indicating stronger attachment, loyalty, etc., or as conformity behavior, whereas *Hitler* might be taken as a more detached form of reference." In this connection, see the discussion herein regarding marked *vs.* unmarked.

[17] This notion has proved fruitful in linguistic analysis. In stating the correlation of two categories A and B, it is said that A signifies a and B signifies a + x rather than that A signifies a and B signifies b (or non-a); in other words, the relationship of B to A is not that between two co-ordinate species but that between genus and species. We may illustrate by comparing the initial phonemes of English *seal* and *zeal.* In this example, s : z : : a : (a + x), the x being the added feature of voicing. From this point of view then, *s* is unmarked and *z* is marked. For further discussion, with examples on the morphological level, cf. T. A. Sebeok, *Finnish and Hungarian Case Systems: Their Form and Function* (Stockholm, 1946), especially pp. 10 ff.

[18] For a discussion of these and similar pairs from a different point of view, see L. Bloomfield, *Language* (New York, 1933), pp. 153-55. He cites, for example, *it's too bad* vs. *it is regrettable, prostitute* vs. *whore, Bob* vs. *Robert,* etc.

equivalent syntactical and morphological patterns, for example *it is me* vs. *it is I*, or *he got taken* vs. *he got took*. Consider for example the ludicrous effect of the "grammatically correct" *boy! am I beaten* instead of the more current *boy! am I beat*.

The following are examples of the kind of structural equivalences which have been suggested for English.[19] It is not always clear which of the members (if either) is to be considered marked; this would vary with the context.

1. John discovered that path   = That path was discovered by John.
                                = John's discovery of the path
   John is clever   = John's cleverness
2. medical training   = training in medicine
   honorable man   = man of honor
3. They escaped, saving nothing = They escaped; they saved nothing.
4. They read the banned books   = They read the books which were banned.
5. The man I phoned was out   = I phoned the man; he was out.
6. to clarify   = to make clear
   to strengthen   = to give strength
7. Equivalent word order
   a) When he comes, I'll see him = I'll see him when he comes.
   b) I saw him in town yesterday = Yesterday, I saw him in town.
   c) an intelligent, attractive girl = an attractive, intelligent girl

Analysis of other languages would, of course, yield other types of equivalent patterns.

To summarize, although it may be established on one particular level of analysis that two sounds or forms or patterns are equivalent, it is nevertheless true that the speaker must choose one of these alternatives. To the extent that the particular alternative is not predictable, the speaker's decision to use one and not the other yields some information[20] on a different level. The linguist's task is to provide statements about which patterns are, from the point of view of the code, in free variation, and the frequency norms for such patterns.[21] Pool has pointed out that the value of such analysis

---

[19] The formal basis for some of the following as well as other patterns is discussed by Harris, "Discourse Analysis," pp. 21-22, and F. W. Harwood and A. M. Wright, "Statistical Study of English Word Formation," *Language*, 32 (1956), 260-73.

[20] For a discussion of the concepts of information and redundancy, see C. E. Shannon and W. Weaver, *The Mathematical Theory of Communication* (Urbana, Ill., 1949). See also Osgood and Sebeok, eds., *Psycholinguistics: A Survey of Theory and Research Problems*, pp. 35-49.

[21] George has suggested (1) the possibility of utilizing as content indicators an individual's deviations from his own general norms, and (2) the possibility of developing norms for specified types of communication.

lies, at least in part, in the unconscious nature of such patterns.[22] It is the task of the content analyst to correlate the choice of one or the other of these free variants with either antecedent events, that is, intentions of the speaker, or subsequent events, that is, effects on the hearer.

THE ANALYSIS OF STRUCTURED MATERIAL

The Limitations of a Quantitative Analysis

Where one deals with other than "spontaneous" communications, for example literary material, an analysis purely in terms of norms and deviations may not prove fruitful. In addition to the choice between alternatives — some kinds of literary language are doubtless characterized by the increased density of marked forms — there is, for example in folklore texts, an additional structure, that is, a set of rules beyond those of the language which further restricts the sequences which occur. It seems that a structural unity characterizes all folklore texts, whether these be such simple forms as proverbs, riddles, weather predictions, dream portents, and the like, or texts of more and frequently intricate complexity, such as some prayers and most folk tales, or forms like the folk song, where the structure of the verse interacts with the musical pattern.[23] Thus for such structured materials "it follows that any quantitative approaches which overlook that unity are likely to be self-stultifying. The variables which are worth quantitative investigation will be those related to a view of the whole system. As a necessary preliminary to identifying these variables a great deal of nonquantitative work must be done. We must identify and clarify our Gestalten

---

[22] On the unconscious, automatic nature of linguistic phenomena as opposed to cultural phenomena, see A. L. Kroeber and C. Kluckhohn, *Culture* (Papers of the Peabody Museum of American Archeology and Ethnology [Cambridge, Mass., 1952]), pp. 123-24.

[23] This section is a partial restatement of T. A. Sebeok, "Toward a Statistical Contingency Method in Folklore Research," *Indiana University Publications, Folklore Series,* 9 (1957), 130-40. On folk tales, cf. the extreme position of the Soviet folklorist V. Propp, according to whom all fairy tales are uniform in their structure; see his *Morphology of the Folktale* (Publication 10, Indiana University Research Center in Anthropology, Folklore, and Linguistics [Bloomington, 1958]). On folk songs, see T. A. Sebeok, "Approaches to the Analysis of Folksong Texts," *Ural-Altaische Jahrbücher,* 31 (1959, in press), where further references are given. On other forms, see the same author's "Structural Analysis in Folklore Research," in *Studies in Cheremis,* Vol. 2, *The Supernatural* (Viking Fund Publications in Anthropology, No. 22 [New York, 1956]).

before we can intelligently measure their frequencies or even consider quantitative relations between their parts."[24]

Previous Applications of Content Analysis to Folk Material

Content analysis is, of course, a technique well known to a variety of social sciences, and has been applied both to a large and diverse group of materials and a large and diverse set of problems; it is less well known to the humanities, and relatively new to folklore research. Variously defined by different workers, we may cite Berelson's definition: "Content analysis is a research technique for the objective, systematic, and quantitative description of the manifest content of communication."[25] Any sort of communication, private or "mass," can be so analyzed. While specific applications have been made in many areas, we call attention here only to the various attempts which have been made in applying content analysis in the study of stylistic features: Berelson's bibliography of such studies includes some 35 references.[26]

This method of content analysis has also been applied to such quasi-folklore media as movies.[27] Also, of course, qualitative content analysis of folklore materials is not uncommon, and has been preferred, perhaps because in a sampling sense the content under analysis tends to be too small or inexact to justify formal and precise counting, or perhaps because its themes have appeared as Gestalten rather than as bundles of measurable features into which such texts can be decomposed. Quantification is useful, however, when precision and objectivity are necessary or desirable, when the materials to be analyzed are many, or for the sake of a high degree of specification in comparing sets of data.[28]

In general, existing methods of content analysis deal only with explicit content, that is, in one way or another they come down to counting the frequency of occurrence of certain items; so, for instance, the relative frequencies of favorable vs. unfavorable evaluations of particular referents are counted. Participants in the interdisciplinary seminar of psychologists and linguists at Cornell

---

[24] J. Ruesch and G. Bateson, "Structure and Process in Social Relations," *Psychiatry*, 12 (1949), 123.

[25] Berelson, *Content Analysis*, p. 18.

[26] Berelson, *Content Analysis*, pp. 66-72, 208-10.

[27] Martha Wolfenstein and N. Leites, *Movies, a Psychological Study* (Glencoe, Ill., 1950).

[28] See H. E. Driver, "Statistics in Anthropology," *American Anthropologist*, 55 (1953), 42-59, for a historical survey of quantification in the various branches of anthropology.

University pointed in their report to three major weaknesses of these current methods of content analysis: "(a) The units of sampling have generally been based upon expediency. . . . (b) The categories employed in deciding when a certain type of content is present or absent in a given unit have been largely arbitrary. . . . (c) Existing methods of content analysis are limited to simple comparisons of frequencies rather than measuring the internal contingencies between categories."[29] It was the feeling of this group that the transitional relations among semantic events are also important for content analysis.

A Structural Characteristic of Nursery Rhymes

We have suggested above that certain types of materials may be characterized by restrictions in their formal structure beyond those imposed by the general grammar of the language. For example, the first lines of nursery rhymes listed below illustrate a similarity in structure which is typical in this genre. The device is obvious; all examples have a reduplicated element.

The reduplicated element may be a vocative (1) or not a vocative (2). If it is a vocative, it may appear with a question (1.1) or an imperative (1.2). If it appears with a question, the element may be initial (1.11) or final (1.12). (The choice of position is perhaps related to the stress pattern of the vocative. If the vocative has loud stress on the initial syllable, for example Cúrlў Lòcks, Pússў Càt, etc., the vocative is initial. If the loud stress occurs on the final syllable, for example Bìllў Bóy, the vocative is final). Examples 1.11a and 2a have in common the use of an appositive after the reduplicated element.

1.11a) Mary, Mary, quite contrary, how does your garden grow?[30]
   b) Curly Locks, Curly Locks, wilt thou be mine?
   c) Pussy Cat, Pussy Cat, where have you been?
1.12) O where have you been, Billy Boy, Billy Boy?
1.2a) Rain, rain, go away!
   b) Lady bug, Lady bug, fly away home!
2a) Peter, Peter, Pumpkin eater;
     had a wife and couldn't keep her.
   b) Three blind mice, three blind mice;
     see how they run, see how they run.

----

[29] J. B. Carroll, F. B. Agard, D. E. Dulany, S. S. Newman, L. Newmark, C. E. Osgood, T. A. Sebeok, and R. L. Solomon, *Report and Recommendations of the Interdisciplinary Summer Seminar in Psychology and Linguistics* (Ithaca, N.Y., 1951), pp. 26-27.

[30] Notice the older pronunciation /kə̀ntréhrĭy/ instead of the current

It is obvious that there is no one-to-one relationship between the structural device and the genre. Not all nursery rhymes have reduplication, nor is reduplication restricted to use in nursery rhymes. But it is equally true that there is *some* relation between the formal characteristics of certain types of messages (in this case nursery rhymes) and the intentions of the speakers and/or the effect of the messages on the hearers. Determining precisely what this relationship is and devising a methodology whereby it can be described constitute a concrete set of research problems requiring much further investigation and collaboration between linguists, content analysts, and perhaps literary critics.[31]

SOME APPLICATIONS OF A STATISTICAL CONTINGENCY METHOD TO FOLKLORE TEXTS

The fundamental logic of the statistical contingency method is quite simple; in fact, it is nothing more than an application of the law of association by contiguity, upon which all theories of learning — and, by the way, also Frazer's theory as to the psychological basis of the principles of magic — are founded in one way or another. Thus, if one idea or concept appears in consciousness, for whatever reason, other ideas or concepts related to it in meaning will also tend to appear, that is, semantic determinants operate upon the sequential patterning of communicative acts. With respect to communicative products it should be possible to find out, by appropriate analysis of the greater-than-chance contingency of units in the products the informant emits, what ideas tend to go together in his thinking. By way of illustration, a much higher-

---

/kántrǒrǐy/ because of the requirements of rhyme. This nursery rhyme also has a version without reduplication: "Mistress Mary, quite contrary," etc.

[31] The current position of many linguists is clearly reflected by the following cautious statement by Harris ("Discourse Analysis," p. 3): ". . . distributional analysis within one discourse yields information about certain correlations of language with other behavior. The reason is that each connected discourse occurs within a particular situation — whether of a person speaking, or of a conversation, or of someone sitting down occasionally over a period of months to write a particular kind of book in a particular literary or scientific tradition. To be sure, this concurrence between situation and discourse does not mean that discourses occurring in similar situations must necessarily have certain formal characteristics in common, while discourses in different situations must have certain formal differences. The concurrence between situation and discourse only makes it understandable, or possible, that such formal correlations should exist.

"It remains to be shown as a matter of empirical fact that such formal correlations do indeed exist, that the discourses of a particular person, social group, or subject-matter exhibit not only particular meanings . . . but also characteristic formal features."

than-chance association was revealed between the notion of writing and the devil in a group of East European folk tales — an insight which is as revealing as it was unexpected.

Let us examine in somewhat greater detail how a contingency analysis of such folk material proceeds in terms of motifs or rather component parts of motifs. A few years ago one of the present authors did a study of dream portents and then one of Cheremis charms.[32] In each case there is a very precise and rigid structure. Charms, of course, must be precise if they are to work. In abstract symbolic form each statement within a charm has a simple formula consisting of two terms connected by an implication sign; for example, "As the apple tree blossoms forth, just so let this wound heal." The analysis of these charms was completed in 1952, at which time the possibility of a contingency analysis had not yet occurred to the author. The model in that study was therefore a traditional frequency analysis, but it is clear that the charms lend themselves to a contingency analysis of what term goes with what. That possibility, suggested at the S.S.R.C.'s Cornell seminar of psychologists and linguists, was adopted in the analysis of other folk materials which we have been doing since, such as a study of prayers which explores, for example, what kinds of themes occur when one addresses a certain type of divinity.

There are five principal steps in such a contingency analysis of content, which are described more fully in Chapter 2. The first of these has to do with the *selection of categories,* which involves a host of empirical considerations, including the comparative reliabilities of different categories, the situation of mutual exclusion between like categories, and so forth. As in all content analysis, so also here one starts with the frequencies of occurrence of certain categorized entities and, usually, the particular categories selected are determined by the analyst's purpose — what information he wants. It is desirable to strike a neat balance between categories broad enough to include all references to the same thing but not so broad that incompatible things are included. Among types of categories with which we have experimented were themes in a corpus of prayer texts and motifs of the folk tale. One result of our research with the folk tale was the observation that the motifs employed in Thompson's index of folk literature[33] already have internal

----

[32] T. A. Sebeok, "Cheremis Dream Portents," *Southwestern Journal of Anthropology,* 6 (1950), 273-85, and T. A. Sebeok and L. H. Orzack, "The Structure and Content of Cheremis Charms," *Anthropos,* 48 (1953), 369-88, 760-72.
[33] S. Thompson, *Motif-Index of Folk Literature,* 2nd ed. (Bloomington, Ind., 1955).

contingencies in different ratios built into them, so that for our purposes we found it necessary to break motifs down into more elementary categories of syntactic classes. Thus, for instance, Q261, "treachery punished," which occurs eight times in the corpus, if counted as a single unit can reveal nothing about whether the co-occurrence of this deed and its punishment is due to chance or whether it is "significant." To learn this it was necessary to calculate separately the relationship of all sorts of actors ("churlish person" or "courteous person," cf. Q2) to various goals, and various actions, and various modifiers, and the like: "deeds rewarded" (Q10-99), "deeds punished" (Q200-399), "kinds of punishment" (Q400-599), and so on.

The second step involves the *selection of units:* contingency is defined by the co-occurrence of two items but, one must add, "within a certain unit." In our case the obvious but not necessarily ideally appropriate unit which suggested itself was the text which had structural unity — say a prayer or a tale. This, of course, was based on a prior assumption — a psychological one — by no means demonstrated, that such a text falls within the temporal span through which the effects of one event persist. However, even in prayers of extreme length and elaborate design, as are those found in certain cultures, this assumption seemed to be borne out, and was supported by statements in the ethnographic literature.[34]

The *coding of material* comes next. A trained analyst (or, preferably, several working independently) reads through the original text (not a translation), noting by symbols the occurrence within the text of the items searched for. This coder's sole task is to judge the presence or absence of reference to a particular item in each unit. For example, in a hypothetical corpus of ten folk tales, Motif A ("mythological") occurred in certain texts, B ("animal") in others, C ("taboo") in others, and so on, as summarized in Table 2.

The determination of *significant contingencies* is the fourth step. As Chapter 2 explains, *chance* contingency is simply the product of the percentages, for example AB ("mythological" times "animal"). The *obtained* contingencies can be evaluated against the chance contingencies in terms of the significance of differences in percent-

----

[34] "Die Hauptbedingung eines Priesterkandidaten ist neben tadellosem Lebenswandel ein gutes Gedächtnis, damit er das lange Gebet, welches fast eine halbe Stunde in Anspruch nimmt, ohne sich zu irren hersagen kann" (H. Paasonen, "Tscheremissische Texte," in P. Siro, ed., *Mémoires de la Société Finno-Ougrienne, LXXVII* [Helsinki, 1939], p. 184).

Table 2

Motif	1	2	3	4	5	6	7	8	9	10	Per Cent of Units
				Text Number							
A	X			X	X		X			X	.50
B	X	X		X	X		X		X	X	.70
C	X		X			X	X		X		.50

age. Thus, it might result that "mythological"-with-"animal" motifs occur significantly more often than would be expected by chance, but that this is not true for either "mythological"-with-"taboo" or "animal"-with-"taboo" motifs. Also, two motifs might appear together less frequently than would be expected by chance, that is, as if the occurrence of one tended to inhibit the occurrence of the other.

While the above information would seem to be useful in itself, we also want to know something about the interrelationship among the entire set of items measured, so that the fifth and last step has reference to contingency ratios. To obtain a matrix of relations which can then be treated so as to yield a cluster analysis, the contingencies must be expressed as ratios which have certain of the properties of correlation coefficients. Osgood and his group are in the process of evaluating several possible indices, one of which is the ratio

$$\frac{A_B + B_A}{A + B},$$

where A_B is the number of units on which A's are contingent upon B's, B_A is the number of units on which B's are contingent upon A's, A is the total number of units for this A item, and B is the total number of units for that B item. It will be seen that if in a given tale in which there are "animal" motifs *no* instances occur of "mythological" motifs, the ratio must be .00; and if *all* occurrences of "mythological" motifs are contingent upon "animal" motifs and vice versa, then the ratio must be 1.00. In the hypothetical illustration above, the "mythological"-with-"animal" contingency ratio is

$$\frac{5 + 5}{5 + 7},$$

or .83.

The final matrix analysis may well provide us with something beyond a mere description of the web of interrelationships that obtains among the set of items being measured. It should, at the very least, afford some information as to the manner in which those items are interrelated in the particular informant's thinking and, further, should allow us to measure the degree of difference between individual informants, say tellers of tales. Such a difference measure, D, has indeed also been developed, actual computations of which generate a D matrix which, when tabulated, gives the "distances" of every item (e.g., motif) from every other item in equivalent units (e.g., versions), and thus makes it possible for us to compare two different items for the same individual, and the same item between two people or between two time points of measurement.

It seems useful in this connection to recall the classic experiments of Bartlett with the repeated and serial reproduction of folk tales,[35] and, a decade later, those of Wolff who, among others, has shown individual determinants that act upon memory when he performed some experiments in the course of which he read his subjects a fairy-tale love story, far from their usual experience but yet evoking their personal participation. The experimenter checked, after a series of reproductions, whether certain "omissions, variations, perseverations, suppressions, and displacements were made by chance," and found that, to the contrary, these were due to deeper motives corresponding to the subject's personality acting in conjunction with certain additional objective processes this investigator called together "structuration."[36]

Thus, such an analysis of folkloristic data may well provide certain insights as to those attitudes of preference of the society in which the informant is a member which are likely to prove centrally characteristic of the culture. While the general trend of such a correspondence, in particular its reflection in folklore, has been well known — Boas, for example, alluded to it[37] — it may now

---

[35] *Remembering.* Bartlett's experiments were twice repeated under conditions more sophisticated from the point of view of folklore theory; the results, however, were analogous, indeed, in part even more drastic; see W. Anderson, *Ein volkskundliches Experiment* (Folklore Fellows Communications, No. 141 [Helsinki, 1951]).

[36] W. Wolff, *The Expression of Personality* (New York, 1943), pp. 203 ff.

[37] So, for instance, in F. Boas, *Kwakiutl Culture as Reflected in Mythology* (American Folk-lore Society Memoirs, Vol. 28 [New York, 1935]), pp. 171-72; "Tsimshian and Kwakiutl mythologies present such a contrast well, for the social structure of the tribes is based on different concepts. . . ."

become possible, with the aid of some such tool as a statistical contingency method, to construct a bridge more solid than has heretofore been available between systems of verbal behavior and the other systems of learned behavior shared by the members of a society.

5 ROBERT PLANT ARMSTRONG
UNIVERSITY OF ARIZONA

CONTENT ANALYSIS IN FOLKLORISTICS

In his work the folklorist typically takes note of the presence of striking dramatic or rhetorical elements in the content of texts he examines. Upon the basis of these distinctive features, he draws at least some of his conclusions, both with respect to the text itself and to relevant cultural or biographical facts.

In the vast majority of instances, the folklorist reaches these conclusions by impressionistic procedures and by a wholistic approach to his materials. Such studies are of considerable value. Their results are often pertinent not only to literary inquiry but also to the study of human behavior in general. Yet it is unfortunate that among some folklorists such procedures constitute the ultimate research techniques. Attempts to be relatively more rigorous, more analytical, and perhaps to give quantitative expression to the results of analysis are dismissed as being "sociological." Such a view must be carefully re-examined.

Ruth Benedict's introduction to *Zuni Mythology* offers a case for examination. Working with raw content,[1] she notes the presence of certain culturally archaic elements, for example the mode of entrance into a dwelling. These elements of behavior are clearly disparate with contemporary Zuni values and behavior. She calls the presence of such elements a kind of "compensatory daydreaming." Such findings are of undoubted significance in understanding the role of myth in Zuni culture, and multiply our insights into the Zuni culture, folkloristics, and myth. Indeed, the genealogical relationship between her "compensatory day-dreaming" and

---

[1] Ruth Benedict, *Zuni Mythology* (New York, 1935), and *Patterns of Culture* (Boston, 1948).

151

Kluckhohn's analysis of myth functioning in such a fashion as to provide adjustive and adaptive mechanisms is clear.[2]

However, inquiry must not be arrested at this point. It is the task of other investigators, building upon Benedict's observations, to ask first whether it is possible to give additional empirical validation to her results, and further to ask if there are not other kinds of information which she failed to discern. All we are maintaining, in effect, is that while some data may be collected by such impressionistic procedures, others, equally significant, will be lost. In all probability, obvious methods most often lead to the identification of none save the most obvious features of a text.

It is therefore the purpose of this chapter to examine content analysis for the benefit of folklorists, and to draw to their attention some techniques which may facilitate the objective description and analysis of the materials with which they are concerned. It is to be hoped further that such remarks will prompt others to extend the effort, and that, in particular, students of the graphic and plastic arts, dance, and music will experiment with similar procedures in order to make increasingly revealing comments on the areas of human behavior with which they are concerned.

Any behavior may be studied either as (1) *mirroring* or as (2) *constituting* a condition in an individual or a society. Such a statement as that of Benedict concerning the method of entering a house referred to above illustrates data used to mirror behavior.

Mirror statements are characteristically derived from the substance of a message. On the other hand, those materials which may be held to be constitutive of conditions within the individual or culture are most frequently derived from the structure of the message. They may also, however, stem from the substance, the difference deriving from the point of view with which the researcher approaches his materials. In mirror statements reference is made to the larger behavioral context within which the message may be conceived to be embedded, while otherwise the message itself constitutes the sole frame of reference. The categories to be used in the last section of this chapter, together with the statistical operations performed upon them, represent statements at this constitutive level.

The writings of folklorists in general, insofar as they attempt to do anything more than present new data, are largely executed on

---

[2] C. Kluckhohn, "Myths and Rituals: A General Theory," *Harvard Theological Review*, 35 (1942), 44-78.

the mirror model, whether they be concerned with an individual or with his cultural milieu. It would seem, accordingly, that perhaps the greatest contribution content analysis can make to folkloristics is not merely to provide a refinement in the procedures yielding such information, although that in itself is of considerable importance, but to afford students the opportunity to improve their descriptions of the constituents of behavior. Studies designed to examine the chief characteristics of an individual or a period as seen in a body of texts represent content analysis used in such a fashion as to mirror that individual or period. On the other hand, pattern studies, showing for example that certain classes of content in a total body of texts are used with a discerned and predictable frequency, or that a given class of behavior exhibits such and such formal characteristics, examine verbal behavior constituting a characteristic of the individual or group.

There are three aspects of messages which may be examined by different kinds of content analysis. Doubtless most studies concern the *substance* of the specimens. Substance, it is apparent, is simply what is manifestly stated in the message. Indeed, content analysis is often confounded with the analysis of substance. The *form* or *structure* of the content and its *condition* are equally amenable to analysis and description, however, though the procedures required may be less apparent and, at first glance, more difficult than those for the analysis of substance. The structure of the content designates its shape, its physical array of elements, determined by means of establishing and describing the parts, however defined, together with their distributions and relationships. These two terms, elements and array, represent two different kinds of analysis, the first corresponding to a morphemic analysis of language, while the second is more nearly similar to the determination of syntax. Structure, in a sense, may be said to designate the physical dimensions of the communication. Finally, the condition of the content refers to such notions as the truth, emotional, and aesthetic values of the segments of the communication.

THE MOTIF INDEX

Any discussion of the analysis of substance of folklore material inevitably invokes initial mention of Stith Thompson's motif index. A motif is a substantive unit (e.g., "the devil falls into the well") which appears frequently in folklore, and is found in very wide cultural distribution. The list of motifs is long. Thompson has presented and discussed them in six large volumes. Here is a system devised for the purpose of cataloging the elements of certain kinds of narrative situations, and it has accrued to itself the great respect to which its breadth of scholarship entitles it. It is, in fact, a kind of trait list, analogous in essence to the lists of cultural traits once in fashion in ethnology, and it is subject to the same criticisms of definition and analytical adequacy as the culture traits themselves. Thus, for the purposes of content analysis there are certain limitations to the motif[3] system, deriving chiefly from the fact that it is an a priori scheme in which each individual motif is externally derived, being whatever Professor Thompson has recognized as one. The grid is so coarse as to let certain kinds of significant data slip through unnoticed.

Over and above this, because there is no clear definition of the limits of a motif, a situation results wherein a motif may in one instance comprise a complete story, while in another it may be only a segment thereof. The motifs are not made commensurate either in terms of structural characteristics of the story (e.g., a certain unit of words or sentences) or with respect to the dramatic magnitude of the action they name. Therefore, it is apparent that the motif cannot be considered a device for successful analysis. To make some such analysis more effective, the problem is to devise a way of defining natural units of the story intermediate between the single word and the total story. Moreover, not only is the motif inadequate for the analysis of substance, but of condition as well, for since the units isolated by motif analysis may perform different dramatic functions, or none at all for that matter, they are analytically valueless.

In all fairness, it must be added that Professor Thompson does not himself present the motif index as an analytical system, but only as a classificatory one. "According to this plan, motifs dealing with one subject are handled together, irrespective of the literary form in which they may appear. No attempt has been made to determine the psychological basis of various motifs or their structural value in narrative art, for though such considerations have great value, they are not, I think, of much practical help toward

---

[3] There is a question involving the "reality" of the motif. The motif, like culture, is a construct, and does not possess any value over and above that fact. It is not a kind of Platonic entity of folklore, it is plain, but rather only an association of behavior traits arbitrarily selected.

the orderly arrangement of the stories and myths of a people."[4]
Accordingly, he is in no wise responsible for the attitude, implicit
in the works of some who use the index in their researches, which
distorts the motif to an analytical unit.

UNITS BASED UPON THE SUBSTANCE OF THE TEXT

It is apparent from the above remarks that a satisfactory
analytical technique must be premised upon the establishment of
relative units — ones defined in terms of the contexts within which
they are found, rather than determined in accordance with the
criteria of an external and arbitrarily postulated system.[5] The
desirability of such a procedure seems so apparent as to recommend
itself. Suffice it to say that when an elastic principle of definition
is achieved, it will prove possible to isolate segments which are at
all times less than the total text and are, in terms of the definition,
equivalent.

Since we are in this section concerned with the substantive aspect
of the text, the defining characteristics for appropriate units will
be found in those modes proper to the substance, for example in
nouns;[6] or in the assertion patterns of the language, as for example
in some carefully established actor-action phase, or in whatever
segment of an utterance flow might be said to constitute a sentence.[7]
The principle may, furthermore, be found in the fictive properties
or dramatic movements of the text,[8] or, if it is nonfictive discourse,
or poetry, then in features of rhetoric, prosody, sense, or device
peculiar to treatment of substance in these types. Finally, such

----

[4] Thompson, *Motif-Index of Folk Literature* (Bloomington, Ind., 1932), p. 3.

[5] See K. L. Pike, *Language in Relation to a Unified Theory of the Structure of Human Behavior*, Pt. 1 (Summer Institute of Linguistics, Glendale,
Calif., 1954), pp. 8-24. The distinctions he presents between the *etic* and
emic levels of analysis are pertinent here. Etic analysis corresponds to the
noncontextual motif, while emic includes the point of view from which the
critical remarks of the motif have been made. While mirror analysis may be
done from either emic or etic points of departure, constitutive analysis may
be cast only in terms of the emic framework.

[6] See A. P. and B. W. Merriam and R. P. Armstrong, "Banyaruanda Proverbs," *Journal of American Folklore*, 67 (1954), No. 265, pp. 267-84. This
study, which infers states in the value system of the Banyaruanda, is an
example of mirror analysis.

[7] Sebeok and Orzack, "The Structure and Content of Cheremis Charms,"
pp. 369-88. This is an example of constitutive analysis.

[8] See Chapter 7 of the present work for remarks on the "interaction phase"
in Russian literature.

units may be established upon the basis of the manifestation of psychological mechanisms, upon economic, political, or religious attitudes, or indeed upon any of the range of points of curiosity which originally led the researcher to the texts. Such procedures in defining content analysis units ensure the delineation of a grid adequate to the subtlety and variety of the cases which will be encountered in the texts. In addition, they will permit generalization at either the individual or cultural level.

Among the above examples of criteria for units there is to be found a kind of natural dichotomy. There are those units whose defining points are based upon the manifest content of the text, that is to say upon what the message objectively conveys. Under this rubric would fall units defined by information actually present concerning the veritable activity of the actors in the text, or by *stated* political activity, judgments, social roles, etc. In the second place, there are units defined by interpretations of the manifest content, such as would be encountered in the search, for example, for instances of personality characteristics or cultural values and attitudes in the text.

If, for example, one were interested in analyzing a body of trickster tales, he might search for (1) whether the trickster dupes, (2) whether these actions contain explicit comments on the relationship between the action and the generally approved values of the group, or (3) whether such attitudes can be inferred from the text. It is clear that in the first two cases the concern is with primary (manifest) substance, while in the third instance it is with secondary (latent) substance. It follows that a different principle of segmentation would be required in each case. In the first of the three, this principle is based solely upon the activity of the trickster, that is, its purpose is to establish units of activity and subsequently to determine whether tricking or duping is involved. In the second analysis the unit becomes simply statements concerning the ethical evaluation of the trickster's acts. In the third case, actor-action phases might be used, or "sentences," or, indeed, the same unit of behavior established for the first analysis. It is also possible, of course, to define a unit based upon the presumed duration of some given kind of attitude.

It is clear that in the above operations the text is differently segmented, not only with reference to the actual spans of material isolated but also with respect to the extent of the textual surface itself. In the second operation, involving the search for explicit evaluations, only portions of the surface of the text would constitute relevant units, while in the first analysis for units of action, and conceivably in the analysis for inferred substance as well, the total surface would be divided into units. But in each case, presumably, the segmentation is adequate to the analytical task which is faced, and, in these terms, one is no more exhaustive than the other.

The segmentation of the total surface of a text, however, affords a certain advantage in behavioral terms insofar as it presents the opportunity to conduct a complete inventory of units. Such an analysis might conceivably be based upon such behavioral units as those suggested above, for example tricking, or else upon some language feature, for example the actor-action phase. The search in the latter case would not be for the presence or absence of tricking merely, but rather for an indication of what, in problem-oriented terms, is the significance of each unit. This is the program which was followed in the analysis of the Suriname materials presented in the concluding section of this chapter.

The determination of unit boundaries, when more than mere presence or absence of a trait is to be noted, and particularly when the complete textual surface is under analysis, is beset with subtle difficulties. Unfortunately, little more than mention of these problems can be made here. Certainly, the problems which are raised are frequently subtle, and involve the exercise of judicious arbitrariness, which, though perhaps tolerable under the hand of a skilled analyst, raises the question of reliability. However, as Pool points out, where a trait is homogeneous in a text, analysts will find it no matter how differently they cut the pie; thus often the matter of reliability of unit definition may be de-emphasized unless there is reason to believe that there is some systematic difference between the subsentence, sentence, and episode levels, or to put this into more familiar terms, a regular difference among the units or among meaningful associations of such units, such that difference rather than similarity would result, and comparability would be lost. Often it is far less important to be able to get consistency in units than it is to get the meaningful unit of interaction. The final criterion for judging the relevance of unit reliability to the particular analysis is, as Osgood pointed out, the independence of results, over several analyses by different analysts, from the units employed.

It is apparent from our consideration of the motif index that the unit of operation must be defined in such a fashion as to be subtotal, equivalent, simple, and unambiguous. The necessity for *subtotal* units (i.e., units shorter than the whole text) is apparent if the unit is to be useful in analysis. As we have seen in the case of the motif, this feature may be absent. Some kind of *equivalence* is also essential, in order that the units eventually isolated may have, with respect to some constant measuring concept, equivalent properties. The basis for equivalence may reside in the fact that two units perform the same function, regardless of variability in other respects; it may be found in structural considerations, as for example if two immediate constituents are to all intents and purposes equivalent when viewed from a certain vantage point. Finally, there is a kind of substantive equivalence, which is to be found when the mere presence of a certain kind of information is of interest. In this latter case all instances of the occurrence of the notion in question may be regarded as equivalent.

The criterion of unit *simplicity* suggests that no more variables than avoidable enter into the unit. An example of the failure to maintain such a control is afforded by the motif with its "built-in contiguities," as Sebeok has noted. It must be stressed that simplicity does not mean consisting of one part only. If one analyzes for dramatic action, for example, the unit will doubtless be comprised of actor, act, and a recipient toward or against whom the action is directed. Simplicity in this particular case derives from building this notion of three parts into the definition of the unit and from subsequently avoiding the establishing of any units in which more than the interaction phase indicated by such terms is included. If one is explicitly aware of the level of operation at which he is to work, and confines himself rigorously to the terms of the definition as stated, he avoids the danger of secluding information. The case is somewhat similar with the level of operation. If one has elected to examine his materials for units of action dramatically defined, he must not permit confusion to enter into the analysis by including raw activity untranslated into the language of dramatic activity as defined. The simple fact of the matter is that, obviously enough, any segment of verbal behavior is a focal point for numerous phenomena: semantic, structural, conditional, dramatic, etc. A clear definition of units and cautious procedure by the analyst will preclude or severely limit the possibility of such interlevel confusion. Either the loose definition of units or the incautious establishing of domain will lead to ambiguity of analysis and, consequently, to invalidation of the results.

One further note must be added to these remarks on the analysis of substance, and it is appropriate that it come at the end of this discussion, since it is involved sometimes with substance and sometimes with structure. Aesthetic properties, along with such questions as truth or falsity, and positive or negative evaluations, are *conditions* of the material. By aesthetic we mean simply the use of devices of substance or structure which are included solely for textural quality of the surface of the message, specifically in terms of developing effect or affect, and which perform no inviolable or inescapable feature of the text as information. While this criterion may be viewed so broadly as to prove inimical to analysis, in practice it may be limited to a consideration of such peculiarly "literary" features as the various manifestations of metaphor (defined as the whole range of verbal stratagems by which the unknown is, through the mediation of an integer somewhat more known, made familiar and interpreted into the experience of those who participate in the literary transaction), and physical principles incorporated to exploit language symmetry, or the piling of activities in the interest of cumulative dramatic import. The relevance of such aesthetic features to content analysis is that they provide another focal point from which research questions may be formulated, principles of segmentation derived, and culturally significant statements eventually made.

STRUCTURAL ANALYSIS

When one is concerned less with substance than with the array of that substance, then his problem becomes one of structure. Structural analysis consists of two activities: delineating units of substance or of condition, and discerning and stating the relationships which obtain among such units.

The first activity, that is the definition and delineation of units, has already been discussed. All that was said there applies equally to the segmentation of the textural surface in structural analysis. Something more remains to be said on this point, however, which is particularly pertinent to analysis for structure. If the logic of the structure is to be seen as clearly as possible, it is necessary that the units of substance or condition be generalized in such a way that the establishing of classes will permit a kind of unity to be perceived in the relatively great variety of raw information. This principle of generalization can be drawn from many areas. Sebeok, in his study of Cheremis charms (discussed in the previous chapter), used the linguistic notion of immediate constituents. Each charm, he finds, is composed of two constituents: those which make purely factual statements about the world, and those which express the "motif of an extremely improbable eventuality." An example will serve to illustrate this: "(morphemes 1-9) As the apple tree blossoms forth, just so let this wound heal! (morphemes 10-13) (All blossoms must be mentioned.) (morphemes 14-21) When water can blossom forth, only then overcome me."[9] It is this last statement (14-21) which constitutes the "motif of the extremely improbable eventuality."

Sebeok first devides this charm into two statements, after the principle concerning their factuality. This yields a division of 1-13 and 14-21. When it is realized that the statement 10-13 actually means "as the [e.g.] peach tree blossoms forth, just so let this wound heal, as the ___n tree blossoms forth," etc., the reason behind this division becomes apparent. In the second step, he notes that with reference only to 1-9 (and by extension therefore to 10-13 as well) there are two actor-action phases, "as the apple-tree blossoms forth," a dependent clause, and "just so let this wound heal," an independent one. He observes further that the modes of the verbs (actions) in the clauses are different in that the verb of the dependent clause is "blossoms," whereas that of the independent clause is "let . . . . heal." It is apparent that the last of these is in the imperative. This distinction is a significant one: it distinguishes the two actor-action phases from one another and provides the principle of generalization for his data, all clauses employing the verb in the indicative mode falling into one class, and those using the verb in the imperative mode into another.

Other principles of generalization may be used as well. Zellig Harris, in his system of discourse analysis, again derives his model from linguistic phenomena, and determines classes based upon positional substitutability. "If we find the sequences AM and AN in our text, we say that M is equivalent to N or that M and N occur in the identical environment A, or that M and N both appear as the environment of the identical element (or sequence of elements) A; and we write M (is equivalent to) N. Then if we find the sequence BM and CN, we say that B is (secondarily) equi-

---

9 Sebeok and Orzack, "The Structure and Content of Cheremis Charms," p. 381. Morpheme numbers refer to the morphemes as found in the original Cheremis.

valent to C, since they occur in the two environments M and N which have been found to be equivalent."[10] The present author, in an unpublished study of some Yoruba riddles, used the formal nature of the riddle to achieve a pair of "immediate constituents" representing the riddle itself, which was viewed as the compounding of a metaphor, and the answer, viewed as a resolution of that metaphor. Since all riddles conform to this pattern, it was possible thus to generalize all specimens in the sample under these two constituents. Categories of substance may be used, as well, as may classes of dramatic function or objective. It is this last point which provides the basis for generalization in the sample study reported in the last section of this chapter.

Generalization requires, of course, that symbols be used to represent the classes of information, and it is this act of simple substitution which seems to have alienated many folklorists from structural studies. Little can be said here to divorce such people from such a predisposition beyond disclaiming any intention upon the part of those who resort to such devices toward obfuscation and spurious accuracy. It is — or should be — apparent that such devices are employed not for their own sake but in the interest of performing operations upon the materials which cannot otherwise be done, and of obtaining "pictures" of the structures which cannot otherwise be obtained.

There is considerable latitude with respect to the specificity of relationships which may be expressed in structural analyses. In Harris' system of discourse analysis, these relationships are merely "before" and "after," and these are not given explicit statement but rather are apparent from the order of the symbols. On the other hand, Sebeok, in the same study we have already discussed, employs the logical relation of implication, $\supset$, to state the nature of the involvement between the terms of his unit. This relationship of implication derives from the occurrence, in the charms, of the "as . . . just so" construction. "As the apple tree blossoms forth, just so let this wound heal," therefore, is recorded as $o_1 \supset s$.

The noted relationship need not be temporal or logical. It can be based, for example, upon dramatic criteria, such as whether a succeeding unit bears toward the preceding one a relationship of forward dramatic movement, whether it arrests that movement, or whether, finally, it is involved with the dramatic point of departure. This would be an example of structure arising from a consideration

---

[10] Harris, "Discourse Analysis," p. 6.

of condition. At a somewhat simpler level of analysis, cultural relationships between the roles of character might be examined. In this event, the relationships might be "approved" or "disapproved." It is clear, in any event, that the choice of such matters depends once again upon the orientation of the researcher. Suffice it to say that the number of alternatives is probably equal to the total number of kinds of problems which can be formulated.

When a statement, such as Sebeok's $O\jmath S$, which is a generalization from his many instances of $o_n\jmath s$, is obtained, it is of cultural significance, since it denotes clearly the structure of all verbal behavior involved in the invocation of charms among the Cheremis. Its value is therefore apparent, and though the behavioral area to which it applies is smaller than a similar structural statement for, let us say, social organization, it is at as high a level of both generalization and significance for the understanding of human behavior. This seems to be one of the directions in which content analysis might, in the future, be profitably extended.

SAMPLE STUDY

In the study which will be described below, some of the points which have been made in the foregoing discussions will be seen in operation. For this study two bodies of folk tales were used, one from the Bush Negroes of Paramaribo, Dutch Guiana, and the other from the Dakota Indians of the United States. The former selection of tales was composed of two kinds, trickster tales about Anansi and selections from another group of Suriname tales more nearly like some of our West European fairy tales than like the trickster stories. The specimens from the Dakota Indians were all of the trickster type.

The purpose of this study was to derive information at once constitutive of culture, and still, at the same time, reflective of culture, at least to the extent that the conclusions reached would be consistent with other ethnographic findings for the two groups.

A dramatic model was used as the basis for the segmentation of the texts. The rationale behind this procedure involved the fact that in stories there is present a certain kind of phenomenon which is not found in any other kind of literary behavior. This unique feature resides in the fact that only in stories does one have "virtual action," that is to say the presence not only of an aesthetic objective, which may be defined as whatever the storyteller may have wished to achieve, but objectives arising from the depicted actors themselves. Furthermore, it must be added that the dramatic model was greatly clarified by the writings of Burke[11] and his analysis of dramatistic behavior.

Following his suggestions, an act was conceived of as consisting of three parts, an actor, an act, and an additional actor toward or against whom the action was directed. The actor was designated with an X, the recipient with a Y, and the action itself with any one of a number of actions which are given in Table 1.

It was early apparent that in defining the unit of concern it had to be (1) subtotal and comparable, (2) concerned with internal rather than external (pragmatic) objectives, and (3) manifest rather than latent. It soon became clear that on the basis of such criteria three magnitudes of units could be discerned: *maximal,* that is to say the total text under consideration; *minimal,* which is the same as Burke's "atoms" of action, and consists of the human body in purposeful action. But since the former proved to be too great, and preclusive of analysis, and the latter too small, since obviously many such atomic elements had been gathered together about themes of common concern, it was necessary to establish a *medial* objective. The duration of this medial objective was premised upon the criteria outlined below.

It was determined that there would be a new medial objective when (1) there occurred an alteration in the actor-constellation of the story, either through a shift in the initiation of the activity, the agents themselves remaining constant, or through the addition or deletion of one or more characters; (2) there was a change in any one of the remaining elements, that is, agency, purpose, scene, or act. The former of these terms seem sufficiently clear; however, some clarification may be given to the latter two. A change in *scene* may be defined as adjustment in the time or the place of the activity. Ordinarily one can say that a new *act* has begun when there is an alteration in the actor constellation. There is, however, an exception to this which may be noted. This exception by definition does not constitute actual alterations of the constellation; it is found in that case where a second actor merely reacts to the move of the initiation actor. In this case, the second actor neither supplements nor resists the activity initiated with respect to him or in his presence. Typically, this situation might result in a ques-

---

[11] K. Burke, *The Philosophy of Literary Form: Studies in Symbolic Action* (Baton Rouge, La., 1941).

tion-and-answer exchange between two characters. (3) Finally, a new objective may be said to have been instituted when there follows a segment of dramatic behavior which is not clearly the consequent of the objective which precedes it. This does not mean, of course, that two contiguous objectives cannot have the relation of event and consequent.

Let us examine a Suriname trickster tale.

Anansi was going to bet with Cockroach to see which could climb

Table 1

OBJECTIVES PERTAINING TO THE DISTRIBUTION OF
REWARD, ASSISTANCE, AND PUNISHMENT

$\overline{A}$	reward
A	aid, befriend, plan good
$\underline{A}$	hinder, prevent, conspire, discourage
$\underline{A}_1$	punish

Praise and Condemnation

$\overline{D}^1$	flatter
$\overline{D}^2$	elevate, exult, praise, boast (reflexive)
D	approve
$\underline{D}_1$	scold, reprimand
$\underline{D}_2$	humiliate, defame, berate, discredit, ridicule, humble oneself (reflexive)
$\underline{D}_3$	condemn, betray, incriminate

OBJECTIVES PERTAINING TO RESISTANCE AND ATTACK

M^1	resist, protest
M^2	save, preserve, protect
M^3	release, free, rescue, escape (reflexive)
M	do justice, vindicate or justify oneself (reflexive)
$\underline{M}$	challenge
$\underline{M}_1$	attack
$\underline{M}_2$	overcome, defeat, conquer, capture
$\underline{M}_3$	kill, destroy, reduce
$\underline{M}_4$	intimidate, accuse
$\underline{M}_5$	accede, acquiesce, surrender

OBJECTIVES PERTAINING TO PERMISSION AND PROHIBITION

$\overline{S}^1$	prescribe, summon, direct
$\overline{S}^2$	insist
$\overline{S}^3$	beg, request
S	permit, invite
$\underline{S}$	proscribe, bar, forbid

OBJECTIVES PERTAINING TO THE ACQUISITION AND
USE OF GOODS AND SERVICES

Gratification and Deprivation

$\bar{C}$	gratify, indulge, enjoy (reflexive)
C	provide, put at ease, alleviate, comfort, please
$\underline{C}$	deny, displease, withhold, disturb, discomfort, torture

Acquisition and Loss of Property

$\bar{O}^1$	retrieve, reclaim, collect
$\bar{O}^2$	acquire, obtain, profit, enrich
$\bar{O}^3$	bargain
O	keep, retain
$\underline{O}$	lose, give

OBJECTIVES PERTAINING TO THE ACQUISITION AND
DISSEMINATION OF INFORMATION

$\bar{R}^1$	prove, convince, verify
$\bar{R}^2$	discover, investigate (get information *from*)
$\bar{R}^3$	enlighten, inform, teach, learn (reflexive) (give information *to*)
$\bar{R}^4$	suggest
$\bar{R}^5$	remember
R	communicate
R^1	believe, agree (this is in contrast with $\underline{M}_5$ which means the acquiescence to power)
$\underline{R}_1$	obscure, keep in ignorance, hide, misinform, falsify
$\underline{R}_2$	disprove
$\underline{R}_3$	forget
$\underline{R}_4$	doubt

OBJECTIVES PERTAINING TO THE CONDUCT OF AFFAIRS

$\bar{E}$	succeed
$\bar{E}^1$	persevere, do one's duty
E	prepare
$\underline{E}_1$	temporize
$\underline{E}_2$	fail

Acceptance and Avoidance of Obligation

$\bar{B}^1$	contract, undertake
$\bar{B}^2$	seek, encounter
B^1	acknowledge, accept
B^2	pay, repay
$\underline{B}_2$	ignore, avoid
$\underline{B}_3$	welch, outwit, deceive
$\underline{B}_4$	cancel

----

higher. But now Cockroach was able to fly, and Anansi was able to climb well. But now, when they went to compete, Cockroach said to him said, "Let us climb to the top of an awara tree." Now Anansi could not fly, and so Cockroach flew up, and went to the top of the tree. He sat down.

Anansi struggled to climb, but the thorns struck him. Soon he cried out, "Friend Cockroach, the tree has ants, I cannot climb it." At once Cockroach cried back from the tree-top, he said, "Well, fly up." Anansi said, "But I do not fly, nor did you beat me, because we did not bet about flying. We were betting about climbing." But now Cockroach said he won, because he was the first to arrive. Then they went to call Cock to settle the dispute.

When Cock came, he saw immediately that Cockroach was his delicacy. At once he cried out, "Ko-Ko-dia-Ko!" Then Cockroach asked Cock, he said, what was the meaning of this cry which he cried? He (Cock) said, if he wanted to hear, then he must walk over to him on foot. So just as Cockroach came toward him, Cock ate him. That is why he eats Cockroach to this day.[12]

In this story three medial units can be distinguished, and these have been indicated by setting them apart into separate physical units. The last line of the story is not characterized by any internal objective, but only a pragmatic one, a condition to be found in many moralistic and etiological tales. Nor does the introductory and orientative material (i.e., "Anansi was going to bet with Cockroach to see which could climb higher. But now Cockroach was able to fly, and Anansi was able to climb well.") contain any internal objective. In view of this fact, such introductory and terminal remarks without any manifest dramatic objective will be included with the units which respectively follow or precede them.

The first medial unit involves the attempt of Cockroach to defeat Anansi. The objective of the second unit concerns Anansi's attempt to convince Cockroach that he has not lived up to the conditions of the wager. The dialogue in this unit may be viewed as establishing the attitudes of the contenders, and as such subordinate to the objective given. Finally, it may be said that the objective of the last unit is clearly that of Cock to capture and devour Cockroach.

After the stories were analyzed and checked, the chi-square test was used to determine whether there were significant differences among the units, or significant similarities.[13] The two Suriname

---

[12] M. J. and F. S. Herskovits, *Suriname Folklore* (New York, 1936), tale 27.

[13] Ordinarily chi-square is used for the purposes of rejecting the hypothesis that an observed difference might be due to chance alone. We start with an expected distribution and a different observed distribution and test whether the difference would occur by chance five or more times out of 100 (p $<.05$).

samples might be examined toward the end of determining whether culture patterning obtains at this level of unconscious selectivity in human behavior, and the trickster samples similarly compared in order to see what characteristics might be said to belong properly to the demands of the trickster stock of situations.

Analysis demonstrated that the two Suriname patterns were extraordinarily alike (thus defining a cultural pattern) in regard to three items: the acquisition of goods (positive O); reprimands, humiliation, defamation, and ridicule (negative D); and obscuring, keeping in ignorance, misinforming, falsifying, forgetting, and doubting (negative R).

In regard to gratifying, indulging, enjoying, providing, comforting, and pleasing (positive C), which may be thought of as being in some sense utilitarian counterparts of acquisition of property, the two kinds of Suriname stories are, however, significantly different (p < .1). Thus, while there would appear to be a patterned, high stress placed upon the acquisition of property in all the Suriname stories, the case is different with gratification, which is unpatterned, being high in Anansi Suriname trickster stories and low in Suriname II, those stories not involving the trickster.

In the Dakota stories, on the other hand, there is little emphasis on the acquisition of goods, and a mid-high emphasis on gratification that leads to no clearly significant differences from the Suriname stories, but to some indications of probable differences. In the comparison of Anansi trickster stories with Dakota trickster stories in regard to acquisition of property (positive O) p > .2. It is at the same level for the comparison of Suriname II stories and Dakota stories in regard to both gratification (positive C) and acquisition or loss of property. While it is not possible on the basis of this evidence to make any very confident inference, it may be pointed out that the general difference indicated in the stories from the two cultures corresponds roughly with the fact that the Suriname Negroes live a settled life favorable to acquisition, and with a pecuniary economy, and also have a patterned high acquisition

---

Here we are reversing the procedure. We start with distributions which are much alike thanks to cultural and literary constraints on them. But conceivably the similarities could be due to chance. We apply the chi-square test to determine the probability that the distributions would be that much alike due to chance alone. Thus, for example, if we report p > .95 it means that the chi-square is small to the point where such a similarity in distribution would happen by chance only five times or less in 100. That will be the level of significance used unless otherwise indicated.

of goods, while the Dakota Indians, semisedentary and without a money economy, are low and unpatterned in this respect.

Condemnation (negative D), including scolding, reprimanding, humiliating, deforming, ridiculing, and incrimination, are, as noted, culturally patterned elements which appear frequently in both kinds of Suriname tales. It is interesting that this category should show up as a cultural pattern in view of the fact that the public expression of censure and ridicule, particularly by indirect allusion, has been elsewhere noted as a characteristic of these as of some West African groups.[14]

The common elements among the two kinds of trickster stories, Anansi and Dakota (which may therefore be presumed to constitute a trickster pattern), pertain to prescribing, summoning, directing, insisting, begging, permitting, and inviting (positive S). Such actions may constitute part of the act of tricking. Both Anansi and Ikto, the Dakota trickster, are frequently found inviting their victims to participate in the affairs which will bring about their undoing.

Oddly enough, that category where one might expect to find the greatest degree of similarity among trickster stories, namely, avoidance of obligations (B), which includes acts of avoiding, welching, outwitting, and deceiving, shows only a weak and not statistically significant trend toward similarity. This reveals the somewhat different functions of the trickster stories in the two cultures. Trickster stories involve a reversal of culturally sanctioned values.

Although there is no general formulation to account for the choice of which values are to be abrogated, and it is beyond the scope of this study to attempt one here, a few observations may be made. In the Dakota stories, Ikto seems pre-eminently concerned with self-gratification at the expense of those who can be duped. Because of his divine nature, chances of contest are precluded. Anansi, on the other hand, while undeniably interested in satisfying his desires, seems to be more intrigued with overcoming those more powerful than he. By virtue of his very size and his humble estate he flaunts power, though cautiously, and ordinarily with marked success.

Specifically, Ikto violates incest taboos, which are of great importance among the Dakota; Anansi violates the pattern of authority, so important in the African cultures from which these people came, though this violation occurs in the world of perhaps

---

[14] Herskovits and Herskovits, *Suriname Folklore*, p. 23.

unconscious allegory. This is not to say that there is laxity in incest regulations in these parts of Africa, or a lack of concern with authority among the Dakota. It may be pointed out, however, that the pattern of political authority among the Dakota is not so faceted and complex as it is in those West African cultures.

On the other hand, there is a certain kind of value which is not, in the large view, reversed. Duties to the gods are not jested at; no more are those to the ancestors. Furthermore, the trickster is not likely to prey upon an individual who is undeserving of such attentions. He dupes the gullible, the foolish, the avaricious. It would seem that the delineation of the character types which the trickster exploits or destroys is as important as the delineation of the trickster himself. Perhaps those who tell these stories are less interested in being like Ikto or Anansi than in avoiding being like his victims.

Finally, there are certain correspondences between the Suriname II and the Dakota samples, among them hindering, preventing, conspiring, discouraging, and punishing (negative A); these objectives occur in both with a similar distribution, but low frequency. Almost significant ($p > .8$) is the similarity shown in praise and condemnation (D). There are also certain differences to be noted between these two groups of stories. Significant differences are to be found in resistance and attack (M), and the acquisition and dissemination of information (R), particularly in the positive categories of these, that is, releasing, resisting, and protecting, and in proving, discovering, and gaining information from another. Rewarding, aiding, befriending (positive A) and prescribing, insisting, and requesting (positive S) also are probably different in pattern ($p < .2$).

The two similarities noted in the paragraph just above should probably not be called a pattern. A pattern is a construct to which — one hypothesizes — future samples of behavior will show some high degree of predictable conformity, and there is no reason to assume a meaningful similarity between these two samples of stories. Any two groups of trickster stories would be expected to show some conformity to the description arrived at, just as any two samples of Suriname tales from the same period would be presumed to adhere to the general description made above. With respect to each other, having neither culture nor genre in common, similarities in the Suriname II and Dakota results are fortuitous. A hypothesis cannot reasonably be made relating them. Given any two samples of stories from any two cultures, one would expect some similarities to emerge from their comparison. For patterned predictable similarities, any two bodies of data must have either common cultural or generic bases.

It has been the purpose of this chapter to acquaint folklorists with a rationale in terms of which they might adapt the procedures of content analysis to their own studies. A perusal of the other essays included in this present collection suggest further procedures and tools to be modified to the needs of the reader's own research program. The comments on Cloze Procedure, touched upon in Chapter 2, may be briefly noted, since the Cloze notion appears to be a particularly fertile one, not only for the folklorist concerned with verbal materials but for those interested in music, dance, and the graphic and plastic arts as well. The usefulness of this procedure in cross-cultural definition of units, for example, is readily apparent.

JOHN A. GARRATY
COLUMBIA UNIVERSITY

THE APPLICATION OF CONTENT ANALYSIS
TO BIOGRAPHY AND HISTORY[1]

"We know very little even of the persons we know most intimately," Somerset Maugham writes in his autobiography, *The Summing Up*. "We do not know them enough to transfer them to the pages of a book and make human beings of them. People are too elusive, too shadowy to be copied."[2] If this is true even for a skillful novelist, a man of unusual imagination, gifted in the manipulation of verbal symbols, pity the poor historian, limited by more modest talents and by the rigid factual restrictions within which he must work! Yet particularly in the field of biography the historian must deal with personality; he must strive not only to describe the career of his subject, but also his character.

In describing the personality of a historical figure the traditional biographer deals with certain specific types of evidence. First of all, he considers whatever insights into himself his subject may have left behind him. These of course may vary greatly from man to man both in number and in validity. More often than might be supposed such evidence has great value. Even a man as reserved as Woodrow Wilson, for example, often explains himself quite frankly:

When I am with anyone in whom I am specially and sincerely interested, the hardest subject for me to broach is just that which is nearest my heart. An unfortunate disposition indeed! I hope to overcome it in time. I can at least speak plainly in writing.

It isn't pleasant or convenient to have strong passions. . . . I have an uncomfortable feeling that I am carrying a volcano about with me. My salvation is in being loved.

----

[1] This chapter in somewhat different form also appears in the author's *The Nature of Biography* (New York, 1957), and is reprinted with permission.

[2] W. S. Maugham, *The Summing Up* (New York, 1938), p. 213.

171

It would be a sheer impossibility for me to confide anything concerning myself — especially any secret of my intellect — to anyone of whose sympathy I could not be absolutely sure beforehand.[3]

Even where such evidence is less frank and revealing than these instances culled from Wilson's letters to his first wife, it is always useful.

A second source of information of this type consists of the comments of contemporaries — persons who knew the subject under investigation and left records of their opinions of him. These opinions can be evaluated more or less scientifically. A careful student will consider all such statements in the light of the closeness of the association between the subject and the commentator. If historical evidence indicates that the person whose opinion has been preserved knew the subject thoroughly and over a long period of time, his judgment will, other things being equal, be assigned greater weight than that of a casual acquaintance. Further, the historian will consider the known bias of the writer. Was he, in life, a friend or a foe of the subject? And what was his reputation as an observer? Did *his* contemporaries consider *him* a good judge of men? Finally, contemporary comments can be checked against specific facts. A writer who offers opinions based on evidence which itself can be proved false cannot (obviously) be considered a reliable judge.

Another traditional method of analyzing the personalities of historical figures is by evaluating their specific actions. Actions speak louder than words. In many ways this adage is true, despite the importance of the unconscious. At least the overt, superficial aspects of personality can be directly observed. Ordinary historical methodology can usually determine, for example, whether or not a man was selfish, honest, or unprincipled.

Finally, the biographer often makes use of the folklore of his subject. The hundreds of tales and stories that make up the Lincoln legend, for example, are mostly beyond historical verification or patently false. Yet the total picture they create has an unquestioned basis in fact. Perhaps they tell the historian more about the times in which Lincoln lived than about the man himself, but they tell *something* of the man. The legends clustered about Lincoln's great rival Stephen A. Douglas, for instance, are quite different.

These "traditional" methods of studying historical personalities,

----

[3] R. S. Baker, *Woodrow Wilson: Life and Letters* (Garden City, N.Y., 1927), 1:110, 2:242, 243.

sound enough so far as they go, leave much to be desired. An individual's self-insights never provide a complete picture of his nature. There are some things he does not know, other things he will not tell. He cannot penetrate what Tennyson called "the abysmal depths of personality." There is also much he merely neglects to tell. "No one," says Maugham, "can tell the whole truth about himself. . . . Rousseau in the course of his *Confessions* narrates incidents that have profoundly shocked the sensibility of mankind. By describing them so frankly he falsified his values and so gave them in his book a greater importance than they had in his life. There were events among a multitude of others, virtuous or at least neutral, that he omitted because they were too ordinary to seem worth recording."[4]

The comments of others are also unsatisfactory, or at least incomplete tools for understanding personality. There is seldom general agreement about the character of any outstanding figure, even among those who knew him best. Consider for a moment the case of Woodrow Wilson. Here are two comments by members of his cabinet: Secretary of the Navy Josephus Daniels: "It has been so rare for a public man to be utterly frank and genuine, to mean wholly what he says, and to carry out his public pledges regardless of all obstacles. . . . He never learned that in public business the longest way round is the nearest way through." Secretary of War Lindley M. Garrison: "I once heard a description which as nearly fits the case of President Wilson as any other I know. In describing someone it was said, 'He was a man of high ideals but no principles.' "[5] Or compare these comments by two close friends: "Those near Wilson never had the least trouble in understanding him perfectly." "Woodrow Wilson died as he lived — unexplained and unrevealed. None — not even his intimates — ever knew the mental processes which crystallized his decisions. . . ."[6]

In addition to the contradictory nature of such evidence, nearly all of it is superficial. It is also in part haphazard. The opinions of intimates are not always preserved — any attempt to quantify comments by contemporaries would be stymied by the impossibility of obtaining a sound sample.

In short, traditional methods of studying historical personalities

----

[4] Maugham, *Summing Up*, p. 10.

[5] J. Daniels, *The Wilson Era* (Chapel Hill, N.C., 1946), 2:3-4; A. S. Link, *Woodrow Wilson and the Progressive Era* (New York, 1954), p. 186n.

[6] Daniels, *Wilson Era*, 2:3; D. Lawrence, *The True Story of Woodrow Wilson* (New York, 1924), p. 13.

are scientific only insofar as they relate to facts and specific actions. Where motives and the internal dynamics of personality are concerned they can provide only impressionistic answers to the student's questions. As was pointed out by the editor of *The Dial* as long ago as 1898, we need "a finer method of analysis than critics have been wont to apply," if we are to "disclose personal elements" in the natures of the great men of history.[7]

If this "finer method" exists anywhere, it must be within the realm of modern psychology. While no psychologist would claim to have mastered the complicated field of human personality, it is obviously true that the profession has made great strides toward that goal. But for the historian or biographer the difficulty lies in the fact that so much of what the psychologist does in his study of personality cannot be accomplished without the co-operation of the subject. It would be most helpful if we could give the Rorschach test to Wilson, get Julius Caesar to look at the pictures of the T.A.T., or put Napoleon on a psychoanalyst's couch, but these things cannot be. Many efforts, or course, have been made to psychoanalyze historical figures, and a few of these have been convincing. But such interpretations can never be more than intelligent guesses. Much of the necessary evidence is always missing, and the Freudian constructs of sublimation and reaction formation make the interpretation of whatever evidence there is a dubious process at best.

Yet there remains much that can be used. The whole field of graphology, for example, is a possible source of insight into the personality of former individuals. Long neglected by American psychologists and thus consigned to the quacks and the Sunday-supplement writers, graphology has recently been developed as an important field of personality research. While it would be dangerous to interpret a historical figure only in terms of his handwriting, it cannot be denied that a person's writing is a form of expressive movement, that it is really "brain writing."

Early experiments, such as those of Alfred Binet nearly half a century ago, made it clear that certain gifted "professional" graphologists could interpret character from handwriting with an accuracy far exceeding chance. Yet these professionals differed among themselves as to how they operated, and untrained individuals who applied the methods that the graphologists claimed they were using could not duplicate their results. However, more recent experi-

----

[7] *The Dial,* 24 (1898), 281.

menters have developed measuring devices that can be applied simply and scientifically, and that correlate highly with other measurements of personality. One graphologist devised a long list of handwriting "variables" and classified the script of a number of individuals according to the prevalence of each one. He then compared these results with personality judgments of the subjects made by a group of psychologists. Many of the "variables" proved useless, but at least six could be related significantly to the psychologists' conclusions. This student makes but modest claims for his experiment, but obviously a study of these "variables" in the handwriting of a historical character might provide a biographer with a number of insights into his subject's personality.[8]

The best modern students, analyzing such things as the form, size, and slant of writing, the upper and lower projections of letters like *t*, *p*, and *f*, the pressure applied by the pen, the relative size of margins, and the way all these complex factors are combined, have made a useful contribution to psychology, and one that historians, especially biographers, might apply to their own specialties.

But the psychological study of handwriting is still not truly scientific. There are, for example, national styles of handwriting which make it impossible to set up universal standards for measuring this personality variable. Further, these styles change over the years, so that to judge any sample the graphologist must know the nationality of the author and the approximate date of the writing. One cannot analyze the writing of a nineteenth-century German and a present-day Englishman by exactly the same criteria. In addition, the differences of opinion among handwriting "authorities" are almost as numerous as the agreements. Measurement can only go so far — style, for example, can be described, but not measured.[9]

But graphology is part of a broader field of personality study — the field of the projective technique. Undoubtedly contrived and standardized projective tools like the Rorschach and the T.A.T. (which unfortunately are of no use for biographical purposes) are the most valuable techniques of this type, but there are others, only

---

[8] G. W. Allport and P. E. Vernon, *Studies in Expressive Movement* (New York, 1933), p. 187; A. Binet, *Les Révélations de l'Écriture* (Paris, 1906); C. L. Hull and R. B. Montgomery, "An Experimental Investigation of Certain Alleged Relations Between Character and Handwriting," *Psychoanalytic Review*, 26 (1919), 63-74; G. R. Pascal, "The Analysis of Handwriting: A Test of Significance," *Character and Personality*, 12 (1943), 123-44.

[9] For a summary of this subject, see H. H. and G. L. Anderson, eds., *Projective Techniques* (New York, 1951), pp. 416-43.

less useful, that can be adapted to historical needs. All of these deal with personal documents, and with content analysis.

In 1920 William Bayard Hale performed, in *The Story of a Style*,[10] a content analysis of the writings of Woodrow Wilson. Hale's approach was completely unscientific — the methods of classification and selection that he used were capricious and unsystematized. His personal view was entirely prejudiced as well, for he hated Wilson and was determined to expose him as a hollow fraud. But even so, Hale threw a great deal of light on Wilson simply by pointing out some simple facts about Wilson's writing, such as his fondness for adjectives. Since Hale's day great advances have been made both in systematizing content analysis and, it may be hoped, in developing a more objective approach among the analyzers. As a result of much work, psychologists have found that the kinds of words a person uses and the frequency with which he employs them are a reflection of his inner nature. A German psychologist, A. Busemann, devised an action quotient (Aq) by dividing the number of active (verbal) ideas in a given passage by the number of qualitative (adjectival) ones. He postulated that an increase in qualitative words was an indication of emotional instability, and found that there was a good correlation between his findings and the results of Rorschach ink-blot tests applied to the same subjects. Busemann's work was further developed by an American, David P. Boder,[11] who studied various types of writing, such as legal documents, fiction, scientific papers, advertisements, and private letters, and arrived at generalizations concerning the ratio of adjectives to verbs in each type. A complicated scientific treatise striving for exactitude will naturally have more adjectives in it than an informal letter, but having standardized the ratios for different types of writing, Boder found it possible to judge emotional instability with some accuracy. Some of his experiments are extremely suggestive for biographers. He took, for example, 132 samples from Emerson's journals over a 50-year period[12] and discovered wide variations in the ratio of adjectives to verbs, though over the years the percentages compared closely to the "standard" for that type of writing. Boder did not attempt to correlate his

---

[10] W. B. Hale, *The Story of a Style* (New York, 1920).

[11] D. P. Boder, "The Adjective-Verb Quotient . . . ," *Psychological Record*, 3 (1940), 310-43.

[12] For each month of the year 1820, and for every fifth year thereafter, he selected a passage of approximately 350 words.

data with the known facts of Emerson's life, but such a comparison would obviously be of interest to a biographer of the man. What is the significance of these figures indicating the number of adjectives per 100 verbs, based on the journals for 1845? July — 21, August — 107, September — 43. Can some event calculated to have stirred Emerson deeply be located in August 1845? Perhaps the cause of such a disturbance will be obvious, but if it is not, a study of adjective-verb ratios could well lead to its discovery. If a high degree of consistency should be found between Emerson's use of adjectives in his journal and his emotional ups and downs, one could assume that Boder's device would prove extremely valuable for obtaining insights into the personality of Emerson or any other subject who has kept a journal, or written letters, or done any other kind of sustained writing over a period of years.

Another of Boder's suggestive studies dealt with the letters of William James. Having determined the number of adjectives per 100 verbs for a series of letters dating from 1882 to 1910, he compared his figures for letters written to men with those written to women at different times of James's life. He found that between the ages of 40 and 50 James's letters to women contained many more adjectives than did the ones he addressed to men, but that in letters written after 60 the opposite was true. The figures are

Table 1

Age	Adjectives per 100 Verbs in Letters		
	To Men	To Women	Total
40-50	43.2	62.7	52.9
60-65	61.5	42.2	51.8

presented in Table 1. The meaning of these statistics may be subject to debate, but they are surely worth debating.[13]

The number of similar studies that might be adapted to the purposes of the biographer is large. Semanticists like Korzybski argue that bad semantic habits are a sign of a cranky, jumpy, even paranoid personality. More than ten years ago a psychologist surveying the whole field concluded: "There is . . . a reasonable

[13] Boder, "The Adjective-Verb Quotient," pp. 329-31.

argument, reinforced by some experimental evidence, that quantitative analysis of written expression can discover individuality," and research since that time has reinforced this view.[14]

There are other tools which might well assist the biographer in digging out the subleties of his subject's personality. Dollard and Mowrer have developed a means of measuring tension as expressed in personal documents.[15] By counting the words revealing some form of discomfort (D), and those indicative of relief or reward (R), they have arrived at a Discomfort-Relief Quotient (DRQ), which can be determined by the equation

$$DRQ = \frac{D}{D + R}.$$

The application of this technique to the written words of a person at different periods of his life might aid in understanding both his general nature and his reactions during the important crises in his career.

Since autobiographies are such important biographical sources, any tool that makes it possible for the biographer to extract additional meaning from this kind of writing would naturally be useful. Such a tool is "value analysis," a method by which autobiographical and other personal data "can be described with a maximum of objectivity and at the same time with a maximum of relevance to the underlying emotional dynamics." This technique, developed by Ralph K. White, was first applied to a study of *Black Boy*, the Negro writer Richard Wright's autobiography.[16]

In order to test the usefulness of the method, White first read *Black Boy* carefully and wrote out his impressions of Wright on the basis of his reading. This is the "normal" way in which any biographer would use such material as a source on the personality of his subject. But then White went over the book again, noting in the margin every value judgment and goal expressed by the author. He developed a set of shorthand symbols to represent these goals and standards of judgment, and counted up the number of times each appeared. Naturally (since White was a competent psychologist to begin with) the conclusions reached in his preliminary ap-

---

[14] F. H. Sandford, "Speech and Personality," *Psychological Bulletin*, 39 (1942), 811-45.

[15] "A Method of Measuring Tension in Written Documents."

[16] R. K. White, *"Black Boy:* A Value-Analysis," *Journal of Abnormal and Social Psychology*, 42 (1947), 440-61.

praisal were duplicated in the counting procedure. The things about Wright that struck the *reader* were the things he mentioned a great deal in his autobiography. The obvious fact that Wright had had an extremely unhappy childhood, for example, was borne out in the counting — the book contained 1,205 examples of frustration and only 349 representing positive satisfactions. White's observance of the author's aggression and his disapproval of others was also verified, for aggression was the second most prevalent value in his book, and 89 per cent of his comments on persons mentioned were unfavorable. Wright's hatred of his father (every mention of him in the book was unfavorable), his ambivalent attitude toward his mother, his relative absence of interest in sex, and his concern with knowledge and truthfulness, were similarly "proved" by the statistical analysis.

But there were several aspects of Wright's personality, often expressed subtly and possibly unconsciously, which did not stand out until they had been counted. By far the most important of these was his emphasis on physical safety. In his preliminary, subjective appraisal, White had not noticed this at all, yet it was by a large margin the most frequently mentioned value in the autobiography, accounting for 18 per cent of all Wright's value judgments! The counting also disclosed the writer's lack of interest in social goals, his failure to identify himself with other Negroes, and his tendency to record *complete* disapproval (as in the case of his father) of persons he disliked.

It might well be that some or all of these characteristics would have been noticed by a different reader. But such a reader might in turn have missed many of the traits that White discovered in his preliminary appraisal. "Value analysis" can definitely act as a check on intuitive judgment. As White has pointed out, the method is useless without the ordinary subjective study which preceded it, and it only assumes its full importance when another subjective analysis of the material is made on the basis of the new ideas brought to light by the counting. The "discovery" of Wright's concern with physical safety, for instance, does not explain the meaning of this pecularity. White weighs the possibility that it may indicate Wright's aggression — *"to accuse others of attacking is itself an effective form of attack."* He also suggests that the author's aggression may have been part of his search for safety, that is, that it was fundamentally defensive, based on the principle that the best defense is a good offense. But the statistical evaluation can even help to discriminate between these two hypotheses. In 122 cases Wright connected some aggressive thought or action with the goal of safety; instances in which he was aggressive for some other reason, such as to gain acceptance by the "gang" in a new school, were relatively rare.

Whatever the conclusion, however, the value of the statistical analysis seems clear. The final interpretation of *Black Boy*, in White's words, was "both broader and sounder because of the inclusion of much critically interpreted statistical material."

One great virtue of this method for the average biographer is its relative simplicity. Ten or 20 hours of training are all that are required to learn the technique, and while the actual scoring of a long autobiography would take a great deal of time, it would not call for any particular background in psychology. The mechanics could even be performed by an assistant — indeed, by having two people score an autobiography separately an admirable check upon the reliability of the results would result. Actually, reliability is not likely to be a problem, for, as White has said, observers will agree as to the facts even if they differ as to the meaning of the facts. Further, it seems clear that this analysis may actually probe into the unconscious mind of the autobiographer in a way that psycholanalytical biographers have always hoped to do but seldom have done. And always the final judgment of the biographer must come into play. He is no slave to the figures. All that they can do is offer him ideas that may not have occurred to him as a result of an ordinary reading of the material.

A similar though slightly more complicated technique has been developed by Baldwin. He performed a minute content analysis on a group of letters written by "Jenny," an old woman, to "Glenn" and "Isabel," a young married couple. Jenny's life story, in rough outline as it might appear in the mind of a biographer, was as follows. She was born in Ireland but had been brought to Canada at an early age. As a young girl she was burdened with the support of her brothers and sisters. Later she married, but the death of her husband left her with a month-old son to care for. For this child, "Ross," she developed an extremely close attachment, skimping and depriving herself in order to give him luxuries incommensurate with her level of income. Their relationship was close and happy until Ross grew up and began to live his own life. Then Jenny became very jealous of his girl friends. When he married she ordered him from her sight forever, but she was not able to adjust to the separation, and after Ross and his wife were divorced, she re-established contact with him. They became friends once more, but continued to quarrel over Ross's interest in various women. But Ross contracted a mastoid infection and died quite suddenly. Jenny then tried a number of different jobs without finding happiness, and finally entered an old ladies' home. At first she seemed satisfied, but soon began to quarrel with the authorities and other inmates. The last years of her life were bitterly unhappy.[17]

This information was pieced together by Baldwin from a series of letters which Jenny wrote to Ross's college roommate and his wife. Baldwin used them, first, to arrive at a subjective analysis of Jenny's personality. His analysis, as he has pointed out, rested upon four types of evidence. He made use of the *frequency* of certain ideas and attitudes expressed in the letters, the *insights* into her own personality which Jenny herself offered, the *contiguity* (Osgood would say "contingency") of various facts and feelings mentioned, and, finally, his own past experience with other cases. This is the method by which any ordinary biographer would arrive at conclusions about the personality of Jenny, and the validity of his conclusions would depend upon his intelligence and his diligence.

But how can the biographer (or his public) be sure that his interpretation is correct? It is this flaw, inherent in even the most brilliant subjective analysis, which Baldwin's second evaluation, a "personal structure analysis," was designed to mend. By *counting* frequencies and contiguities[18] in Jenny's letters, he sought to validate his subjective analysis of her personality.

Of course the objective content analysis was in itself partly subjective. Baldwin, for example, broke down Jenny's behavior into categories, according to certain subjects that she discussed. Some subjects were not classified at all; others were lumped together into general classifications, a few were treated separately. This involved decision making that was entirely subjective. He had a category, "Men," and another, "Women." Yet he placed Ross in a separate category, and considered Glenn and Isabel as a unit in themselves, ignoring the sex differential. Each decision was based upon the

----

[17] Baldwin, "Personal Structure Analysis," pp. 164-65. For "Jenny's" letters see G. W. Allport, "Letters from Jenny," *Journal of Abnormal and Social Psychology*, 41 (1946), 315-50, 449-80.

[18] Jenny's insights into herself are actually examples of contiguity. Thus, when she says she feels sorry for a child in an institution where she is working because he reminds her of her son Ross, her sympathy and her memory are contiguous, and they are also an example of self-insight.

understanding of Jenny which he had obtained through subjective study. In all he selected 15 topics,[19] each broken down into the different attitudes that Jenny expressed in connection with them. Under "Ross," for instance, all references were classified generally as favorable, unfavorable, or neutral, and then further defined under such headings as attacked, selfish, lazy, and dishonest, and their opposites. But in this way judgments based on frequency could be mechanically checked.

To test the accuracy of conclusions based on contiguity, the letters were subdivided into general periods, covering broad sections of the subject's life, and then into incidents, "small temporal segment[s] of the letters during which Jenny is writing about one general topic." Again, the decision as to what was a "period" or an "incident" was a subjective one. All of the categories referred to in a given incident were judged to be contiguous. Thus, if the categories "Ross-unfavorable" and "Money-saved" appear within the same incident with a frequency exceeding chance, it can be assumed that these two concepts had some relationship in Jenny's mind, just as their individual mention a great number of times (i.e., their frequency) indicates something about her personality.

When all the "incidents" in the letters had been thus categorized, and the information transferred to punch cards, it was possible with the aid of an I.B.M. machine to determine quickly both the number of times that any person, goal, or idea was mentioned, and the number of favorable, unfavorable, etc., references to it in proportion to the total references. Further, the cards produced information on the relationship of ideas and persons in the mind of the writer. The mere existence of a relationship, of course, means little unless it can be shown that the frequency of the relationship is statistically significant. But this can be done by using a relatively simple mathematical formula (the chi-square method) which can be applied, if not necessarily understood, by anyone who can handle long division. And once a significant relationship has been established, valuable insights may come to light. The frequency with which Jenny associated favorable references to her son and references to "The Past-relived" in the same incident, for example, points up her wish to return to the happy days when Ross was growing up and completely dependent upon her.

----

[19] Ross, Women, Men, Her Family, Herself, Money, Death, Health, Jobs, Religion, Nature and Art, Gifts and Purchases, Children, Homes, and The Past.

Baldwin found that certain groups of categories tended to relate themselves in clusters, which he was able to describe schematically. Here is one of his clusters, together with his interpretation of it:

MONEY–sought

JOBS–sought   JOBS–rejected

HERSELF–innocent victim

HEALTH–dramatized

This cluster, Baldwin writes,

contains the categories with the highest frequencies. The large frequencies suggest that the search for a job was the most important problem in Jenny's life during period one [covering her life up to the time of her reconciliation with Ross]. . . . The presence of two opposite attitudes in the same cluster suggests an ambivalence. There is not sufficient information . . . to determine the reason why she needed a job (although *money-sought* certainly gives a clue), nor why she rejected them. From the fact that *herself-innocent-victim* is related to both attitudes toward jobs, it is clear that Jenny externalized the source of her difficulty and felt that she was not at fault in requiring work and at the same time being unable to work. It also appears in this cluster that Jenny's health was bad. At least she considered her health to be part of her unfortunate condition.[20]

Another cluster illustrates both the strength and the weakness of the method:

DEATH–planned for

MONEY–scrupulously regarded ———————————— MONEY–suspiciously guarded

This suggested to Baldwin that Jenny expected to die, and therefore guarded her money with great care, but he could not explain her *suspicious* guarding. Neither was the connection between Death and her scrupulous regard for money apparent. But the fact that a statistically significant correspondence existed between these seemingly unrelated attitudes led the experimenter to re-examine the letters subjectively "to discover more details about Jenny's attitude toward death." He then noticed things he had previously passed over as insignificant — her emphasis on making sure that her money fell into the hands of friends when she passed on (she even sewed money into her corset, lest some stranger steal her purse in the event she should drop dead in the street), and her fear of dying with unpaid debts on her hands, which led her on one occasion to send some cash to Glenn before leaving on a trip to

---

[20] Baldwin, "Personal Structure Analysis," p. 177.

cover the expense of burying her in case she should die while away. While Baldwin had noted Jenny's scrupulous regard for money and her careful protection of her assets, and had therefore included these categories in his analysis, he had missed their relationship to her attitude toward death. As a result of the counting process "a mysterious pattern of correspondences" produced "the insight which was previously missing."[21]

Baldwin was also able to establish the practical value of personal structure analysis by comparing his own evaluation of Jenny's personality with those of five other persons, all trained in the field, who studied the letters only subjectively. Only one of these experts extracted as much information from the letters as the experimenter, and all agreed that the conclusions reached by the statistical study seemed sound. In addition, Baldwin had another psychologist perform a "blind analysis" by studying the statistical results without reading the letters, and then writing a description of Jenny. His characterization agreed substantially with Baldwin's and with those of all the others. Indeed, only two of the subjective analyses contained any essential information that he had missed.

As in the case of value analysis, Baldwin's "Personal Structure Analysis" requires a considerable mass of material if its conclusions are to be statistically reliable, and much tedious effort in scoring the record. And it will not in itself explain personality. Significant relationships having been uncovered, it is the analyst's task to understand and interpret these relationships. Thus, the biographer can find in such methods no simple answer to his questions about the personality of his subject. But if he applies this kind of technique he can buttress his opinions with really weighty evidence, based on "quantitative, systematic, objective . . . interpretation."[22] In a field where so many conclusions tend to rest on impulse and prejudice, this type of "proof" has great value.

Within the limits described, content analysis might also be applied to certain broad historical questions involving masses of people rather than individuals. Our present age, for example, has been frequently referred to as an age of anxiety, whereas other periods have been called by such titles as "The Age of Faith" and "The Age of Reason." It might be enlightening to collect a sample of certain kinds of writing in two periods widely separated in time and subject them to, say, the Dollard and Mowrer DRQ analysis.

---

[21] Baldwin, "Personal Structure Analysis," p. 178.
[22] Baldwin, "Personal Structure Analysis," p. 183.

Similar studies of all sorts of questions relating to intellectual history might be envisioned. Surely it would be just as easy to set up categories of ideas as categories of personality traits. Historians write of the "American mind" or the "mind of the Middle Ages" in very unscientific terms. Frequently, as Pool has pointed out, they are more concerned with the location of the *first* expression of an idea than with its prevalence at a particular time. A conscious effort to be systematic both in their sampling of the evidence and their analysis of its content might not lead them to more accurate conclusions, but it would, at least, make it possible for others to check their conclusions with relative ease. An example of what is involved is offered by Thomas C. Cochran's *Railroad Leaders*.[23] Cochran analyzed some 100,000 letters of railroad executives in the last half of the nineteenth century in order to determine their collective points of view on such questions as their concepts of the role of government in the economy and their attitudes toward labor. While his sampling technique appears to have been far from scientific, and his specific results therefore questionable, his study is interesting methodologically, and could readily be adapted to all sorts of historical questions.

Discussion at the conference helped to clarify both the advantages and the disadvantages of content analysis in historical and biographical research. There was general agreement that insofar as content analysis is a device for measuring personality and ideologies it produces a scientific check on intuitive, subjective judgments. Too often historians have seized upon isolated instances or expressions and generalized from them. Reputable historians would agree that such practices are unsound. They have little respect, for example, for the procedure of writers like biographer Emil Ludwig, who once explained that his method of understanding the personality of a subject was to brood over a picture of the man until he "discovered" the "key" to his character. Only then did Ludwig turn to the documents for what he called "corroboration" of his insight. But while most historians make sure that their generalizations follow rather than precede their study of evidence, they do not always weigh the evidence on any scientifically testable balance. Content analysis can sometimes provide just this kind of balance.

It was also clear from the discussion of this subject that content analysis can help in the resolution of conflicting biographical and

----

[23] T. C. Cochran, *Railroad Leaders: 1845-1890* (Cambridge, Mass., 1953).

historical interpretations either by clarifying doubtful issues or by illustrating ambivalences in the subject. Further, most of the conferees agreed that contiguity was a more significant factor in the content analysis of personal documents than frequency, in that it was more likely to reflect relationships hidden even from the subject himself; but, alas, they also agreed that contiguity was more difficult to measure, interpret, and control objectively than simple frequency relationships. When are two ideas or traits actually contiguous? Must they appear in the same sentence? The same paragraph or thought unit? Osgood in another chapter describes a study in which all ideas expressed in a single speech were considered to reflect contiguity. The choice of units for the study of these relationships is highly subjective — yet the size of the units may affect the results.

The discussion of the use of content analysis in history and biography continually highlighted such essentially subjective aspects of the technique. The interpretation of the results of any counting must depend upon the mind of the investigator, and his prejudices and preconceptions may influence his conclusions. The very decision as to what to count must also affect the outcome. The value of the results is completely dependent upon the setting up of proper categories, and of the accurate coding of the material. The reliability of the coding process, of course, is subject to testing, but the validity of the conclusions depends upon the soundness of the basic subjective decisions of the experimenter.

Much of this difficulty could be eliminated by the development of "precut" categories which the student could apply to his particular problem. While admitting that it would be advantageous to provide a predetermined set of categories (such as White's) for the classification of personality traits, the conferees also agreed that no extant set was universally adaptable. The difficulty, as Osgood somewhat ruefully remarked, is that this would call for an "adequate theory of personality," which is something that simply does not exist as yet.

Another weakness in the use of content analysis in historical and biographical research was brought out through the remarks of Mahl on the problem of representational vs. instrumental models. In a sense the problem is related to the use of the Freudian concepts of sublimation and reaction formation, which the psychoanalytical biographers have used with reckless abandon. Content analysis can call responses to the attention of the investigator, but it cannot prove to him that they are representational rather than instrumental responses. Yet it is essential that the investigator know which type of response he is dealing with.

Another factor (in the more complicated forms of analysis) that seems purely subjective and relatively unscientific involves the weighing of certain statements more heavily than others. In value analysis, for example, White assigned five emphasis units to each strongly expressed value. It is not clear how this weighing was determined, yet in any mechanical process such a decision may profoundly affect the results. White also urges the experimenter to be constantly on the lookout for subleties and for over-all meanings (a point emphasized at the conference by Alexander George), which again involves highly subjective factors.

Finally, there are certain weaknesses in the use of content analysis from the historical point of view. Published personal writings (especially speeches and autobiographies) are often the product of other pens than the official author's. Would a content analysis of President Eisenhower's radio speeches — or of his book, *Crusade in Europe* — offer valid evidence about his personality or about the personalities of his ghost writers? Then there is the question of reticence. While it is true that the theory of projective techniques postulates that no one can help expressing himself when he writes, there are degrees and degrees of expressiveness. Many public figures reveal very little of themselves in their letters and autobiographies, held back either by personal inhibitions or by their ideas of conventionality. Also, psychologists have not resolved the problem of literary style as distinct from personal style as an influence on personal writings. In one sense style may be revealing, in another it may undermine the usefulness of content analysis by introducing artistically contrived distortions into the record. It is also true, as Mahl pointed out, that style and other forms of expression are culturally bound to some extent, and that culture changes over time as well as from place to place. One of the greatest difficulties in using content analysis in historical study would be, therefore, the establishment of "norms" for different cultures at different periods of time.

In conclusion, it seems clear that content analysis offers history and biography a fruitful field for research. Careful, imaginative use of the method ought to reduce the historian's dependence upon subjective judgments, enable him to resolve doubts rising from conflicting evidence, and, in general, add confidence to his conclusions by reducing them to measurable, reproducible limits.

7 ITHIEL DE SOLA POOL
MASSACHUSETTS INSTITUTE OF TECHNOLOGY

TRENDS IN CONTENT ANALYSIS TODAY:
A SUMMARY

The previous chapters in this book have each dealt with the use of content analysis in a particular field of knowledge and usually in a particular way. The present chapter is an attempt to report what the men who wrote these chapters said when they confronted each other and each other's problems at the Allerton House conference. It is in short an attempt to seek out the areas of consensus, the common problems, the directions in which workers in the field of content analysis seemed to be moving. But this chapter is not a committee report. It is one man's view of what came out of the conference, and as such it will be stated as the author's exposition of the group's ideas with only occasional references to the conference as such or credits to the members and their individual divergences or individually derived thoughts which the author has freely and gratefully borrowed.

WHAT THE VOLUME COVERS

For all the breadth of the topics discussed, their focus has been on one small area of the total range of problems with which content analysis may deal. Table 1 illustrates what we have discussed intensively and what we have skirted in discussion or touched on in at most one chapter.

Our interest has been in inference. That need not have been the case. We could have discussed the problem of summarizing vast masses of material by succinct statistical measures. We could have discussed the problem of counting to make descriptive statements about texts more precise. For example, linguists want to know the

Table 1[a]

| Uses of Content Analysis | Type of Analysis | | | |
| | Quantitative, measuring: | | | Qualitative |
	Fre-quencies	Contin-gencies	Inten-sities	Qualitative
To describe texts	0	0	0	0
To draw inferences from texts as to their antecedents	+	+	+	0
To draw inferences from texts as to their effects	0	0	0	0

[a] + = Discussed intensively.
  0 = Not discussed intensively.

frequency with which different language forms are used. That is a useful descriptive kind of content analysis, but not one with which we concerned ourselves. Librarians want to know what the flow of books and articles is in each discipline. To do this they analyze the content of each text, classifying it under established headings, and count the frequencies so arising. That, too, is descriptive frequency content analysis and a useful enterprise.

Another type of purely descriptive analysis was discussed extensively at a more recent conference sponsored by the same S.S.R.C. Committee on Psychology and Linguistics. That conference on the description and analysis of style brought together literary persons, linguists, and social scientists interested in finding ways to describe the style of a text as such. Its results, which are also due for publication under the title *Aspects of Style in Language,* will in some sense be a companion volume to this one. The present work, however, explores problems of description only as a step toward inference. Our concern has been with inferences from the content of a text to what was going on in the environment in which the text appeared.

These inferences can go two ways. There can be inferences which ask what it was that *led* to a statement appearing, and there can be inferences which ask what was likely to *follow* from the appearance of a statement.

The latter kind of inference we also discussed a little. It may be illustrated by copy testing for example, where one may analyze the characteristics of various texts and then see which ones produce which reactions. The same sort of effect inference is made when one notes different reactions to different advertisements or propaganda pieces, and then searches the texts to find what produced these responses. Other examples of inferences regarding effects may be found in psychological experiments in which the stimulus material is a text. The texts used for the different conditions of an experiment may be analyzed for inferences about the determinants of the response behavior. Osgood in his chapter pays some attention to what he calls "decoding dependencies," that is, "dependencies of events in listeners and readers . . . upon the content and structure of messages." But on the whole our emphasis has been on inferences about the sources, not the receivers, of messages.

Thus the uses of content analysis which we did discuss for the most part were those where the inference to be drawn concerns the antecedents of the text itself and conditions of its production. For that kind of research the logic of inference has been most fully analyzed by Alexander George (Chap. 1). He was concerned with inferences derived from propaganda issued in World War II and concerning the propagandists' military intentions. But in a strictly analogous way John Garraty was concerned, in Chapter 6, with inferences from the statements of a great man in history to his state of tension at the time of writing or speaking. George Mahl, in Chapter 3, was concerned with inferences from a patient's speech disturbances to his degree of anxiety. Charles Osgood, in Chapter 2, wanted to draw inferences from a man's statements to his underlying evaluations and associations. These are examples of the kinds of inferences from texts to antecedents with which most current content analysis seems to be concerned.

We have now looked along the rows of the table above and we find current content analysis work focused in one of them. Now let us look down the columns. Not only is our focus of attention limited to one use of content analysis, it is also limited to but a few of the types of analysis which could be used to serve that purpose.

QUALITATIVE ANALYSIS

We have not discussed qualitative content analysis in most of the chapters in this volume. True, qualitative methods have been forcefully put forward in the chapter by Alexander George. His conclusion as to the futility of trying to be rigorously numerical in some of the kinds of policy-oriented research with which he was concerned provoked little disagreement among the conferees. But there was a desire to define the areas where his argument applied and the areas where numerical quantification makes sense.

The problem with which George deals is that of explaining the behavior of particular actors in a particular situation. He discusses a kind of detective work. And the best detective, he tells us, is the one with a prepared but open mind ready to spark to any clue which gives the game away, though it occurs but once. George's careful study of intelligence analysis in World War II has fully documented that some such detectives can do very well using "nonfrequency" methods of content analysis. He has also shown that they did much better than their wartime colleagues who tried *ad hoc* to set up mechanical quantitative procedures for doing the same detective work. Garraty, in similar vein, notes with approval White's procedure in his analysis of Richard Wright's *Black Boy* and Baldwin's in his analysis of Jenny. Each started with an intuitive analysis of a kind that would be familiar to historians or psychiatrists. Certain inferences were successfully made at that stage about the personality and problems of each author. But in each study this preliminary qualitative analysis provided the set of categories to be explored in a more novel and rigorous kind of quantitative content analysis. The latter was then performed and in each of the two cases brought forth truly important insights which the more traditional reading had failed to elicit.[1] It is with this further quantitative step for improving the results of historical research that Garraty was concerned, and each of us was concerned with the analogous problem for his own discipline, the problem of pushing back the frontiers through careful if arduous counting which might add to what we can learn by intelligent intuitive observation. George's point is not in contradiction. He demonstrates why the initial hypothesis-forming phase of a study is essential if one is later to count what is relevant to count, why "nonfrequency" qualitative analysis (to use George's term) also produces some

---

[1] It should not be assumed that qualitative methods are insightful, and quantitative ones merely mechanical methods for checking hypotheses. The relationship is a circular one; each provides new insights on which the other can feed. New insights about a text gained by a quantitative content analysis, once discovered, become obvious and can be used in further intuitive examination of the text. Discovering by quantitative analysis the unsuspected fact that Richard Wright is preoccupied with personal safety, one will then not miss such allusions in an ordinary reading of his works. Indeed, it was suggested at the conference that a good way to train qualitative content analysts was to make them do quantitative analyses, for the rigor of the latter makes them aware of aspects of communication which they might otherwise miss.

things which a quantitative analysis cannot, why in a practical operation such as intelligence, where time is of the essence and one must choose rather than doing both, an impressionistic analysis is usually preferable to a formal count. However, the logic of the process of inference which George examines leads the scientific researcher to a conclusion different from that of the intelligence operator. It leads him to embrace the rigors and promise of quantitative measurement as a step enabling him to go beyond where he could go otherwise. If, despite the incisive discussion by George of qualitative content analysis for intelligence purposes, we do not put a plus sign in that cell of the table describing our book, it is because nonfrequency analysis was not an area in which the rest of the conferees were working. George's discussion of non-frequency methods served to make us define the limits of our common problems rather than to pinpoint that as a common one. Most of us were concerned with content analysis for scientific generalization, not for intelligence purposes. And those of us (e.g., Garraty) who were concerned with developing methods applicable to specific situations were seeking exact, quantitative, standardizable ones with which to check and supplement intuitive judgments. Thus we define the area of content analysis in this volume as the counting or measuring of features of a text, and that for purposes of inference.

But the things in a text which can be counted or measured are many and we do not attempt here to discuss them all. The characteristic of the conference was that we discussed measurement of contingencies a great deal. We discussed the measurement of symbol frequencies somewhat less. We discussed the measurement of intensity least of all. Only one paper, Osgood's, deals with that extensively.

INTENSITY

The desire to measure the intensity of attitudes has been with us from the earliest days of content analysis. One of the first issues explored was the degree of bias in journalistic treatments of partisan issues: which party got more column inches; which got the bigger headlines; which got the better pictures; which got the loaded words. But there are so many ways of slanting a text that measurement of them all has defeated every researcher who has tried it. The usual operational solution has been to settle for the measurement of column inches or some such frequency. There was

an underlying assumption that frequency of mention would correlate with intensity of expressed attitude, and so a straightforward
frequency count of either inches or symbols, supplemented at most
by a positive or negative valence distinction, might provide a useful index of the intensity of feeling. The most common single
content analysis categories of past years have been "pro-x,"
"anti-x," "pro-y," "anti-y," where x and y were opposed sides; and
the most common statistic in the results has been proportion of
favorable or unfavorable references to x or y.

The assumption that the frequency of statements provides a good
index of intensity of attitude is probably reasonable for a large
class of cases. By "attitude" here, of course, we mean the attitude
expressed in the body of the text, not the covert feelings of the
author. Even with this limitation the assumption baldly spelled out
sounds absurd, because it is perfectly clear that frequency is only
one of a variety of devices by which feeling is expressed. But the
experience of more than one analyst who has tried refinements in
measuring intensity has been that nothing much is added by other
measures than the frequency one. That would suggest that at least
in a large class of forms of verbal expression much of the total
variance in intensity is accounted for by the one component,
frequency.

True, this is simply an allegation or a hypothesis. It is chal-
lenged by George and by Mahl, who questions the "assumption
that there is an isomorphic relation between behavioral states and
quantitative properties of lexical content." The data does not now
exist to establish the classes of cases where the assumption is valid,
and the classes where it is not, and by how much. We do not want
to become victims of our convenient assumption by using it blindly
as though it always applied, but it works well enough so that those
now working in the field of content analysis have not found it an
immediate stumbling block to be removed from the road.

The problem of measurement of intensity is one to which Osgood's
chapter addresses itself, particularly in the section on evaluative
assertion analysis. The objective of evaluative assertion analysis
is to arrive at a measurement of the attitude of the source toward
certain attitude objects. It is an attempt to obtain a measure of
evaluation, not frequency. The basic data are derived from judges
who use a seven-point scale. However, the judgments are made on
texts from which all identifying context has been removed, and the
resulting evaluations are then used in turn as measures for the final

evaluations of each other. This ingenious measure of attitude does not rest upon frequency of appearance, except for the way in which it uses the seven-point scale. It does assume that "an intense connector ($\pm$ 3) is treated as equivalent to an ordinary assertion ($\pm$ 1) made three times. . . ." Clearly, it is not easy to measure intensity quite independently of frequency, though evaluative assertion analysis is a start. It is entirely conceivable that similar measures could also be devised for other aspects of intensity besides intensity of evaluation, for example intensity of emphasis, intensity of belief in facts, etc.

Evaluative assertion analysis is the exception to what we have been saying about the complete dependence of content analysts on the assumption that intensity is simply a function of frequency. The fact that that assumption was generally used was made explicit by several of the conference participants and in several of the papers. For example, in dealing with the problem of the intensity of contingencies between symbols Osgood said: "reflecting the basic psychological principle relating habit strength to frequency of response, the method does indirectly reflect the strength of associations. . . . The stronger the association between two ideas in the thinking of the source, the more regularly will the occurrence of one be the condition for the occurrence . . . of the other."

If we are to drop this assumption that frequency will measure intensity, either because the assumption is inadequate or simply to test its adequacy by independent observations, we are led either to the use of judges, as above, or to the use of some linguistic knowledge. Saporta and Sebeok, in their discussion of "marked" and "unmarked" forms, introduce the problem of identifying lexical equivalents which differ only in certain of their connotations, which would include such matters as intensity. The content analyst would like the aid of linguistics in enumerating the lexical and structural forms through which nuances of intensity are conveyed. This is one area where the interests of content analysis and linguistics meet.

FREQUENCY

Counting frequencies was the main activity of content analysts in the 1930's and 1940's. Indeed, for many people that is how content analysis was defined. Berelson's book minus one chapter is almost wholly devoted to such frequency counts. Lasswell's content analyses were frequency counts of symbols; so for the most part were the RADIR studies at the Hoover Institute. The units could vary greatly: there were counts of column inches, of key words, of themes, of literary forms, of types of characters, etc. But up to ten years ago almost all studies had for their basic logic a comparison of the *frequency* of certain types of symbolic expression in different segments of text. The comparison might be of texts produced at different times, or by different authors, or in different ideological conditions, or in different states of feeling, or for different purposes; but for each comparison the test was that symbols of type x were significantly more frequent in one body of text than in another.

Such analyses continue to be discussed in this volume,[2] but the striking thing is that somehow a new kind of quantitative analysis had simultaneously occurred to many of the researchers at our conference. We found that we had each in his own way become much more interested in contingencies than in straight frequencies. It was a striking illustration of parallel but independent development in science.

CONTINGENCIES

Contingency analysis is a quantitative procedure. It involves counting. But the form of the hypothesis and of the critical observations is different from that in a simple frequency analysis. Contingency analysis asks not how often a given symbolic form appears in each of several bodies of text, but how often it appears in conjunction with other symbolic units.[3] The difference can be expressed

----

[2] For a recent example of a frequency content analysis, see Karin Dovring's chapter on land reform as a propaganda theme in F. Dovring, *Land and Labor in Europe, 1900-1950* (The Hague, 1956).

[3] In Osgood's chapter, in which contingency analysis receives its fullest and best-elaborated statement, he presents it in a pure form which sharply distinguishes it from frequency analysis. Following his procedure one ends up at a certain point with a matrix containing only plusses and minuses representing presence above a critical level (or not) of each symbol in each unit of tabulation. It should be noted, however, that it is quite possible to combine frequency and contingency measurement. We could ask how far the number of occurrences of symbol A departs from the ordinarily expected number if symbol B happens to be present in the environment. Such data would be conveyed if Osgood's Figure 3A or Raw Data Matrix had scale numbers in it instead of just plusses and minuses. Another combination of contingency and frequency data is found in this author's *Symbols of Democracy* (Stanford, Calif., 1952), in which normal equations are computed for predicting the frequency of one symbol given a certain frequency of certain other symbols in the environment, and then departures of frequency from the expected level are measured.

both most rigorously and most clearly as the difference between a simple probability statement and a conditional probability statement. Traditional frequency analysis sought to determine the probability that a specified symbol would be drawn in each unit trial as one examined a particular set of texts. Contingency analysis seeks to determine the probability that a specified symbol will be drawn, given that other specified symbols are in that or related units.

An early example, perhaps the earliest, is Baldwin's study of the letters of an old woman to which we have already referred.[4] This study, which appeared in 1942, showed the pattern of the woman's associations. It is quite fully described in Garraty's chapter. Ten years later the present author in one of the RADIR studies published a contingency analysis of the contexts in which the word "democracy" occurred, with a view to noting in which periods and countries it appeared along with words signifying representative government, or along with words signifying the common people, or along with words signifying freedom, these being three distinctive strands in democratic ideology. Although the units of analysis, because of their breadth, were not well suited to the purpose of contingency analysis, the contingency method seemed to open up interesting possibilities for analyzing the data. It did in fact show important differences between the Continental mass tradition of democracy and the Anglo-American libertarian tradition. Reporting a straight frequency count of the word "democracy" would under those circumstances have confounded the different ideological traditions.

In the same period, during the years just before our conference, the idea of contingency analysis was independently occurring to a number of us. In 1951 there appeared a report of an interdisciplinary seminar of psychologists and linguists held at Cornell in which two of the present authors, Osgood and Sebeok, participated. Its critique of existing methods of content analysis contained the statement that they "are limited to simple comparisons of frequencies rather than measuring the internal contingencies between categories."[5] Osgood has now devised a set of procedures for measuring such contingencies, and these he describes in Chapter 2.

In that chapter he presents three illustrative reports of applica-

---

[4] Baldwin, "Personal Structure Analysis," pp. 164-65.
[5] Carroll, Agard, Dulany, Newman, Newmark, Osgood, Sebeok, and Solomon, *Interdisciplinary Summer Seminar in Psychology and Linguistics*, p. 27.

tions of contingency analysis, one on radio speeches by W. J. Cameron, one on Goebbels' diary, and one on a psychotherapy protocol. He found, for example, that whenever Goebbels talked about factional conflicts among the Nazi elite he was more apt to refer to Hitler than when he talked about other relevant subjects. The Fuehrer came to his mind perhaps in the role of judge and arbiter of Goebbels' conflicts with other leaders. Osgood also found, to cite another example, that the particular psychotherapy patient whose interviews he analyzed talked a good deal about both his mother and heterosexual relations but did not talk about them together. When he talked about one he avoided talking about the other.

Sebeok and Saporta also report in their chapter another current use of contingency methods — on folklore material. They report, for example, a contingency in one culture between the notion of writing and the notion of the devil.

One might add that those of the conference participants who made a strong case for the instrumental model of communication were approaching the same set of problems to the extent that the context which they wished to take into account in assessing meanings was the verbal context provided by the rest of the communication. (Needless to say, this is only one part of the context they wished considered.) Mahl, for example, remarks that "The general classification of silences by all patients at all times in the interview as 'anxious' . . . would be uninterpretive. . . ." (Silence, of course, is a symbol which can be used in content analysis just as much as any noise which is a symbol. Indeed, the analysis of it as part of grammar goes back to Panini.) But silence is clearly a symbol with different meanings depending on its context. It means different things when it comes from a man who is relaxed than when it comes from one who is tense. Either state may lead him to interrupt his verbal flow, but silence in the context of a large number of broken sentences, errors, and slips is different from silence in their absence. The analyst who wishes to interpret a silence may look to evidence about the state of the author outside the communication, if he has such evidence. But if he has no such evidence, then it is the other symbols in the context of which a symbol occurs that enable him to choose between interpretations. Clearly it is those symbolic contexts that the analyst of contingencies is also examining. The problem of context, thus generally stated, was of interest to all the participants at the conference.

One may speculate as to what were the influences which account for the simultaneous emergence of interest in contingency relations by a number of content analysts previously working independently. Three sources of influence seem fairly clear: the psychological theory of association, the mathematical theory of information, and linguistics.

One of the conference participants commented that the contingency method as used in psychotherapy "is Freud's basic law of association." The subject under discussion when that point was made was the RADIR finding of a contingency in Russian editorials between affect for authority and affect for freedom; the RADIR analyst had interpreted that association as an indication of conflict. The analogy to the procedure of an analyst in psychotherapy is clear. The relevance of the principle of association (in its stimulus response version) to contingency analysis is also discussed in Osgood's chapter. Osgood formulates a principle for the appropriate length of the unit in which to count co-occurrences. The unit, he believes, should be such that associative connections may still be presumed to operate within it. That principle applies, assuming a purpose in which Osgood is indeed interested, that of studying the psychological process of association in the communicator. There was some discussion at the conference of how far this principle would apply where the matter of interest was policy, that is, an attempt to produce a certain effect upon the audience. If, for example, it is the policy of a newspaper to create a certain image of a public official, then the span within which appropriate items might be clustered would be that which might be assumed to affect the association structure of the reader, and that might be a different span from that appropriate to the associational structure of the author. On the other hand, doubt was expressed as to how far policy would be capable of modifying the contingency structure of a text or at least of eliminating contingencies. Osgood suggested that deliberate suppression of a contingency would create a negative contingency. A chance relation might be almost impossible to produce by plan. All these issues are unresolved and remain for future research to explore. However, the discussion of the issue among the participants in the conference makes clear that the idea of contingency analysis was derived by them in part from the analogy of association.

The influence of information theory as formulated by Claude Shannon is equally clear. The publicity which that development gave in academic circles to the method of deciphering verbal codes by means of transitional probabilities of symbols suggested to content analysts solutions to problems that had previously seemed insoluable. That is not to say that contingency analysis is an application of information theory; it is not. It is only an analogous development, sparked by the metaphor of information theory jargon. Still, the genealogy is clear. In *Symbols of Democracy* this author specifically credited Shannon and Weaver as the source of his idea for analysis and justified it as follows: "Words occur in clusters, not at random. A sentence, a paragraph, or an article containing the word 'caste' is more likely to contain the word 'India' than is one containing the word 'reindeer'. . . . A cryptanalyst can guess from the known words what the unknown words may be. He does this by establishing an actuarial model of the language. The model states the frequencies with which given words appear in association with other given words."

Osgood, who has carried the development of contingency analysis farther than anyone else, also shows the impact of the same set of concepts. He and his colleagues at the University of Illinois, where Shannon's book was published,[6] have worked on the application of information theory to psychology. The Cloze Procedure developed by Wilson Taylor is directly based upon its suggestions. Thus, we have an example of a familiar event in the history of science: a seminal idea in one field sparks an analogous development in another.

The third of the overdetermining influences in the development of contingency analysis was structural linguistics (see Chap. 4). The appropriateness of contingency analysis as a method for dealing with texts arises from the very structure of language, the common medium which all content analysts study. Human communication is accomplished by way of a large number of basic units (morphemes) put together in accordance with structural rules.

Recognition of this fact has led structural linguistics to the method of distributional analysis. This may be illustrated by Harris' "Discourse Analysis," published in 1952, which comes very close to being itself a contingency content analysis. "Descriptive linguistics," he says, "which sets out to describe the occurrence of elements in any stretch of speech, ends up by describing it primarily

---

[6] *Mathematical Theory of Communication.*

in respect to other elements of the same sentence."[7] Thus if a given morpheme, say "ran," appears in the identical context with another morpheme, say "ate" (e.g., the dog ran; the dog ate), then these are treated as equivalent in linguistic category (clearly not in meaning). These equivalences can in turn lead to secondary equivalences by analogy with the familiar mathematical axiom that things equal to the same thing are equal to each other. By applying such principles beyond the sentence to whole texts, Harris suggested a way of identifying characteristic formal features of a particular writer, or type of literature, or situation of writing. He developed only the method, merely suggesting its usefulness to social science. He said, "It remains to be shown as a matter of empirical fact that such formal correlations do indeed exist, that the discourses of a particular person, social group, style, or subject-matter exhibit not only particular meanings (in their selection of morphemes) but also characteristic formal features."[8] This is a challenge which social scientists have yet to pick up fully. In the chapters comprising the present volume there are several references to the advantages of studying formal features of a person's discourse rather than meanings if one would infer sensitive facts about him, for the former are far less consciously controlled than is his selection of morphemes. (This point is mentioned in almost every chapter.) But the content analyst does not wish to limit himself to the formal features of language alone. He concerns himself both with those and with the meanings selected. As Harris put it, "Any analysis which aimed to find out whether certain words, selected by the investigator, occur in the text or not, would be an investigation of the CONTENT of the text and would be ultimately based on the MEANINGS of the words selected."[9] While Harris excluded that kind of investigation from his own task as a linguist, what he did with regard to the co-occurrence of formal features was so obviously relevant to the problems of the content analyst, and his method so obviously appropriate in some respects to the meaning aspects of language too, that it would have been extraordinary if there had been no impact on content analysis.

As an example of the relevance of "Discourse Analysis" to content analysis let us mention the 12 sample grammatical rules of equivalence which Harris listed. Many forms of content analysis

---

[7] Harris, "Discourse Analysis," p. 2.

[8] Harris, "Discourse Analysis," p. 3.

[9] Harris, "Discourse Analysis," p. 5.

require the reduction of elaborate sentences to a limited number of simple assertions. See, for example, Chapter 2 on evaluative assertion analysis, which requires this kind of reduction (e.g., "The unruly prisoner shouted" becomes "the prisoner was unruly" and "the prisoner shouted"). Scores of content analysts have each independently struggled with making a grammar to meet their coding needs with regard to such cases, yet we find that the problem has largely been solved by the structural linguists, and in particular one can turn to Harris' 12 rules designed for the almost identical purpose in discourse analysis.

Linguistics thus suggested to content analysts the way to take account of the structures and contexts in which symbols occur by way of noting the symbolic environments of the symbols of interest. The meaning units which the content analyst counts are themselves not unambiguous. They are multipurpose, and when removed from their contexts are capable of a variety of interpretations. Critics have denigrated frequency analysis for a long time for precisely that reason — it fails to take account of the context and the different things a given symbol may mean. Content analysts have recognized this as a major problem. Taking a cue from linguistics, contingency analysis turns out to be a first step toward incorporating into content analysis some relevant data about the structures with which units are put together.

THE SELECTION OF UNITS OF ANALYSIS

The unit items which the content analyst counts can be of various kinds, for example words, phrases, ideas, sentences, paragraphs, columns, whole articles. Conceivably he might turn for units to the linguist, who for his purposes has the task of "identification of the minimal units in the code — the phonemes and morphemes" (Chap. 4). The conferees discussed whether there is a basic unit of meaning relevant to content analysis and if so what it is. Clearly, it is not the single word as determined by spaces on the page, though analyses can be and have often been conducted with the word as unit.[10] The morpheme is a smaller unit than content analysts

----

[10] The precise linguistic definition of a word is far from easy to state. Which of the following does one treat as the same or different words: come, coming; will, shall, won't; good-by; status quo; United States, America (meaning U.S.A.), America (meaning continent); rat (meaning rodent), rat (meaning bad man); bear (meaning animal), bear (meaning carry), bear (meaning have a child), bare.

normally care to work with. Both experimental work on how people read and write and theoretical work in linguistics suggest that there may be units more closely geared to the actual processes of communication than the single word. In the previous sentence the phrase "the single word" and not "the" or "single" or "word" was in some sense a unit of meaning. It was the phrase which the writer considered in the process of composition. If he had rearranged the sentence, it is that phrase as a unit which he would have moved. It was presumably that whole phrase, too, which the reader's eye saw as a unit and about which he thought, if he stopped to consider what was being said.

Clearly what we mean by a basic unit of meaning is that there is relatively little freedom for variation within it, but much freedom at its boundaries. Habit strengths are strong, transitional probabilities high within it but low across its boundaries. Such a unit, if it exists, is a kind of building block.

Such a unit is not necessarily the same for all purposes. An actual building block contains molecules which are the unit for the chemist and nuclear particles which are the unit for the physicist, yet the building block is itself a unit for the builder. The unit which we have been discussing under the metaphor of "building block" is the unit of semantic structure, the unit of meaningful discourse. For an analysis of pausal phenomena the unit might be different. One cannot stop for an "er" or "ah" in the middle of a syllable, but one can in the middle of a word. So the unit for a study of such pausal breaks is at least a syllable, and perhaps it is much longer than that. There may be definable points in the phrasing where such breaks occur. (Most often they do not occur at the syntactical breaking points.) For still other kinds of analysis the appropriate unit may be a much longer one such as the sentence or paragraph or article.

What this implies is that the unit counted should be at least as long as the unit in whatever is assumed to be the relevant psychological process in the communicating organism, and not so much longer as to lose sensitivity. Berelson[11] has reviewed the few studies that have been made of length of unit, and his description suggests that within a reasonable range it may not make too much difference.

We leave this matter of "basic units" vague. It is not one to which satisfactory answers yet exist. It is a problem the conferees discussed, but not one they could resolve. It is one of the problems

----

[11] *Content Analysis*, pp. 143 ff.

of content analysis to which psycholinguistics may help produce an answer. But as of now it is not clear how one identifies a basic unit of meaning.

To identify the basic atom of meaning would of course be a great help in content analysis, but it by no means follows that all analyses would proceed with such "atomic" units. Just as "the basic unit," whatever that is, is determined by the rules of linguistic structure, so other units may be determined by other relevant structures. The theme or slogan may be the appropriate unit for analyzing a propagandistic tract, the actor or the character may be the appropriate unit for analyzing an image, or the incident of action the appropriate unit for analyzing a story with a plot.

We are here implying a particularly important point made by a number of the authors of this volume: categories of analysis should be related to the structure of the material under discussion. Armstrong makes this point about literary materials, objecting to some earlier content analyses of literary materials in which the items counted had nothing to do with literature as such. George makes this point about propaganda analysis: he finds that symbol counts which took no account of the structure of strategic planning in the propaganda yielded few inferences of use. For example, a count of critical references to Britain was not likely to reveal much of the intentions of Nazi propaganda, for it might make critical references for many different purposes and in many different ways. Saporta and Sebeok make the same point with regard to such material as charms, riddles, portents, etc., which conform to strict formal rules; the appropriate unit to use in such cases is a unit of the structure.

Since most inferences are based on which of alternative symbolic forms actually appear, and since structural constraints partly determine the range of alternative possible forms, it is clear that for most purposes what one counts needs to have some relation to the structure of the piece examined. A song, a poem, a folk story, a charm, an editorial, a five-minute radio talk, each has its set literary form. A psychiatric hour has a beginning, a middle, and an end. A story has a plot and a poem has meter and rhyme form. An analysis of the content of any of these has to take account of such structures. So, too, analysis of propaganda may need to take account of the strategies of persuasion. Mark Anthony's famous speech in *Julius Caesar* is an example: a structural constraint on the speech was the need to start from the predispositions of the audience in order to move them gradually to the desired position. A mode of analysis which does not permit one to take account of such structural considerations but requires the treatment of statements at all points as alike is likely to be a failure.

Armstrong, in his chapter, makes this case particularly strongly. The units he uses for the analysis of folk stories from the Dakotas and from Suriname are units of story action. They conform to his criterion that the units be directly related to the hypotheses which research is investigating. Their limits are set by changes in the situation described. They are units of behavior of characters in the story, not units of the language in which the story is told.

Too little use has been made of such behavioral units. To explain why such units are useful, let me cite an example of a study with units similar to that of Armstrong's though not nearly so well defined. This author once did an analysis of a series of Russian short stories. The unit was an incident of interaction of two persons, for example a single conversational exchange. Typically there would be three to six of these on a page. The striking result was the high proportion of inappropriate or noncomplementary behaviors of the two actors, for instance actor 1 saying "I love you," actor 2 saying "I hate you," or actor 1 saying "I love you," actor 2 remaining impassive, etc. Absent from the stories were the normal expected responses to a stimulus. We cite this analysis precisely because the unit was subject to criticism for vagueness. That would be serious, however, only if there were some systematic relationship between noncomplementary behavior and the precise demarcation of the beginnings and ends of units. That is unlikely. Noncomplementarity probably pervaded the spirit of the texts, and would have appeared no matter what size of action unit within a wide range had been selected. Probably if two coders came up with quite different identifications of interactions they would still make the same substantive finding. On the other hand, it is likely that any attempt to impose a rigid verbal unit would have obscured the finding. Noncomplementarity would not be found in any randomly selected page, or 100 words, or perhaps even paragraph, for these would cut across the episodes of interaction. It would be extremely hard to define a unit of verbal forms that would conform to the limits of an interaction. That illustrates why, if our hypothesis involves an inference from the actions described in a text to some other social variable, the action itself is usually the appropriate unit, not some more convenient verbal unit in which the finding may not hold.

From the point we have just made, it should be clear that one focus of the conference was on the problem of how to make the items counted relevant to the inferences with which the researcher is concerned. In this connection we considered, besides the matter of unit definition, two other matters: (1) the differences between instrumental and representational communications, and (2) the prospect of finding general categories which would be relevant to more than one study.

REPRESENTATIONAL AND INSTRUMENTAL COMMUNICATIONS

There is something important at which the conferees were driving in the distinction between representational and instrumental communication. It crops up in several chapters of the present work. What do we mean by these words? There was undoubtedly some difference of opinion. A rough definition was presented in the Introduction[12] and we have noted other definitions in the chapters by George, Osgood, and Mahl. Clearly the terms can refer to at least three different things: a kind of communication, an aspect of a communication, and a model for analysis. Let us illustrate.

Kind of communication. The scream "ouch" in pain is representational communication — it accurately represents the state of its author. A lie is instrumental communication.

Aspect of communication. The single communication "Friends, Romans, countrymen, lend me your ears" had a representational aspect as a demand to be heard (it said what it meant), and an instrumental aspect in its use of terms of identification.

Model for analysis. The counting of the frequency of a name as an index of interest in the person named is analysis according to a representational model — it assumes that the text represents the state of its author. Reading between the lines is analysis according to the instrumental model.

Cutting across these distinctions are some others. The notion that an author is somehow represented by his communication may

----

[12] "Representational" means that something in the words of the message may have indicatorial validity regardless of circumstances, and it is at the message that the analyst looks. "Instrumental" in a rough way signifies that the important point is not what the message says on the face of it but what it conveys, given context and circumstances.

refer to representation of different levels of the author's complex psyche. The communication may *represent* his most basic associative processes, or his "true" conscious attitudes, or the overt attitudes which he wishes to communicate.

Cutting across all of these distinctions is another important one. Sometimes above we take "representation" to mean that something in a communication indexes in a stable, recurrent fashion something about the author — what Alexander George would call "direct" content indicators. In that sense the anxiety-revealing speech disturbances which Mahl (who introduced the distinction) analyzes are representations. At other times, however, the term "representational" is taken to refer to "the face validity of the manifest lexical content of a message" (George), or in other words the dictionary meaning of a sentence. In that usage, if we take the symbols present to index anything else than what they say (even if the indexing relation is completely stable), or if for an index we use any aspects of the communication other than the lexical items, we characterize the operation as "instrumental."

All of these somewhat different usages were applied by the conferees in the discussion of a common core of problems. Our task now is to summarize this discussion, and to do so we must obviously choose one set of definitions and stick with it. In the discussion to follow we take as "representational" any content feature which across the body of text with which we are concerned indexes ("directly" in George's terminology) something (anything) about the source. "Instrumental" we take to be that which is manipulated (and thus varied in its relation to the thing being indexed so as to achieve the author's objectives).[13] We have in short accepted the first of the two options in the paragraph just above. The crux of the distinction there lies in how far strategy by the author modifies the indicatorial value of the communications feature we are observing.

Turning back to the three options in the first paragraph of this section, we shall choose to define here not two different kinds of communications but two different aspects of a communication. A man is hot and sweaty; he would like a drink. He wipes his brow and says to his host, "My, it's hot." The representational aspect of the communication is that the man is hot; its instrumental but unspoken purpose is not to convey this fact to the world but to pro-

----

[13] This differs from Mahl's usage since an indicator deviating from manifest lexical content may be quite stable as an indicator. Mahl, in short, selects the second of the options mentioned in the paragraph just above.

duce the answer "Would you like something to drink?" If it fails
to produce the desired result the hot man may vary his strategy
and make his communication explicit. He may say "Please give
me a drink." That statement is not only instrumental to achieving
a certain result; it also represents once more the fact that the
speaker is hot and thirsty, for it indicates in a well-established
way a fact about the speaker which his strategy did not hide.

The rather complicated statements above about our usage of the
terms instrumental and representational may be summarized with
some precision if we introduce a formal terminology and set of
formal rules. A source may have n states $(s_1, s_2 \ldots s_n)$. The
source may independently of these states adopt any one of m
manipulative strategies $(m_1, m_2 \ldots m_m)$. The universe may independently be in any one of p states $(u_1, u_2 \ldots u_p)$. Finally the
content emitted by the source may be in any one of r states $(c_1, c_2$
$\ldots c_r)$. The terms representational and instrumental were used to
discuss assertions about dependency of states in C on states in S
and/or M and/or U.

A representational assertion maps some element c_k into some
element s_i. More broadly we may also call an assertion representational if it maps some element c_k into some combination s_iu_j.
The definition of representational assertions which Mahl uses im-
poses a further constraint. He calls an assertion representational
only if the semantic meaning of an element c_k which maps into an
element s_i is the assertion that s_i is a fact.

An instrumental assertion maps some element c_k into some element m_h. A broader definition would call an assertion instrumental
if it mapped some element c_k into some combination $m_h u_j$ or (even
broader) into some combination $m_hs_iu_j$.

Since we have asserted M to be independent of S, it is clear that
any assertion mapping an element c_k into some m_h (an instrumental
assertion in the narrow sense) implies the absence of a stable relationship of c_k to any s_i (cf. the example of a mathematical proof
in the discussion below).

Obviously, the only complete analysis is one mapping elements c_k
into combinations $m_hs_iu_j$. However, we are often lacking in good
evidence of which state in M exists. Thus it would often be desirable to find relationships of C (content) and S (source) which are
negligibly affected by M (manipulative strategy). That is the
justification of seeking to establish representational assertions even

about communications which we know to be in many respects consciously manipulated.

Almost every communication has both representational and instrumental aspects. The weight given each may vary. We can set up a scale. A mathematical proof is close to a purely instrumental communication. It is designed to achieve a certain objective, in this case a cognitive one. That objective is controlling. Without making the proof wrong there are but few aspects of it which one can vary to represent one's own peculiar psychic conditions. The state of the speaker is indeed conveyed in some minor ways, but relatively few. On the whole, any two statements of the proof will be much alike regardless of where or when they are given, for the strategies are limited and purpose is controlling. Since the text of the proof is that stable, its relation to the state of the source is highly unstable.

At the other extreme there is obsessional behavior of certain kinds in which the calculated use of communication to achieve a result is less easily discernible than is its quality as conveying the state of the communicator.

This example, however, immediately cries out for qualification. It is perfectly clear that obsessional behavior is not unmotivated. One of Freud's major contributions may be considered to be the application of instrumental interpretations to unconscious processes. The Freudian interpretation of dreams, for example, gives a central position to purpose, designated as wish. The representational symbols are bent to the fulfillment of the wish. So, too, during a psychiatric interview, as Mahl points out, the patient's statements are not interpretable as pure representations of his state, but are rather devices being used to achieve certain objectives, often with regard to the psychiatrist. The patient tries to attract his attention or to get his sympathy and says what will serve these purposes.

So the instrumental aspect appears in all communications, not just in manipulative propaganda of the kind which Alexander George analyzed, though its role in that may be greater. Likewise, a representational element exists and may be sought in the most calculated of instrumental communications. An example of an analysis which uses the representational element in highly manipulated communications is *Movies*, by Wolfenstein and Leites. It is a content analysis designed to identify national myths in one of the most calculated of the mass media. Movies are made for the box office. Every shot is designed to appeal to an imagined audience. It does not represent the aesthetic taste or the emotional states of the authors or directors in any immediate way. Individual idiosyncrasies are ironed out in the collective process of production. Yet in the very process of collectively producing an expression of what the producers conceive to be the fantasy life of their audience, they are representing something about their own image of the culture in which they live. In that lies the creative element in the making of a movie, which emerges despite the influence of box-office considerations. There are choices to be made which express the character and environment of the chooser. There is a story to be thought up, pieces to be put together; there is room for associations to float, controlled of course by one's image of the audience's associations. And in this process the fantasies and values of the culture somehow get expressed. There is thus room for analysis of movies, not only in terms of the instrumental calculations which go into them but also as representations of their makers.

Similarly, the fact that a propagandist is given instructions does not eliminate a representational element in his propaganda. A Soviet propagandist, for example, may be told that neutralism in a third country is useful to the Soviets at the moment, and that attacks should be replaced by flattery and encouragement. It is still his problem to decide what constitutes flattery and encouragement, what neutrals will like and respond to. There is thus for him a realm of initiative undetermined by policy, and in that he may reveal some of his images of life.

It may be hard sometimes to know whether an instrumental or a representational assumption gives us a more correct inference as to the reasons for particular symbolic behavior. The contingency noted earlier between symbols of freedom and symbols of authority in *Pravda* editorials was there interpreted as *representing* a conflict within Soviet ideology. It could be taken, however, that symbols of freedom were introduced *instrumentally* to make authoritarian statements more palatable to the readers. There is a third and most likely alternative, namely, that both things were happening at once. But even if we choose to look for representational behavior, we must, as Alexander George has pointed out, be aware of the bounds set by instrumental considerations within which representation of the communicator can operate.

A content analysis which deals with highly instrumental material such as propaganda may work well for a while with certain categories and then break down when the symbolic strategy of the communicator changes. The uses made of given symbols may change in the middle of the count in response to strategy's demands, and entirely new indices may become the important ones for the behavior in which we are interested. Thus in a psychotherapeutic interview the patient's strategy objective may be to get the therapist to talk at a time when the therapist is not so inclined. The patient may try silence, attempting to outwait the therapist. When this does not work he can try telling a funny story to arouse a response. If this does not work he can try being insulting and provocative. The purpose may remain constant as the strategies change. The count of any one symbolic behavior among those chosen for instrumental purposes will be fruitless.

The same thing may be true in the political sphere. A standard pattern of Soviet strategy has been to accuse opponents of exactly that which they intended to do themselves. Stalin used this device extensively and, as Myron Rush has shown in his insightful content analysis of recent Soviet documents,[14] Khrushchev has also used it extensively. For example, Malenkov was accused of being responsible for agricultural policies of which Khrushchev himself was the author. Here is a strategy. Clearly one cannot devise a simple counting procedure in the presence of it. One cannot count everything that Soviet leaders criticize and conclude that really they are for them. That would lead us to conclude that really the Soviet leaders are in favor of capitalism, the United States, production failures, etc. Nor, however, can one count the things that Soviet leaders criticize and assume that those are the things they are against, for from time to time they adopt the strategy of disarming opposition to what they favor by attacking that very thing and blaming it on the enemy of the moment. As Alexander George has argued, the context must be the guide to the strategy being used. Rush's book is an illuminating example of the use of all possible contextual clues for the selection of the appropriate symbols to look for at any given time.

Contingency analysis is a different, more rigorously quantitative way of trying to get at some contextual factors. It of course limits the contexts considered to those in the text. It does, however, permit one to interpret symbol A differently when it appears accompanied by symbol B than when it appears accompanied by symbol C. This

---

[14] M. Rush, *The Rise of Khrushchev* (Washington, D.C., 1958). See also Leites, Bernaut, and Garthoff, "Politburo Images of Stalin," for a similar analysis of the speeches on Stalin's seventieth birthday.

is one way to take account of changes in strategy. However he does it, the analyst who is dealing with instrumental texts must take account of the fluctuating strategies of the moment.

While in principle all strategies can fluctuate to meet changing conditions, it is not in practice the case that all strategies do fluctuate within delimited sectors which may be of interest. There are situations within which a uniform set of categories can successfully be applied to a body of texts to make inferences even regarding strategy. But we should remain clearly aware that where that is done we are making a hidden assumption of continuity of strategy. An example would be a study of testimonials in magazine advertisements. Within the institutional context of the American market system it is generally pretty clear that the objective of testimonials is to increase the number of customers buying a product by communicating to them the fact of a positive evaluation of it from someone with whom they identify positively. There is little reason to expect this strategy to change in any normal course of events, although a little imagination can produce hypothetical exceptions, for example using testimonials to change the image of a product so as to avoid government regulatory actions. Normally, however, one can operate in terms of the inference that the appearance of a testimonial represents the desire of a firm to sell more of its product to sectors of the public who could be expected to identify favorably with the kind of person issuing the testimonial. Categories based on these instrumental assumptions could be designed and used in a highly uniform and standardized fashion.

Thus there are situations where even with highly instrumental materials fairly standard categories may enable us to make some inferences as to the intentions of the communicator, but the problem always remains with the analyst to consider whether the assumptions he is using are still valid, or whether instrumental constraints are leading the author to use different symbols at different times for the same purpose and the same symbols at different times for different purposes.

STANDARDIZED CATEGORIES FOR CONTENT ANALYSIS

The above considerations lead us directly to another issue on which the conferees did not fully agree. That is the issue of the desirability of finding standardized content analysis categories that could be used by different researchers in different studies to the end that studies would become more comparable and additive. Clearly this is a laudable aspiration and one that has been with content analysts from the beginning. Lasswell popularized the often-copied categories of "pro-self," "pro-other," "anti-self," "anti-other." White's value analysis provides another set of standardized categories. Thompson's motif index is widely used though Sebeok, Saporta, and Armstrong found it unsatisfactory for lack of theoretical basis.

In other fields of social science general tools of a similar kind have proved of great use. The intelligence quotient is such a standardized measure. In studies of the relation of intelligence to some other variable, it is most convenient that there is a standardized measure of at least one of the variables. Garraty noted how useful it would be for historians if relevant "precut" content analysis categories existed.

It is questionable, however, how ready we are to establish standard measures of that sort in content analysis. Such a measure is convenient when a considerable number of researchers are working on the same variable, and when someone succeeds in working out good categories for that variable. It is doubtful that either of those criteria can be met in most areas of content analysis.

Let us take for the moment Osgood's contingency analysis of Mr. Cameron's Ford Hour speeches. It is a study of the structure of an ideology. We may want to ask ourselves what general categories of ideology there are which we want to use in the characterization not only of Mr. Cameron's but of other ideological statements. Certainly a most obvious one is the category of conservative. A number of scholars have conducted studies of ideological texts in terms of conservatism-liberalism. But conservatism is not a single coherent thing; as a category it is a catchall. Intelligence is a catchall, too. As measured it consists of a number of weighted discrete components. Perhaps then we could look at the clusters revealed in the contingency relationships among symbols in the Cameron speeches and come up with a proposed definition of conservatism in terms of contingencies of set symbols. "Perhaps," however, is the word to be underlined. It seems highly dubious that what one would want to call anyone else's conservatism, even if one restricted oneself to contemporary American culture, would be expressed in the same set of symbols and in the same relationships among them. We are probably not yet at the point where we know how to construct a useful content index of conservatism. But here the word to underline is "probably." The way we will know when we can construct a good enough index so that many people will use it is when someone actually develops one.

Until that time there is a good deal to be said for *ad hoc* categories. Armstrong's classification of objectives in folk stories is such a set of categories. If one asks why the items discovered were grouped under a particular heading to form a category, there is no answer except Armstrong's feeling that they were somehow alike. Another example of that sort of content analysis is Nicholas Vakar's analysis of *Pravda* editorials.[15] What Vakar did was to take the most common nouns from *Pravda* editorials; this gave him a list to compare with the most common nouns in standardized word lists of French, German, English, and pre-Soviet Russian. He then grouped the words in each list to show differences in emphasis on concepts of different types. For example, he found that the pre-Soviet Russian vocabulary and to some extent the French gave "greater emphasis to the expressive aspects of the self" than did the English and German. But such words (feeling, soul, thought, faith, mind) have disappeared from *Pravda*'s main vocabulary. On the other hand, in the *Pravda* vocabulary verbs implying domination or manipulation number eight out of the top 20 and appear elsewhere only in two examples from the German list.

One of the conferees was troubled by this procedure, for, to put it in his words, "If another analyst were to do the same thing, he would come up with a different grouping of words and thus a different set of categories of analysis. That is what makes it hard to accept." One can only agree that that is the fact; two persons looking at the same list of words will choose to group them under different central concepts. They will in short be looking for different things. Not all the conferees, however, agreed that that was bad. To some of us it seemed quite legitimate, in the absence of a prior theory, to make up the theory as one went along, grouping together symbolic elements which seemed in some sense to go together. If one is struck by the predominance of a certain kind of symbolic behavior in a text, it seems an abnegation of one's critical intelligence to refuse to note that behavior as a category because one has not started out realizing its significance or because it has not been identified in other social theories or pieces of social research.

----

[15] N. Vakar, "The Mass Communication Index: Some Observations on Communist Russian Discourse," *Symposium,* 10 (1956), 42-59.

What the analyst does who uses *ad hoc* categories is to form his hypotheses and validate them out of the same set of data.[16] One can only agree that this is not so good a scientific procedure as getting one's hypotheses first from one set of data or experiences, and then validating them on another. But it is by no means an unknown or totally invalid procedure. There are indeed situations where one has no choice. There may exist only a single set of data. One is then engaged in a kind of detective work. One studies the data, rearranges them, and puts them together in different ways until one finds that hypothesis which explains the puzzling aspects of them. Examples of this kind of procedure are common in natural history. One examines a set of bones to try to reconstruct a pre-historic animal. One may hope to find later another specimen that may confirm or disprove one's reconstruction, but for the moment the validation of the hypothesized reconstruction is in the degree to which it accounts for all the facts in the same set of bones which was used to get the idea.

So, too, the content analyst who has a set of texts which in the fullness of their circumstances are historically unique may be justified in coding them under whatever categories seem best to bring out the significant differences within them. An analysis of the speeches of Mr. Cameron, a unique and unreproducible individual, may well tabulate those symbols which Mr. Cameron himself used regardless of the generality of these categories.

In the Cameron study the list of symbols tabulated in the first place was *ad hoc*, but the grouping of them into clusters was objectively validated by contingency analysis. That is why the study and the contingency method it represents are such great advances over previous methods. In previous studies the symbols initially counted were determined *ad hoc*. They would then be grouped into broader classes relevant to interesting hypotheses. These groupings were also *ad hoc*. Thus one might decide that concern with progress would be indexed by a list of counted terms including progress, advance, modern, old-fashioned, forward-looking, change, conservatism, etc. But there was no rigorous standard for inclusion or exclusion. Contingency analysis, while it does not tell us what to look for in the first place (that still requires either intuition or exhaustiveness), does enable us to determine what symbols do in

---

[16] Alexander George discusses in some detail the relation of hypothesis formation and hypothesis testing. See his *Propaganda Analysis*.

point of fact go together in any given body of text.[17] It therefore begins to open the way toward developing standardized categories by making it feasible to justify and test the relevance of component elements empirically.

There is no single simple answer to the problem of the standardization of content analysis categories. There are gains and losses in standardization. There are times for standardization, there are times for rigorous but unique categories, and there are even times for the free play of the analyst's intuition on what goes with what.

Nevertheless it is clear that for many purposes the development of some kinds of standardized categories is both desirable and sure to come as content analysis progresses. Linguistic uniformities in the medium of communication are likely to provide some of the bases for standardized categories. We noted above, for example, a list of 12 rules of grammatical equivalence developed by Harris. These could become such a set of standard coding rules as they become more widely known by content analysts.

In this conference discussion three areas were identified where attempts at standardized procedures seem likely to be justified soon by reason of both needs and possibilities. These areas in which there was felt to be a possibility of developing standard categories were measuring tensions, valence, and, finally, linguistic categories.

MEASURING TENSION

It might prove possible to develop a set of categories designed to test whether a speaker or writer — the categories might be different for oral and written communication — is under tension at the moment of communicating. George Mahl's speech disturbance analysis is directed toward finding such a measure of anxiety in psychotherapeutic interviews, and it does indeed seem that certain forms of hesitation and speech imperfection do give anxiety away. During World War II there were attempts made to apply to Hitler's speeches similar analyses of clues of tensions. Since the confer-

---

[17] Up to now, in the absence of any means for testing what symbols properly formed a cluster, it has been hard to avoid lumping together things that were different, or counting equivalent categories as separate. One of the problems in content analysis has been that almost any category can be made to seem the most frequent by subdividing the others finely enough. There is no natural standard for fineness of categories. A contingency analysis enables us to set such standards because it provides a measurement of distance between symbols. We can establish a specific distance criterion for a category.

ence Charles Osgood has been working on a set of suicide notes which promises interesting results. John Garraty indicates how valuable a similar measure would be to a historian studying the documents of a past great man. He himself reported attempts at using such devices as the adjective-verb ratio on letters written by Theodore Roosevelt, Wilson, and others, at moments when he knew them to be under tension. He would like to be able to look at historical documents, at least of the more spontaneous kinds such as handwritten letters, and be able to say that at that time Wilson, or whoever it might be, was under stress.[18] Alexander George discussed the usefulness of being able to look at a propaganda document, pick out some topic, and say of it, "This is something they are really concerned about." James Jenkins reported an experimental finding that subjects with high anxiety scores produced unusual word associations and wrote things with unusual linguistic structures.

Thus the interest exists in a variety of fields, and at least for some types of material the problem may be soluble. A standardized measure of tension for materials of a specified kind is conceivable.

Let us consider briefly some of the conditions for the successful development of a measure of that sort. We noted above that invariant verbal categories were not likely to be useful where the message was being instrumentally manipulated. Therefore, in this connection the first and most important thing we can say is that the measure must be of things outside the realm of conscious manipulation. No measure of tension based, for example, on explicit statements about being worried is likely to work, as Mahl points out in his chapter. There are alternative strategies of rehearsing and denying anxiety, and except with the help of clues in a rather extensive context it is not possible to say whether presence or absence of statements of worry attests to its presence or attests to its absence.

Mahl's speech disturbance measure meets this criterion. Try as they may, most persons are not able to control verbal slips, sentence breaks, "ah's," and stutters when they are tense.

Other measures may seek not that which is uncontrollable, but that which people make no attempt to control. Linguistic categories

---

[18] Both George and Garraty have published on Wilson, George specifically attempting to elucidate the psychology of the man from the historical records. See A. L. and J. George, *Woodrow Wilson and Col. House: A Personality Study* (New York, 1956), and J. A. Garraty, *Woodrow Wilson: A Great Life in Brief* (New York, 1956).

may provide examples of that. Our culture attaches little social value to such things as word order. If we had data on the frequency distribution of the syntactical alternatives in language we might be able to spot mood changes by changes in the choices among them. Generally speaking, if one can find indices in realms which persons do not attempt to control, then standardized measures of the author's state of feeling may prove possible.

MEASURING VALENCE

Similar considerations apply to categories for measuring valence, though with at least one important qualification. For reasons which will prove quite instructive, one is likely to be interested in measuring the explicit judgments expressed in a text, regardless of whether they represent the true feelings of the communicator. (In the case of tension we are normally interested in the source rather than the text.) In short, we may be interested here in making an inference not about the true feelings of the communicator but in measuring the explicit valence in the text he emits. Why that is so we shall examine in some detail in a moment, but before we do so let us consider the interest in and feasibility of valence measures.

Probably the majority of all content analysis studies done to date have used some valence measure. Campaign tracts are characterized as for or against a given side. International propaganda is characterized as friendly or hostile to national entities. Open-ended interview responses are characterized as for or against. The Lasswellian categories of "pro-self," "anti-self," "pro-other," and "anti-other" are widely used. Yet the methods used in most studies for judging valence leave something to be desired by way of rigor. Reliability may turn out to be reasonably good because human beings are so sensitively geared to this dimension of intercourse and because the texts analyzed are often quite blatantly partisan. Yet there are always subtle marginal cases, texts not easily characterized, and biases arising from the context. The problem of validly measuring valence in texts remains an important one.

That is the problem which Osgood attacked with the method he calls evaluative assertion analysis, which is described in Chapter 2. It is an extension of interests represented by his work on the semantic differential. Semantic differential data always bring out the evaluative factor as the most important of all. Osgood's evaluative assertion analysis applies this finding about the connotations of words to the analysis of texts. He uses the evaluative leaning of common words to measure attitudes toward objects referred to in a text while hiding from the coder the proper names which would give clues to the context in which the object was named. The method is successful. Thus we now have at least one established standardized measure of valence in communication content independent of the context.

The feasibility and usefulness of such a measure applied to a text regardless of instrumental use may suggest to the reader that some of our earlier comments were overstated. The careful reader may have noted that the above remarks asserted that context-free measurement of symbolic forms which are instrumentally manipulated is apt to be misleading, and that therefore standardization of content measures is most feasible for behaviors below the level of conscious manipulation. Yet now we are pointing to the practicability and value of measuring explicit valences which appear on the face of a text, and nothing is more often manipulated instrumentally than expressions of evaluation. Clearly there is a range of issues here which need clarification, and it is on these issues that much of the discussion among the assembled content analysts focused. We can clarify our conclusions if we make explicit the different purposes we try to serve by content analysis. In trying to lay down rules for use of a tool we must specify what we are trying to do with it. The rules for swinging an ax are different when one is chopping than they are when one is using the back end of it as a hammer.

In Table 2 we once again list at the left, as we did in Table 1, the major uses of content analysis: description, inference to ante-

Table 2

	Possibility of Standardized Categories			
	Symbolic Characteristics			
	Variable		Invariant	
Uses of Content Analysis	Instru-mental	Represen-tational	Instru-mental	Represen-tational
Description	+	+	+	+
Inferences to Antecedents	0	0	+	+
Inferences to Effects	+	+	+	+

cedents, inferences to effects. This time, however, we match these uses not against kinds of analysis but against kinds of texts, or, more accurately, kinds of textual characteristics to which the analysis can be applied. We distinguish now between those symbolic characteristics which are manipulated or varied with circumstances and those which in any particular situation emerge as a kind of automatic reflex. This is substantially but not exactly the distinction between instrumental or purposively controlled communication and representational communication. We noted that there could be within institutional limits instrumental behaviors either so obviously useful for a given purpose (e.g., testimonials) or so dogmatized that their presence justifies a uniform inference. So, too, there can be communication which, though representational in a limited time span, is unstable over a longer one even though not calculated for a purpose. A fad is an example. Different slang expressions express the same mood over relatively short intervals. What our generation would have described as "hot" our children describe as "cool." Thus, variations in usage which require attention to the context and which limit what can be learned by counts of uniform categories arise even in noninstrumental uses of language. Yet for many practical purposes the important variabilities in use of symbols are the instrumental ones, and the invariant patterns are representational.

The question we attempt to answer with Table 2 is where standardized categories are apt to be effectively used and where they are not. Clearly they can be useful, as we have noted, where the patterns of symbolic use are stable, but they can also be used, even if the material is instrumentally manipulated, where the purpose is purely description. The interesting issues on which the conferees focused arise in the situations represented by the lower left portion of the table, the application of standardized categories to inferences about instrumentally manipulated material.

The proposition implied by the table is that quantitative techniques of content analysis with highly standardized categories are not likely to be useful for inferences about the antecedents of instrumentally manipulated communications but that they might be useful for inferences about responses to them. This is an assertion which is not self-evident; it needs justification. The implicit assumption here is that we are dealing with a mass media system. Content analysis, as all of social science, is so much a part of literate civilization that we are apt to take that assumption for granted and to forget that we are doing so. The assumption is that the act of producing a communication is the act of an individual or of a single and identifiable organized group, while the act of responding to a communication may well be a repeated and scattered act of many different individuals located in many different contexts. One can imagine a reverse situation; then the conclusions in the table would be reversed. An example of this reversal would be a study of American English as perceived and responded to by British travelers in the United States. Here there would be a mass source and individual, easily identified respondents. But in most of our studies it is the other way around. In the usual situation, if we study a text with a view to making an inference about its antecedents, we are studying it in order to learn something about one specific group of persons who can be located in time and place and whose history, prejudices, purposes, and operational code can be identified. Variations in the text can and should be interpreted in terms of their particular strategy.

If on the other hand we look at a text with a view to making inferences about its consequences, we sometimes, in fact often, must think of the words as having a life of their own abstracted from context, for the contexts in which they operate are so varied that we cannot summarize them. Millions of persons may hear the words in as many different contexts. The questions put to ourselves will therefore often have to be about the effects of the text itself as an isolated factor, regardless of the various contexts in which it may occur.

Not everyone who studies communication effects uses this mass media model in which the message received is an anonymous nondescript or rather "multidescript" entity. The psychiatrist, for example, is concerned with a particular person's responses. Even the propaganda analyst who is concerned with mass media may nevertheless find that he has to classify responses by broad categories of situations into which the message comes. Some of the most important findings of modern communications research have been on the ways in which the predispositions of the respondent shape his attention to, perception of, and response to a message.[19] Nevertheless, the multiplicity of ways in which a message is received in
----
[19] See C. Hovland, A. Lumsdaine, and F. Sheffield, *Experiments on Mass Communication* (Princeton, N.J., 1949); C. Hovland, I. L. Janis, and H. Kelly, *Communication and Persuasion* (New Haven, Conn., 1953); B. Berelson, P. F. Lazarsfeld, and W. McPhee, *Voting* (Chicago, 1954).

a mass media situation means that it makes more sense to describe the message itself as an independent variable than it would if we were concerned with a single receiver and could describe the message as received instead of the message itself.

Clearly the message itself is a separate entity from either its antecedents or its consequences. One could conceivably do a content analysis of messages washed ashore in sealed bottles dropped overboard by unknown persons. Inferences about the antecedents of the messages would be quite free from the helpful warping provided by knowledge of the author. But in real life it seldom makes sense to proceed in that way; one can gain a great deal by taking account of all the instrumental considerations which went into the unique event of composition. The author of mass media materials, however, to some small degree approaches the situation of the sailor dropping the bottle over the side. He does not know who will listen. For the analyst of effects it therefore makes sense to make what inferences he can on the basis of the text alone, regardless of the context of the receipt. It follows that for greater generality our table should really be relabeled. The second row should be labeled "Inferences about identified communicators, whether senders or receivers," and the third row should be labeled "Inferences about unidentifiable communicators."

We were alerted to this set of considerations in the first place by the conclusion that measures of tension could best be made with invariant noninstrumental aspects of communications, while measures of valence seemed useful even where applied to symbols that were instrumentally manipulated. The reason is now clear. The measure of tension is a measure designed to learn something about the specific author of the communication. The measure of valence, among its other uses, is one for the purpose of estimating what is coming into a diverse audience of interest to us. An evaluative assertion analysis of newspaper bias in a campaign, for example, might be for the purpose of learning whether the audience is receiving equivalent stimulus material from the different sides. Its finding might be entirely wrong for any one reader because of his deliberate exercise of selection among reading materials. But we have to wash out that kind of idiosyncrasy if we are trying to generalize about communication to a large and diverse audience.

The general rule is simply that the more one can conveniently learn about the specific language use of the persons of interest, the less sense it makes to rely on standardized categories based on the language itself without interpretation of its private significance to him. On the other hand, the less one is able to say about the specifics of the language use of the persons of interest in the case of interest, the more sense do standardized categories make. There seems to be no issue of principle beyond that.

Valence seems to be something which can be reasonably well judged without reference to the context in which a statement is made. Osgood finds relatively high reliability of coding of masked evaluative material. In that respect expressions of valence seem to be relatively closely geared to the linguistic code in which communication takes place. One of the characteristics of language of which linguists have made a good deal is that there can be agreement on what the code is in the presence of sharp differences in the uses to which it is put. Thus one of the common assertions of linguists is that they do not need a sample from a culture, but only one good informant to tell them about a language. For if a symbol does not communicate to the informant, regardless of whether it is one he would accept or like, then it is not an effective part of the code. In the same way, judgments of valence communicated may have a validity quite apart from the context.

Osgood's evaluative assertion analysis relies upon judges who are users of the linguistic code in which the communication takes place. For the reasons just noted, the judges succeed in making reliable judgments. One wonders whether it is not possible to take a further step and identify the factors which lead the judges to judge as they do. Since in evaluative assertion analysis the judges see only the text and not the context, there must be something in the words themselves which conveys the valence. That which communicates the valence may lie in part in the evaluative loading of particular words; the semantic differential technique can document that. But it must also lie in part in the linguistic structure of the message, for one can presumably make sentences of different intensities by rearranging the same evaluative words. The problem is to identify the different ways within the linguistic code in which evaluation can be expressed. This brings us directly to the central problem in the relation of linguistics and content analysis: how can we relate categories of the language to categories of meaning; what are the different ways in which a single idea can be expressed?

LINGUISTICS AND CONTENT ANALYSIS

On the face of it, the relation of linguistics to content analysis should be a close one, but historically it has not been. Both linguists and content analysts analyze texts and are concerned with language patterns, but two differences in their approaches have kept them apart.

Linguists have not been interested in meanings, but only in "the distribution of forms, that is, their privilege of occurrence in relation to other forms . . ." (Chap. 4). Content analysts have not been interested in forms, but only in the meanings which these forms convey.

Linguists historically have not been interested in frequencies. They have tended to consider only whether it was allowable for a given structure to appear, not how often it appeared. Content analysts have been interested only in quantities, not in the difference between that which was not possible of occurrence in the language and that which was possible but occurred in their sample with almost zero frequency.

Both these differences of approach seem likely to be bridged in the near future. The bridges may be built from both directions. Linguistic methods may shed some light on analysis of meanings. Note, for example, the suggestion by Saporta and Sebeok that at least some aspects of the semantic relationship between pairs of related terms could be deduced from distributional data by noting the difference in the distributions within limited texts and in the language as a whole (e.g., *Capitalism* and *Communism* occur in identical linguistic environments in the language as a whole but not in a single author's statements). On the other hand, even if linguistic methods continue to be applied exclusively to formal matters, content analysts can usefully inform themselves of what the available equivalent forms are through which any given meaning can be expressed. The usefulness to content analysts of knowledge of linguistic forms has been put clearly by a psycholinguist, John B. Carroll: "Linguistic and psycholinguistic studies could aid in the formulation of more reliable and valid content analysis categories. Linguistic analysis suggests the possibility of establishing categories based on form classes or substitution groups (for example, the range of ways in which a particular country could be referred to might be described in this way)."[20]

----
[20] J. B. Carroll, *The Study of Language* (Cambridge, Mass., 1953), p. 120.

The difference between the nonstatistical approach of the linguist and the statistical approach of the content analyst is already being bridged. Some linguistic scholars, notably B. Mandelbrot, have been working with probability models.[21] The main interest has been on the degree of concentration in the forms used, that is, what proportion of all form usages are provided by any given proportion of the available forms.[22] Most linguists still are satisfied to distinguish roughly between major and minor patterns of the language, but there is a beginning of more quantitative work.

Thus the barriers between linguistics and content analysis seem likely to give way, and it seems probable at least that content analysis methods will be increasingly enriched by knowledge of the findings of linguistic research. Four likely lines of influence suggest themselves. Linguistics is likely to be useful to content analysts (1) by providing a model of a discipline which has successfully treated certain problems of textual analysis, (2) by providing methods for establishing the semantic identity of different forms, (3) by providing methods for stating the relationships between semantic entities in a text, and (4) by suggesting some not otherwise obvious behavioral indicators of the communicator's state at the time of communication.

1. *Linguistics as a model.* We have already noted above that contingency analysis was in part suggested by the notions of distributional linguistic analysis. Linguists observe the environments in which a given form appears. The contingency content analyst in much the same way asks in what semantic environment any given semantic entity appears. It seems probable that the methods used in coping with the former problem may have some suggestive relevance to the latter. Linguistic analysis, for example, treats two forms as identical if they may appear in identical environments. But as Saporta and Sebeok point out, one might treat the probabilities of their appearing in identical environments as in some respects a measure of their meaning. Thus, to use their example, *eye doctor*

---

[21] B. Mandelbrot, "An Informational Theory of the Structure of Language Based upon the Statistical Matching of Messages and Coding," in W. Jackson, ed., *Proceedings of a Symposium on Information Theory* (Royal Society, London, 1950), and "Structure formelle des Textes et Communication," *Word*, 10 (1954), 1-27. See also G. Herdan, *Language as Choice and Chance* (Groningen, 1956), and the critique of Herdan by M. Halle in *Kratylos*, 3 (1958), 20-28.

[22] See J. Whatmough, *Language, a Modern Synthesis* (London, 1956), Chap. 11, and G. U. Yule, *The Statistical Study of Literary Vocabulary* (London, 1944).

and *oculist* are closer than *oculist* and *lawyer,* in that there are more meaningful environments in which either of the former pair could appear than in which either of the latter pair could appear.

2. *Establishing the semantic identity of different forms.* Content analysis categories are seldom single morphemes or uniquely defined groups of morphemes. They are usually concepts capable of being expressed in a number of different ways. On the face of it, the counting of verbal expressions to ascertain the extent of or emphasis on certain concepts might be thought to require that we identify the precise verbal forms which convey those concepts. Historically, however, that has seldom been done. Most content analysis procedures use the coder as a judge of what lexical forms convey what meanings of interest. They have relied on the common sense of a coder who was, of course, a user of the language in which the analysis was being done. His common sense enables him to recognize, for example, that the phrases "a man of courage," "a brave man," and "a guy with guts" all mean the same thing.

We noted above Carroll's suggestion that linguistics might provide useful and more objective ways to define categories of equivalent meanings, as for instance the different ways of referring to a country. This author and most of his fellow conferees share this view, but it is not self-evident that there is much to be gained by such linguistic definition of categories. One may wonder how much improvement is to be expected from the substitution of formal linguistic rules of equivalence for common sense in content analysis. With a certain amount of care, reliability can be achieved between coders who are ordinary users of a language. One might argue that the probability of improving upon such human judges is small. Even if that turns out to be true, linguistic analysis can help us to understand what the coder is doing. Even if we do not improve on the "human computer," we want to learn how that computer works when it recognizes quite different forms as equivalent.

Furthermore, it may well be that a better understanding of the alternative forms of expression available for any given meaning will enable us to devise more sensitive and parsimonious content analysis categories for human coders to use. Categories designed by persons lacking sophistication in linguistic forms tend to catch different meanings within the same category and fail to catch the relevant ones. The more refined and rigorous the content analysis the more that is apt to be true. Refinement and rigor come at the expense of the coder's intuitions, as Alexander George emphasized in his chapter. Thus, as content analyses become more refined and rigorous it may well be that analysts need to become linguistically more sophisticated if they are to avoid the dangers of mechanical absurdity. An example of the kind of thing which would be most useful to content analysts, to which we have already referred more than once, is Harris' rules of grammatical equivalence.

3. *Establishing semantic relationships.* An example of a refinement for which some linguistic analysis would be quite useful comes to mind as we think of the next steps in contingency analysis. To establish a contingency we need a unit of space, and then if we find within that unit both of two symbolic elements we say that we have a contingency. That, however, is a rather simple measure. To note only that two words or two ideas appear in the same paragraph or sentence is not fully indicative of what is communicated. We may want also to know their structural relationship. Mr. Cameron, for example, tends to associate *youth* and *disease*. These terms appear in the same speeches. But clearly they are counterposed; they are poles on a single continuum in Cameron's thinking, even though they are not semantically antonyms. On the other hand, it is entirely possible that the antonym of *youth*, namely, *old age*, might show up as *not* part of a contingency with *youth* and *disease* precisely because it is an alternative label for the end of the continuum for which Cameron actually uses the label *disease*. Thus a negative contingency finding might indicate homonyms, one of which was preferred. Osgood, as well as Saporta and Sebeok, note that an empirical contingency can be interpreted in different ways depending on whether the entities related are synonyms, antonyms, or independent of each other.

Clearly it is possible to conceive of a new and more refined kind of contingency analysis which would take account not merely of the co-presence of items, but would code them differently according to whether the linguistic structures relating them showed them to be joined, counterposed, or independent. In such an analysis one would code the symbols *Jack* and *Jill* differently in each of the following semantic relationships. Joined: "Jack and Jill went up the hill"; counterposed: "Jack was a boy, Jill was a girl"; independent: successive entries in a telephone book, "Jack Smith, Jill Smith." Such coding of direction and intensity of connectedness was used, it will be recalled, in evaluative assertion analysis.

The value of such combined contingency and structural coding may be brought out by reference to the discussion of the relation of contingency and meaning.

A number of persons, among them Zellig Harris and the present author, have attempted to use intersymbol contingencies or formal distribution as a definition or index of meaning for empirical studies.[23] The assertion is that the meaning of a word may be considered as approximated or explicated by the probability of its appearance given the other words of the context. That this can lead to an oversimple interpretation of meaning has been shown by Saporta and Sebeok in their chapter and by Saporta more fully in a recent article.[24] Let us quote Saporta: "Harris' thesis is perhaps best summarized in his statement that 'if we consider words or morphemes A and B to be more different in meaning than A and C, then we will often find that the distributions of A and B are more different than the distributions of A and C. In other words difference of meaning correlates with difference in distribution.' . . . Although Harris' hypothesis may turn out to be valid, i.e., that there are distributional correlates of meaning difference, some refinement is necessary before the hypothesis can be stated in a testable form."[25] Harris discusses various kinds of pairs of forms "where presumably distributional correlates may be established for differences in meaning."[26] Among these are stylistic alternatives, for example *ain't* and *am not;* synonyms, for example *eye doctor* and *oculist;* pairs from the same grammatical class, for example *oculist* and *lawyer;* and members of two different grammatical classes. The last of these may be defined as never having the same environments. Pairs of the penultimate kind, for example *oculist* and *lawyer,* may differ in meaning corresponding to the amount of difference in their environments.

With regard to these matters Saporta points out several things. For one, opposites tend to share common environments. "Bad and naughty are closer in meaning than bad and good. And yet, the relatively restricted use of naughty might result in its sharing fewer environments with bad than good does."[27] Secondly, members of different grammatical classes, for example *chair* and *sit,* may share more in meaning than pairs from within the same gram-

---

[23] I. de Sola Pool, "Symbols, Meanings and Social Science," in L. Bryson, *Symbols and Values* (New York, 1954). Also Harris, "Distributional Structure."

[24] "A Note on the Relation Between Meaning and Distribution."

[25] Saporta, "A Note on the Relation Between Meaning and Distribution," p. 22.

[26] Saporta, "A Note on the Relation Between Meaning and Distribution," p. 22.

[27] Saporta, "A Note on the Relation Between Meaning and Distribution," p. 23.

matical class. Third, note that two words such as *ser* and *estar* in Spanish may be rather strictly specified for different situations, yet have a single translation (to be) in another language. Finally, the choice of measures of degree of difference in distributions "will in large part determine the degree of correlation."[28]

Thus there are problems in identifying meaning with distribution in the linguists' sense. Some of these same considerations apply to the identification of meaning and contingency, though contingency is a looser concept than distribution, and thus avoids some of the difficulties regarding grammatical class, since forms of different grammatical classes appear freely in the same contingency analysis unit.

If we are to clarify the relation of contingency and meaning, it is perhaps desirable to distinguish three levels of description of lexical practices. The simplest descriptions concern mere contingencies. *Youth* and *disease* are contingent for Mr. Cameron. At the next level we introduce other structural facts. *Youth* and *disease* are contingent but structurally joined by dissociative connectors rather than by associative ones. (Note that that could not necessarily be established simply by the co-contingency of dissociative terms with *youth* and *disease,* if, for example, Cameron always counterposed *youth and vigor* to *disease,* for then there would be many associative "ands" in the unit, too.) At the third level we introduce descriptions of aspects of meaning, *if there are any,* which are not indexed by structural facts at all.

The confusion of these levels in its most extreme form would consist of the assertion, already shown to be wrong, that positive contingency between two words implies similarity in their meaning. A more sophisticated statement asserts that if one described completely the contingencies between any one word and all other words taken not singly but in all possible groupings (the groupings being of course without reference to order), one would have in effect a complete description of the distribution of the word. For the reason noted in the previous paragraph, even that is probably not strictly true, but is an arguable version of the notion that the meaning of a word is the company it keeps. As an abstract proposition it is at least a close approximation. But as a practical matter it is not of much use. It is far more practicable to consider contingency data only for pairs or small groups of words at a time, and to take account of the semantic facts which make the interpretation of

---

[28] Saporta, "A Note on the Relation Between Meaning and Distribution," p. 26.

identical contingency data on *youth* and *disease, youth* and *old age,* and *old age* and *disease,* for example, all quite different.

In the interesting discussion of these matters by Saporta and Sebeok we are left with a further unanswered but interesting question concerning the relation of the second and third of the above levels of description of lexical facts. Are there semantic facts which cannot be described by distributional facts at all, and how can those semantic facts be objectively described? Can we hypothetically conceive of words having identical distributions and yet different meanings? If so, is there any objective index of the nondistributional element of their meaning? Does the semantic differential technique index such an element, and if so, fully or only in part? Clarification of this order of highly abstract questions about the relationship of linguistic codes and meaning may prove of considerable practical significance for the designing of content analysis categories.

4. *Linguistic indicators of behavior.* Finally, one of the contributions of linguistics to content analysis is to indicate which characteristics of language use are fixed characteristics of the code and therefore constant between persons and situations, and which characteristics are particular to a speaker or situation and therefore useful as psycholinguistic indices. For example, in a tonal language tone is partly fixed and cannot be used as an index of mood, as freely as it can in English.

Pausal phenomena and speech disturbances (which Mahl described), word order, syllable-word quotients, word-sentence quotients, parts of speech quotients, common words, uncommon words, and many other linguistic phenomena were mentioned as worthy of exploration as psychological indices. The suggestions for indices and their use were numerous and varied. Let us summarize some of the suggestions which came out at the conference.

Newman: It seems to be a natural phenomenon of language to have polar terms [e.g., hot, cold; good, bad; etc.]. That breaks through all the differences you get in linguistic structure between cultures; but the way in which particular concepts are polarized in different cultures varies.

Casagrande and Osgood: Bilinguals under some circumstances revert to constructions which are characteristic of their first language. In a psychiatric interview this may also be revealing of association to childhood. More generally, with respect to age level there are shifting probabilities of different constructions. When a patient is talking spontaneously, those are not something he is likely to control. Does he talk within the patterns of the level to which he is associating?

Saporta: There are also different social levels of a language, formal, standard colloquial, substandard colloquial, etc.; also geographic dialects. What do shifts between these indicate about the state of a speaker?

Osgood: These may also index social relations. Forms of politeness index relationships between people.

Pool: Such choice of language type also indexes the role in which a person conceives of himself or his activity. The fact that we discuss content analysis in academese indicates the class of things to which we conceive of it as belonging. One might find politics belonging to the realm of the ideological or the personal according to the language chosen to discuss it.

Osgood: One might in an experiment have subjects write letters to hypothetical persons having different social roles with respect to the writer.

Saporta: A study has been made of the language that mothers use to children. Mothering language is quite different from normal language.

Casagrande: The use of that would be a clue to emotional states in therapy.

Newman: The width of difference in a subject's spoken and written language might throw light on the control of the individual in assuming roles.

Note that all these suggestions required of the linguists that they study the distinctive features of certain types of language. Some of that sort of work has been done; much remains to be done. The discussion of "marked members" in the chapter by Saporta and Sebeok is a treatment of this problem. The marked elements are equivalent to unmarked elements and sometimes to alternative marked elements except that they convey special connotations. These are not only about the referent, but also about the discourse situation. Thus *he arrived prematurely* for *he came too soon* is a choice of formal language which might index psychological states of the speaker or the social relation in which he is talking. Further linguistic study of such marked forms, particularly statistical linguistic study of their use, would be of utmost help to content analysts.

All of the above comments concern variations in types of discourse within a single language code. Clearly the job of analysis of the available variations and their significance must be done separately for each language. Thus the problems of cross-cultural content analysis are all of the above multiplied by the different language codes involved. Historically a good deal of content analysis research has been cross-cultural.

Most of Lasswell's work and the work of those influenced by him has concerned the parallelisms and divergences of trends in attention to major political symbols in different countries. It has been possible to do that sort of comparative analysis at least within the West because the major political concepts have been shared across linguistic boundaries. Democracy, Communism, socialism, parliaments, political parties, peace, war, are the central ideological entities of political discussion in all of Western civilization. Nuances certainly vary, and problems of translation have existed for this kind of analysis, but they were not of such magnitude as to invalidate the procedure (e.g., political issues are much the same in all parts of Switzerland; the definition of the issues is hardly a function of the language in which they are discussed). That is clearly true for as homogeneous a culture area as the West, and is probably, though not certainly, also true for much wider areas. At least in national politics, the major symbolisms of Western ideologies have taken hold fairly extensively all over the world. Miss Martha Jane Smith of New York University recently did a comparative content analysis of Soviet and Chinese Communist propaganda to the United States,[29] modeling her technique on the Library of Congress and RADIR studies. There were interesting divergences as well as parallelisms, some probably cultural in explanation and some political. For example, the Chinese put more emphasis on symbols for the people, and imperialism; the Russians did not discuss the Korean War. But none of the divergences would seem to be a product of the fact that the political concepts had been originally framed in different languages. The Chinese have managed to take over the baggage of Marxism-Leninism.

The above comments, however, are impressionistic statements, and open up one more large and important area of psycholinguistic investigation which would be of much use to content analysts. How far do language codes affect the content of the messages conveyable and conveyed in them? That is the question most generally associated with the name of Benjamin Whorf.[30] The discussion

---

[29] Martha J. Smith, "Key Symbols in U.S.S.R. and Chinese Propaganda to the U.S.A." (Ph.D. thesis, New York University, New York, 1958).

[30] J. B. Whorf and J. B. Carroll, *Language, Thought, and Reality* (New York, 1956).

which he stimulated has given rise to much of the most interesting recent psycholinguistic research. There is now some fairly strong evidence that the code is not totally without effect at least on such elementary matters as color recall.[31] But the magnitude and scope of influence of the code remains a matter for study and one in which content analysts are bound to have an interest.

All of this suggests that though psycholinguistic indicators will be different in different languages, yet there may be some important cross-language uniformities. There may be some real universals. Perhaps sentence breaks and slips increase with anxiety in every culture and language. Perhaps there are some universal significances to shrill or rumbling sounds. The onomatopoeic quality of sounds can be interpreted with better-than-chance results by nonusers of a language. Aside from any such true universals which may exist, there are also universal categories, the precise indicators of which vary between languages but which can be translated. Newman noted that all languages seem to have polar terms. Osgood's research on the semantic differential suggests that the evaluative dimension is dominant in all. If so, polarity and specifically evaluative polarity could be used cross-culturally in a content analysis study though the indicatorial symbols would be different and differently grouped in each language. Formal language, colloquial language, rude language, mothering language, upper-class language, lower-class language, men's language, women's language, children's language, are probably categories for every language. The linguist, however, must identify the elements in different languages which are equivalent, not semantically, but in serving to identify these varieties of speech. These elements may be very different and not even formally alike. But they help to define universal categories in which the content analyst is interested. The problem is in many ways not unlike that of finding the lexical indicators which in different languages serve to identify the same universal semantic concept. Thus the content analyst interested in cross-cultural research stands to benefit from any progress which linguistics makes on problems of translation. It would seem that the fruitful interchange between content analysis and linguistics is only beginning.

----

[31] E. H. Lenneberg, "Cognition in Ethnolinguistics," *Language*, 29 (1953), 463-71, and E. H. Lenneberg and J. M. Roberts, *Language of Experience* (Indiana University Publications in Anthropology and Linguistics [Bloomington, 1956]).

SELECTIVE BIBLIOGRAPHY

BOOKS

Allport, G. W., and P. E. Vernon, *Studies in Expressive Movement,* Macmillan, New York, 1933.

Anderson, H. H. and G. L., eds., *An Introduction to Projective Techniques and Other Devices for Understanding the Dynamics of Human Behavior,* Prentice-Hall, New York, 1951.

Anderson, W., *Ein Volkskundliches Experiment,* Folklore Fellows Communications, No. 141, Helsinki, 1951.

Baker, R. S., *Woodrow Wilson: Life and Letters,* Doubleday, Garden City, N.Y., 1927.

Bartlett, F. C., *Remembering: A Study in Experimental and Social Psychology,* Cambridge University Press, New York, 1932.

Benedict, Ruth, *Patterns of Culture,* Houghton Mifflin, Boston, 1934.

———, *Zuni Mythology,* Columbia University Press, New York, 1935.

Berelson, B., *Content Analysis in Communication Research,* Free Press, Glencoe, Ill., 1952.

———, P. F. Lazarsfeld, and W. McPhee, *Voting,* University of Chicago Press, Chicago, 1954.

Binet, A., *Les Révélations de l'Écriture,* F. Alcan, Paris, 1906.

Bloomfield, L., *Language,* H. Holt, New York, 1933.

Boas, F., *Kwakiutl Culture as Reflected in Mythology,* American Folklore Society Memoirs, Vol. 28, Stechert, New York, 1935.

Burke, K., *The Philosophy of Literary Form: Studies in Symbolic Action,* Louisiana State University Press, Baton Rouge, 1941.

Carroll, J. B., *The Study of Language: A Survey of Linguistics and Related Disciplines in America,* Harvard University Press, Cambridge, Mass., 1953.

Cochran, T. C., *Railroad Leaders: 1845-1890; the Business Mind in Action,* Harvard University Press, Cambridge, Mass., 1953.

Daniels, J., *The Wilson Era,* University of North Carolina Press, Chapel Hill, 1946.

Dollard, J., and N. E. Miller, *Personality and Psychotherapy; an Analysis in Terms of Learning, Thinking, and Culture,* McGraw-Hill, New York, 1950.

Garraty, J. A., *The Nature of Biography,* Knopf, New York, 1957.

Garraty, J. A., *Woodrow Wilson: A Great Life in Brief*, Knopf, New York, 1956.

George, A. L., *Propaganda Analysis: A Study of Inferences Made from Nazi Propaganda in World War II*, Row, Peterson, Evanston, Ill., 1959.

—— and Juliette George, *Woodrow Wilson and Colonel House: A Personality Study*, Day, New York, 1956.

Hale, W. B., *The Story of a Style*, Viking, New York, 1920.

Herdan, G., *Language as Choice and Chance*, P. Noordhoff, Groningen, 1956.

Herskovits, M. J. and F. S., *Suriname Folklore*, Columbia University Press, New York, 1936.

Holt, E. B., *Animal Drive and the Learning Process*, Williams and Norgate, London, 1931.

Hovland, C., I. L. Janis, and H. Kelly, *Communication and Persuasion*, Yale University Press, New Haven, Conn., 1953.

——, A. Lumsdaine, and F. Sheffield, *Experiments on Mass Communication*, Princeton University Press, Princeton, N.J., 1949.

Kecskemeti, P., *Meaning, Communication, and Value*, University of Chicago Press, Chicago, 1952.

Kroeber, A. L., and C. Kluckhohn, *Culture*, Papers of the Peabody Museum of American Archeology and Ethnology, Cambridge, Mass., 1952.

Lasswell, H. D., N. Leites, and associates, *Language of Politics; Studies in Quantitative Semantics*, George W. Stewart, New York, 1949.

——, D. Lerner, and I. de Sola Pool, *The Comparative Study of Symbols*, Hoover Institute Studies; Ser. C: Symbols, No. 1, Stanford University Press, Stanford, Calif., 1952.

Lawrence, D., *The True Story of Woodrow Wilson*, Doran, New York, 1924.

Lenneberg, E. H., and J. M. Roberts, *Language of Experience*, Indiana University Publications in Anthropology and Linguistics, Bloomington, 1956.

Link, A. S., *Woodrow Wilson and the Progressive Era*, Harper, New York, 1954.

Lochner, L., ed., *The Goebbels Diaries, 1942-1943*, Doubleday, Garden City, N.Y., 1948.

Maugham, W. S., *The Summing Up*, Ryerson Press, New York, 1938.

Mead, G. H., *Mind, Self, and Society*, University of Chicago Press, Chicago, 1934.

Miller, G. A., *Language and Communication*, McGraw-Hill, New York, 1951.

Morris, C. W., *Signs, Language, and Behavior*, Prentice-Hall, New York, 1946.

Osgood, C. E., *Method and Theory in Experimental Psychology*, Oxford, New York, 1953.

——, G. J. Suci, and P. H. Tannenbaum, *The Measurement of Meaning*, University of Illinois Press, Urbana, 1957.

Pool, I. de Sola, *Symbols of Democracy*, Stanford University Press, Stanford, Calif., 1952.

Propp, V., *Morphology of the Folktale*, Publication 10, Indiana University Research Center in Anthropology, Folklore, and Linguistics, Bloomington, 1958.

Rush, M., *The Rise of Khrushchev*, Public Affairs Press, Washington, D.C., 1958.

Sebeok, T. A., ed., *Aspects of Style in Language* (in press).

————, *Finnish and Hungarian Case Systems: Their Form and Function*, Acta Instituti Hungarici Universitatis, Högskolan, Ungerska Institutet, Stockholm, 1946.

Shannon, C. E., and W. Weaver, *The Mathematical Theory of Communication*, University of Illinois Press, Urbana, 1949.

Skinner, B. F., *Verbal Behavior*, Appleton, New York, 1957.

Thompson, S., *Motif-Index of Folk Literature*, 1st and 2nd eds., Indiana University Press, Bloomington, 1932, 1955.

Whatmough, J., *Language, a Modern Synthesis*, Secker and Warburg, London, 1956.

Whorf, J. B., and J. B. Carroll, *Language, Thought, and Reality*, Wiley, New York, 1956.

Wolfenstein, Martha, and N. Leites, *Movies, a Psychological Study*, Free Press, Glencoe, Ill., 1950.

Wolff, W., *The Expression of Personality; Experimental Depth Psychology*, Harper, New York, 1943.

Yule, G. U., *The Statistical Study of Literary Vocabulary*, Cambridge University Press, London, 1944.

ARTICLES

Allport, G. W., "Letters from Jenny," *Journal of Abnormal and Social Psychology*, 41 (1946), 315-50, 449-80.

Auld, F., Jr., and E. J. Murray, "Content-Analysis Studies of Psychotherapy," *Psychological Bulletin*, 52 (1955), 377-95.

Baldwin, A. L., "Personal Structure Analysis: A Statistical Method for Investigating the Single Personality," *Journal of Abnormal and Social Psychology*, 37 (1942), 163-83.

Bloch, B., "Linguistic Structure and Linguistic Analysis," in *Report of the Fourth Annual Round Table Meeting on Linguistics and Language Teaching*, Washington, D.C., 1953, pp. 40-44.

Boder, D. P., "The Adjective-Verb Quotient . . . ," *Psychological Record*, 3 (1940), 310-43.

Carroll, J. B., F. B. Agard, D. E. Dulany, S. S. Newman, L. Newmark, C. E. Osgood, T. A. Sebeok, and R. L. Solomon, *Report and Recommendations of the Interdisciplinary Summer Seminar in Psychology and Linguistics*, Ithaca, New York, 1951.

Cartwright, D. P., "Analysis of Qualitative Material," in L. Festinger and D. Katz, eds., *Research Methods in the Behavioral Sciences*, Dryden, New York, 1953.

Diderichsen, P., "The Importance of Distribution versus Other Criteria in Linguistic Analysis," *Proceedings of the Eighth International Congress of Linguists*, Oslo, 1958, pp. 156-82.

Dollard, J., and O. H. Mowrer, "A Method of Measuring Tension in Written Documents," *Journal of Abnormal and Social Psychology*, 42 (1947), 3-32.

Dovring, Karin, "Land Reform as a Propaganda Theme," in F. Dovring, *Land and Labor in Europe, 1900-1950*, M. Nijhoff, The Hague, 1956.

Driver, H. E., "Statistics in Anthropology," *American Anthropologist*, 55 (1953), 42-59.

George, A. L., "Prediction of Political Action by Means of Propaganda Analysis," *Public Opinion Quarterly*, 20 (1956), 334-45.

Goldstein, J., "Content Analysis: A Propaganda and Opinion Study," Ph.D. thesis, New School for Social Research, New York, 1942.

Green, T. S., Jr., "Mr. Cameron and the Ford House," *Public Opinion Quarterly*, 3 (1939), 669-75.

Halle, M., "Criticism of Herdan's *Language as Choice and Chance*," *Kratylos*, 3 (1958), 20-28.

Harris, Z. S., "Discourse Analysis," *Language*, 28 (1952), 1-30.

———, "Distributional Structure," *Word*, 10 (1954), 146-62.

Harwood, F. W., and A. M. Wright, "Statistical Study of English Word Formation," *Language*, 32 (1956), 260-73.

Hockett, C. F., "Two Models of Grammatical Description," *Word*, 10 (1954), 210-34.

Hull, C. L., and R. B. Montgomery, "An Experimental Investigation of Certain Alleged Relations Between Character and Handwriting," *Psychoanalytic Review*, 26 (1919), 63-74.

Janis, I. L., "Meaning and the Study of Symbolic Behavior," *Psychiatry*, 6 (1943), 425-39.

———, "The Problem of Validating Content Analysis," in H. D. Lasswell, N. Leites, and associates, *Language of Politics; Studies in Quantitative Semantics*, George W. Stewart, New York, 1949.

Kasl, S. V., and G. F. Mahl, "Experimentally Induced Anxiety and Speech Disturbances," *American Psychologist*, 13 (1958), 349.

Kluckhohn, C., "Myths and Rituals: A General Theory," *Harvard Theological Review*, 35 (1942), 44-78.

Lazarsfeld, P. F., and A. H. Barton, "Qualitative Measurement in the Social Sciences: Classification, Typologies, and Indices," in D. Lerner and H. D. Lasswell, eds., *The Policy Sciences: Recent Developments in Scope and Method*, Stanford University Press, Stanford, Calif., 1951.

Leites, N., Elsa Bernaut, and R. L. Garthoff, "Politburo Images of Stalin," *World Politics*, 3 (1951), 317-39.

Lenneberg, E. H., "Cognition in Ethnolinguistics," *Language*, 29 (1953), 463-71.

Mahl, G. F., "Disturbances and Silences in the Patient's Speech in Psychotherapy," *Journal of Abnormal and Social Psychology*, 53 (1956), 1-15.

————, "Disturbances in the Patient's Speech as a Function of Anxiety," a paper delivered before the Eastern Psychological Association, Atlantic City, N.J., 1956.

————, "Measuring the Patient's Anxiety During Interviews from 'Expressive' Aspects of His Speech," *Transactions of the New York Academy of Science*, 21 (1959), 249-57.

————, " 'Normal' Disturbances in Spontaneous Speech: General Quantitative Aspects," a paper delivered before the American Psychological Association, Chicago, 1956.

Mandelbrot, B., "An Informational Theory of the Structure of Language Based upon the Statistical Matching of Messages and Coding," in W. Jackson, ed., *Proceedings of a Symposium on Information Theory*, Royal Society, London, 1950.

————, "Structure formelle des Textes et Communications," *Word*, 10 (1954), 1-27.

Merriam, A. P. and B. W., and R. P. Armstrong, "Banyaruanda Proverbs," *Journal of American Folklore*, 67 (1954), No. 265, pp. 267-84.

Miller, G. A., "Psycholinguistics," in G. Lindzey, ed., *Handbook of Social Psychology*, Addison-Wesley, Cambridge, Mass., 1954.

———— and J. A. Selfridge, "Verbal Context and the Recall of Meaningful Material," *American Journal of Psychology*, 63 (1950), 176-85.

Osgood, C. E., "Aptitude and Comprehension Correlates of 'Cloze' Readability Scores," a paper delivered before the American Psychological Association, Chicago, 1956.

———— and Lois Anderson, "Certain Relations Between Experienced Contingencies, Association Structure, and Contingencies in Encoded Messages," *American Journal of Psychology*, 70 (1957), 411-20.

————, S. Saporta, and J. C. Nunnally, "Evaluative Assertion Analysis," *Litera*, 3 (1956), 47-102.

———— and T. A. Sebeok, eds., "Psycholinguistics: A Survey of Theory and Research Problems," *Journal of Abnormal and Social Psychology*, 49, Supp. (1954); Indiana University Publications in Anthropology and Linguistics, Memoir 10, Bloomington, 1954.

———— and G. J. Suci, "A Measure of Relation Determined by Both Mean Difference and Profile Information," *Psychological Bulletin*, 49 (1952), 251-62.

———— and P. H. Tannenbaum, "The Principle of Congruity in the Prediction of Attitude Change," *Psychological Review*, 62 (1955), 42-55.

Paasonen, H., "Tscheremissische Texte," in P. Siro, ed., *Memoires de la Société Finno-Ougrienne, LXXVII*, Suomalaisugrilainen seura, Helsinki, 1939.

Pascal, G. R., "The Analysis of Handwriting: A Test of Significance," *Character and Personality*, 12 (1943), 123-44.

Pike, K. L., *Language in Relation to a Unified Theory of the Structure of Human Behavior*, Pt. 1, Summer Institute of Linguistics, Glendale, Calif., 1954.

Pool, I. de Sola, "Symbols, Meanings and Social Science," in L. Bryson, *Symbols and Values*, Harper, New York, 1954.

Reich, W., "On Character Analysis," in R. Fliess, ed., *The Psychoanalytic Reader*, International Universities Press, New York, 1948.

Rubenstein, H., review of Miller's *Language and Communication*, *Language*, 28 (1952), 116.

Ruesch, J., and G. Bateson, "Structure and Process in Social Relations," *Psychiatry*, 12 (1949), 105-24.

Sandford, F. H., "Speech and Personality," *Psychological Bulletin*, 39 (1942), 811-45.

Saporta, S., "A Note on the Relation Between Meaning and Distribution," *Litera*, 4 (1957), 22-26.

Sebeok, T. A., "Approaches to the Analysis of Folksong Texts," *Ural-Altaische Jahrbücher*, 31 (1959, in press).

———, "Cheremis Dream Portents," *Southwestern Journal of Anthropology*, 6 (1950), 273-85.

———, "Structural Analysis in Folklore Research," in *Studies in Cheremis*, Vol. 2, *The Supernatural*, Viking Fund Publications in Anthropology, No. 22, New York, 1956.

———, "Toward a Statistical Contingency Method in Folklore Research," *Indiana University Publications, Folklore Series*, 9 (1957), 130-40.

——— and L. H. Orzack, "The Structure and Content of Cheremis Charms," *Anthropos*, 48 (1953), 369-88, 760-72.

Smith, H. L., Jr., "An Outline of Metalinguistic Analysis," in *Report of the Third Annual Round Table Meeting on Linguistics and Language Teaching*, Washington, D.C., 1952, pp. 59-66.

Smith, Martha J., "Key Symbols in U.S.S.R. and Chinese Propaganda to the U.S.A.," Ph.D. thesis, New York University, New York, 1958.

Spang-Hanssen, H., "Typological and Statistical Aspects of Distribution as a Criterion in Linguistic Analysis," *Proceedings of the Eighth International Congress of Linguists*, Oslo, 1958, pp. 182-94.

Taylor, W. L., "Application of Cloze and Entropy Measures to the Study of Contextual Constraints in Samples of Continuous Prose," Ph.D. thesis, University of Illinois, Urbana, 1954; *Dissertation Abstracts*, 15 (1955), 464-65.

———, " 'Cloze Procedure': A New Tool for Measuring Readability," *Journalism Quarterly*, 30 (1953), 415-33.

———, "Recent Developments in the Use of 'Cloze Procedure,' " *Journalism Quarterly*, 33 (1956), No. 1.

Vakar, N., "The Mass Communication Index: Some Observations on Communist Russian Discourse," *Symposium*, 10 (1956), 42-59.

White, R. K., "*Black Boy:* A Value-Analysis," *Journal of Abnormal and Social Psychology*, 42 (1947), 440-61.

NAME INDEX

Agard, F. B., 144n, 197n
Allport, G. W., 175n, 181n
Anderson, G. L., 175n
Anderson, H. H., 175n
Anderson, Lois, 55n, 59n, 69
Anderson, W., 149n
Armstrong, R. P., 5, 6, 78, 88, 155n, 161, 204, 205, 214
Auld, F., Jr., 16, 17n, 90, 107
Baker, R. S., 172n
Baldwin, A. L., 54, 180, 181, 183, 184, 192, 197
Bartlett, F. C., 86n, 149
Barton, A. H., 9n
Bateson, G., 143n
Benedict, Ruth, 151, 152
Berelson, B., 1, 8n, 15n, 23n, 26, 143, 195, 203
Bernaut, Elsa, 98n, 211n
Binet, A., 174, 175n
Bloch, B., 134n
Bloomfield, L., 140n
Boas, F., 149
Boder, D. P., 176, 177
Bryson, L., 228n
Burke, K., 163
Busemann, A., 176
Cameron, W. J., 5, 66, 67, 73, 74, 198, 213, 215, 227, 229
Carroll, J. B., 6, 144n, 197n, 224, 226, 232n
Cartwright, D. P., 9n, 28
Casagrande, J. B., 6, 86, 230-31
Chall, Jeanne S., 80, 82

Cochran, T. C., 185
Dale, E., 80, 82
Daniels, J., 173
Diderichsen, P., 135n
Dollard, J., 17, 99n, 106n, 178, 184
Dovring, F., 196n
Dovring, Karin, 196n
Driver, H. E., 143n
Dulany, D. E., 144n, 197n
Dulles, J. F., 44
Eden, Sir A., 44
Eisenhower, D. D., 50, 187
Fadner, R., 41
Festinger, L., 9n
Flesch, R., 80, 82
Frazer, Sir J. G., 145
Freud, S., 199, 209
Fritzsche, H., 12, 13
Gardner, J. W., 6
Garraty, J. A., 5, 6, 77, 87, 89, 171n, 191, 192, 193, 197, 217
Garthoff, R. L., 98n, 211n
George, A. L., 2, 5, 6, 7, 27n, 31n, 73, 85, 86, 87, 89, 103, 104, 134n, 139n, 141n, 187, 191, 192, 193, 194, 204, 206, 207, 209, 210, 211, 215n, 217, 226
Goebbels, J. P., 5, 12, 14n, 22, 55, 69-70, 73, 75, 198
Goldstein, J., 22n
Green, T. S., Jr., 67
Greenberg, J., 132n
Hale, W. B., 176
Halle, M., 225n

241

SUBJECT INDEX

Cloze Procedure, 5, 37, 41, 78-88, 136n, 170, 200

Contingency analysis, 2, 37, 39, 41, 54-78, 90, 135, 144, 145, 146, 147, 148, 150, 181, 182, 186, 190, 193, 196-202, 211, 213, 215, 225, 227, 229

Evaluative assertion analysis, 5, 35, 37, 40, 41, 43, 48, 49-54, 156, 172, 179, 184, 187, 194, 195, 202, 218, 222, 223, 227

Folklore, content analysis of, 5, 134, 142, 143, 145, 146, 147, 148, 149, 151-70, 172, 198, 204, 205

Frequency analysis, 2, 9, 10-11, 12, 13, 18, 23, 24, 32, 37, 41, 54, 56, 58, 59, 60, 61, 67, 69, 71, 76, 90, 113, 131, 134, 139, 141, 143, 144, 146, 169, 181, 182, 183, 186, 190, 192, 193, 194, 195-96, 197

Inferences to antecedents of contents, 2, 17, 18, 19, 20, 29-31, 35, 189-90, 191, 205-6, 219-20, 221, 222

Inferences to consequences of contents, 13-14, 15, 18, 19, 20, 29-31, 35, 37, 189, 190, 191, 205-6, 219-20, 221, 222

Instrumental model, 2, 3, 4, 14, 16, 52, 75, 89, 90, 91-96, 97, 99, 100, 103, 104, 105, 107, 109, 134n, 186, 187, 198, 206-12, 219, 220

Intensity, measurement of, 48, 49, 50, 52, 76, 90, 190, 193-95

Linguistics, content analysis of, 1, 5, 23, 27, 78, 102, 104, 105, 106, 107, 109, 131-50, 160, 189-90, 195, 200, 201, 202, 203, 223, 224-33

Propaganda, content analysis of, 7, 12-25, 28, 30-32, 52, 54, 55, 71, 73, 77, 87, 100, 204, 210, 218, 221

Psychotherapy, content analysis of, 5, 16, 18, 33, 52, 54, 55, 71-73, 74, 77, 89-130, 134, 137, 191, 198, 199, 204, 209, 211, 221, 230

Qualitative content analysis, 7-32, 191, 192, 193

RADIR studies, 11, 196, 197, 199, 232

Representational model, 2, 3, 33-88, 89, 90, 92, 95, 96, 97, 99, 101, 104, 134n, 186, 187, 206-12, 219, 220

Units for content analysis, 5, 11, 22, 41, 56, 61-62, 69, 78, 90, 93, 99, 132, 144, 145, 147, 148, 153, 154, 155-59, 163, 166, 170, 186, 187, 203, 204, 205, 206, 227